Austin and Boxerman's

Information Systems
for Healthcare Management

SEVENTH EDITION

Austin and Boxerman's

Information Systems
for Healthcare Management

Gerald L. Glandon
Detlev H. Smaltz
Donna J. Slovensky

SEVENTH EDITION

Health Administration Press, Chicago
Association of University Programs in Health Administration, VA

AUPHA

Your board, staff, or clients may also benefit from this book's insight. For more information on quantity discounts, contact the Health Administration Press Marketing Manager at (312) 424-9470.

Reprinting April 2011

Library of Congress Cataloging-in-Publication Data

Glandon, Gerald L.
     Austin and Boxerman's information systems for healthcare management / Gerald L. Glandon, Detlev H. Smaltz, Donna J. Slovensky.—7th ed.
         p. ; cm.
     Rev. ed. of: Information systems for healthcare management / Charles J. Austin, Stuart B. Boxerman. 6th ed. c2003.
     Includes bibliographical references and index.
     ISBN-13: 978-1-56793-297-3 (alk. paper)
     ISBN-10: 1-56793-297-5 (alk paper)
1. Health services administration—Computer networks. 2. Health services administration—Data processing. 3. Information storage and retrieval systems—Hospitals. I. Smaltz, Detlev H. (Detlev Herb) II. Slovensky, Donna J. (Donna Jean) III. Austin, Charles J. Information systems for healthcare management. IV. Association of University Programs in Health Administration. V. Title. VI. Title: Information systems for healthcare management.
     [DNLM: 1. Management Information Systems. 2. Health Services Administration. 3. Medical Informatics Computing. W 26.5 G545a 2008]
     RA971.23.A976 2008
     362.11068—dc22

                                                                                 2008017469

The paper used in this publication meets the minimum requirements of American National Standard for Information Sciences—Permanence of Paper for Printed Library Materials, ANSI Z39.48-1984. ⊚™

Project manager: Amanda Bove; Acquisitions editor: Audrey Kaufman; Cover designer: Anne LoCascio.

Health Administration Press
A division of the Foundation
   of the American College of
   Healthcare Executives
One North Franklin Street
Suite 1700
Chicago, IL 60606
(312) 424-2800

Association of University Programs
   in Health Administration
2000 14th Street North
Suite 780
Arlington, VA 22201
(703) 894-0940

CONTENTS

DETAILED CONTENTS

FOREWORD

I was very pleased when representatives of Health Administration Press notified me that the Press planned to publish a seventh edition of *Information Systems for Healthcare Management*. Since retiring from active teaching and research, I have been anxious to see this work continue to help students and healthcare managers learn about the effective application and management of information technology. I was doubly pleased with the selection of three highly qualified coauthors for the new edition. Gerald Glandon holds the position that I once occupied at the University of Alabama at Birmingham (UAB). Donna Slovensky is a former colleague of mine on the UAB faculty. Detlev Smaltz adds an important new perspective as chief information officer of the Ohio State University Medical Center.

This new edition provides more than just updated material from previous editions. Major revisions and additions to the text provide a broad focus on all components of information systems in healthcare organizations. These changes are described in the preface. Yet the overall focus remains the same: "how the management of healthcare organizations can be improved by the intelligent use of information."

A large number of people have been instrumental in keeping this book alive through 28 years and seven editions. In addition to the highly capable staff at Health Administration Press, numerous contributors, research assistants, proofreaders, and editors have assisted me. Special thanks go to my friend and colleague, Stuart Boxerman, who served as coauthor for editions five and six.

—Charles J. Austin, Ph.D.
Hilton Head Island, SC

PREFACE AND ACKNOWLEDGMENTS

Despite the rapid and persistent changes in information technology and its applications to healthcare problems, issues of quality, cost, and access have been with us for more than half a century. As we struggle with solutions to these fundamental problems, we are forced to reexamine and update our use of the information necessary to support management and clinical decision making. In past years, teaching the management of information services could be delegated to a small section of management education. Now, it has become central to all that we do and teach. The chief information officer (CIO) now has a seat with the executive committee for many healthcare delivery organizations. Fortunately for those in the field, the development of new information technologies has raced far ahead of their use in healthcare. The challenge that the CIO and his or her leadership team faces is to understand the potential applications of technology, strategically plan for the selection and implementation of that technology, make sure the participants of the system receive sufficient training to adequately use the technology, and find a way to pay for it.

This text provides an overview of information management and information technology for practicing healthcare executives and managers and for students interested in information technology in healthcare management. Many of these readers will never work directly in information technology, and very few will ever become CIOs. Yet these current and future leaders must understand the basic concepts of this core element of healthcare delivery. To address this need, the text reflects a new approach to addressing leadership needs by providing current and future leaders with the knowledge, skills, and competencies necessary to effectively manage healthcare information systems. These leaders must exhibit competencies in core technologies, including hardware, software, and communication systems; clinical applications of these technologies; and fundamental organizational management. Consequently, we employ terminology to reflect this book's broad vision that information systems must include the management of technology, information, and human resources. The book is suitable as a textbook for a one-semester graduate or advanced undergraduate course in health information systems. It can also serve as a reference for healthcare managers and others involved in the selection and use of health information systems. Extensive lists of Internet sources are included to provide supplemental information on the major topics covered.

Changes made in this seventh edition will render the organization of this text almost unrecognizable to many. Among the many challenges in writing a textbook on information systems for healthcare management is the absence of widely accepted, consistent terminology defining the nature and scope of information systems. To some, information systems consist of computer hardware and software, communication networks, and other technology. Others insist that it is the software that supports clinical processes. Still others concentrate on the definition, collection, storage, retrieval, analysis, and distribution of clinical and/or administrative healthcare information. These are all valid and vital elements of information systems.

Throughout this book, we employ a broad concept of information systems to include the management of technology, information, and human resources. We will use the term *information management/information technology (IM/IT)* to focus our attention on all major components of information systems. It is this perspective of information systems that has given rise to chapters on leadership, governance, and value delivery that are not often part of textbooks in this area. We recognize that not everybody will agree with this perspective, but we hope that by clarifying the concepts up front, readers will understand our approach.

Consequently, this book is about management and how the management of healthcare organizations can be improved by the *intelligent* use of information. The intelligent use of information in healthcare management does not just happen. The manager must ensure that it occurs in a systematic, formally planned manner. This book, then, deals with two important matters:

1. the management of information resources in healthcare organizations; and
2. the effective use of information for patient care and organizational management.

Part I, "Aligning IM/IT and Organizational Strategy," contains five chapters that demonstrate the following:

- How healthcare IM/IT supports business objectives
- How the IM/IT function is led
- Governance models of IM/IT
- The role of IM/IT in coordinating business practices within an organization
- The relationship of healthcare IM/IT to the external environment

Part II, "Blocking and Tackling," contains two chapters describing the fundamental operations of healthcare IM/IT, including the architecture of IM/IT infrastructure and the delivery of services by Information Technology.

Part III, "Achieving Strategic Competitive Advantage," imparts in its three chapters the next stage of IM/IT delivery by discussing evolving IM/IT applications, transforming to a knowledge-enabled organization, assessing IM/IT value delivery, and speculating on future issues.

For instructors who choose to use this book in their courses, accompanying resources are available online. For access information, e-mail hap1@ache.org. Contained in these resources are PowerPoint presentations for each chapter, answers to the discussion questions, a test bank for each chapter, and a complex case regarding the design of an electronic medical record in a multispecialty group practice environment.

As in decades past, pressures for more comprehensive, more timely, more accurate, and more relevant management of information continue as the U.S. healthcare system faces the following recurrent problems:

- Healthcare services constitute an ever-increasing portion of the goods and services we produce (the gross domestic product).
- The number of uninsured people living in the United States continues to grow.
- The healthcare system does not consistently produce high-quality care.

Managing the triangle of cost, quality, and access, a national health policy priority, increasingly translates into pressure on individual providers. The system responds with market-driven healthcare reform efforts that have many consequences but, importantly, have led to the development of integrated delivery systems through mergers and acquisitions and to changes in systems of payment for services. Healthcare organizations have grown larger and more complex, and information systems must keep pace with the effects of organizational complexity, continued advances in medical technology, and growing demand for accountability from within and outside the healthcare organization (Gauthier and Serber 2005).

In this pursuit, some jargon often gets in the way of communication and understanding. Throughout this book, careful distinctions are drawn between data and information. As used in this book, *data* are raw facts and figures collected by the organization. *Information*, on the other hand, is defined as data that have been processed and analyzed in a formal, intelligent way so that the results are directly useful to clinicians and managers. All too often, computerized data banks are available, but they are little used because of inadequate planning of information content and structure needed to support management planning and control—organizations become data rich but information poor (Smaltz et al. 2005).

Acknowledgments

The development of such a complex text requires the input and support of a host of individuals. Primarily, we owe Charles Austin and Stuart Boxerman a substantial debt. It is deceptively easy to look at any text and find potential areas of change. Once you start implementing that change, however, you learn that the prior authors had good reason for what they produced. We all gained a profound respect for their contributions. JaNean Whitlow spent endless hours gathering background information from the Web and maintained our comprehensive set of references. Lorrinda Khan added great value to the design and structure of the text with her impressive editorial skills, and Angela Grace provided high-quality secretarial support. In addition, Dr. Smaltz would like to thank his entire team at the Ohio State University Medical Center for their dedication to continuously improving the practice of IM/IT management. In particular, Ben Walters and Ron Kibbe provided excellent counsel on IM/IT service management. Additionally, Phil Skinner, Benita Gilliard, Kevin Jones, and Jyoti Kamal, all of the Ohio State University Medical Center, as well as Randy Carpenter, of HealthSouth, provided sample exhibits and/or invaluable insight. The responsibility for remaining errors or oversights in this edition lies entirely with the authors.

References

Gauthier, A., and M. Serber. 2005. *A Need to Transform the U.S. Healthcare System: Improving Access, Quality, and Efficiency.* New York: Commonwealth Fund.

Smaltz, D., J. Glaser, R. Skinner, and T. Cunningham III (eds.). 2005. *The CEO-CIO Partnership: Harnessing the Value of Information Technology in Healthcare.* Chicago: Healthcare Information and Management Systems Society.

ALIGNING IM/IT
AND ORGANIZATIONAL STRATEGY

CONNECTING THE STRATEGIC DOTS: DOES IM/IT MATTER?

Learning Objectives

1. Describe the challenges of cost, quality, and access currently facing the U.S. healthcare system.
2. Analyze the implications of the cost, quality, and access challenges for the management of healthcare information systems.
3. Illustrate the history and current state of healthcare information systems development.
4. Analyze the importance of the key priorities that healthcare information systems will face in the future.
5. Assess how well healthcare system challenges and their implications align with healthcare information system priorities.

Healthcare Information Technology: The Future Is Now

Healthcare delivery continues to be an information-intensive set of processes. A series of Institute of Medicine (1999, 2001) studies suggests that high-quality patient care relies on careful documentation of each patient's medical history, health status, current medical conditions, and treatment plans. Financial information is essential for strategic planning and efficient operational support of the patient care process. Management of healthcare organizations requires reliable, accurate, current, secure, and relevant clinical and administrative information. A strong argument can be made that the healthcare field is one of the most information-intensive sectors of the U.S. economy.

Information technology has advanced to a high level of sophistication. However, technology can only provide tools to aid in the accomplishment of a wider set of organizational goals. Analysis of information requirements in the broader organizational context should always take precedence over a rush to computerize. Information technology by itself is not the answer to management problems; technology must be part of a broader restructuring of the organization, including reengineering of business processes. Alignment of information technology strategy with management goals of the healthcare organization is essential. Despite these cautions, effective design, implementation, and management of healthcare information management/information technology (IM/IT) show great promise (De Angelo 2000; Glaser and Garets 2005; Kaushal, Barker, and Bates 2001; Smaltz et al. 2005).

An essential element in a successful information systems implementation is carefully planned teamwork by clinicians, managers, and technical systems specialists. Information systems developed in isolation by technicians may be technically pure and elegant in design, but rarely will they pass the test of reality in meeting organizational requirements. On the other hand, very few managers and clinicians possess the equally important technical knowledge and skills of systems analysis and design, and the amateur analyst cannot hope to avoid the havoc that can result from a poorly designed system. A balanced effort is required: Operational personnel contribute ideas on system requirements and organizational realities, and technical personnel employ their skills in analysis and design.

This chapter sets the stage for what will appear throughout the rest of the book. It begins with a brief overview of the current healthcare environment as a driver of healthcare IM/IT and then presents the future trends in healthcare related to IM/IT. Next is a history of healthcare systems and healthcare priorities today. The last part of the chapter develops a framework of categories of information systems.

The Current Healthcare Environment

While nothing is more dangerous than predicting the future, Goldsmith (1980) looked into the future of healthcare for the late 1980s. He foresaw a vastly different landscape for the delivery of care than existed at the time. He documented a number of demographic, secular, and organizational changes that would shape that future. Such changes included the growing elderly population, the decline of the hospital as the center of the healthcare delivery universe, the oversupply of physicians, the expanded role of government in financing healthcare, the shift of financial risk from payers to providers, the expansion of health maintenance organizations (HMOs) in various forms, and problems related to the uninsured. He observed that to address issues such as continuity, linkage, coordination, and accountability, changes in the organization of the healthcare delivery system would be required. One can question the accuracy of specific predictions made in his forecast, but most would not deny that he was correct in the change in focus. Looking back, it is clear that these issues require added emphasis on improving the management of both healthcare information and its technology.

Three overriding factors are driving change in healthcare: the costs of care, evidence-based management, and organizational change.

Healthcare Costs

Healthcare costs continue to grow unabated. National health spending reached $2 trillion in 2005 and consumed about 16 percent of the U.S. gross domestic product (GDP) (see data in Table 1.1). Because the magnitude of this number is beyond comprehension by most people, Figure 1.1 presents this data over time (from 1960 to 2005, including a projection to 2010) on a per person (per capita) basis. The United States spent $6,697 per person on healthcare in 2005, the result of a steady increase for more than 45 years. Figure 1.1 also shows spending as a percentage of GDP for the same time frame. Healthcare goods and services are taking an ever-increasing portion of the goods and services produced in the United States, increasing from only 5.2 percent in 1960 to 16 percent in 2005 and an expected 17.2 percent by 2010.

Figure 1.2 analyzes the spending by decade by presenting annualized increases. Health spending increased faster than GDP in all periods presented, although not always by the same amounts. These data suggest that during good economic times, poor times, Republican presidents, Democratic presidents, and so forth, the result has been the same: Health spending continues to grow.

Figure 1.3 looks at the aggregate data in more detail for 2005. It displays the spending by major health delivery category for 2005. Hospital services (30.8 percent) was the largest single category, but physician services (21.2 percent), prescription drugs (10.1 percent), and nursing home care (6.1 percent) were also substantial in that year.

Next, the spending for major categories over time is presented in Figure 1.4. For the most recent period, from 2000 to 2005, overall national health expenditures increased at an annualized rate of 7.7 percent per year. Hospital services increased slightly more than that aggregate rate for the period (7.9 percent per year), while prescription drugs increased by more (10 percent per year) and nursing home care by much less (4.9 percent per year). To put all of this in perspective, one can decompose these overall changes into key component parts to help determine the true magnitude of this overall change in healthcare spending and to aid in seeking solutions. Looking at the 2000–2005 period, the data in Table 1.1 can be used to decompose the overall health expenditure changes (see Figure 1.5 for a summary of the decomposition results):

- Population increases are expected to contribute to an increase in overall healthcare spending. During this period, the U.S. population increased about 0.7 percent per year. Therefore, health spending per capita increased only 7.0 percent (7.7 percent–0.7 percent) per year during the period. Population increases accounted for 8.7 percent of overall health spending.
- Inflation for the economy as a whole (measured by the Consumer Price Index) also contributes to overall healthcare expenditure increases. Inflation was 2.5 percent per year during the 2000–2005 period. Therefore, real or inflation-adjusted health spending per capita increased 4.5 percent per year (7.7 percent–0.7 percent–2.5 percent). Overall

TABLE 1.1
Select National Health Expenditures, GDP, Population, and Price Indexes: 1960–2010

Component	Level 1960	Level 1970	Level 1980	Level 1990	Level 2000	Level 2004	Level 2005	Level 2010*
National Health Expenditures (NHE)	**$27.5**	**$74.9**	$253.9	$714.0	$1,353.3	$1,858.9	$1,987.7	$2,776.4
Research and Construction	$2.6	$7.8	$12.3	$26.4	$94.0	$120.0	$126.8	$175.6
Health Services and Supplies	$24.9	$67.1	$233.5	$669.6	$1,260.9	$1,738.9	$1,860.9	$2,600.8
Government Administration and								
Net Private Insurance	$1.2	$2.8	$12.2	$40.0	$81.0	$135.2	$143.0	$206.2
Government Public Health Act	$0.4	$1.4	$6.7	$20.2	$43.9	$52.5	$56.6	$81.7
Personal Healthcare	$23.3	$62.9	$214.6	$609.4	$1,136.1	$1,551.3	$1,661.4	$2,312.9
Hospital	$9.2	$27.6	$101.5	$253.9	$413.1	$566.9	$611.6	$860.9
Professional Services								
Physician Services	$5.4	$14.0	$47.1	$157.5	$290.2	$393.7	$421.2	$577.1
Dental Services	$2.0	$4.7	$13.3	$31.5	$60.7	$81.5	$86.6	$118.4
Other Professional Services	$0.4	$0.7	$3.6	$18.2	$39.0	$52.6	$56.7	$78.0
Other Personal Healthcare	$0.6	$1.2	$3.3	$9.6	$36.7	$53.3	$57.2	$88.8
Home Health Care	$0.1	$0.2	$2.4	$12.6	$31.6	$42.7	$47.5	$72.7
Nursing Homes	$0.8	$4.0	$17.7	$52.7	$95.3	$115.0	$121.9	$153.4
Retail Outlet Sales								
Prescription Drugs	$2.7	$5.5	$12.0	$40.3	$121.8	$189.7	$200.7	$291.5
Durable Medical Equipment	$0.6	$1.6	$3.9	$10.6	$17.7	$23.1	$24.0	$29.4
Other Nondurable Items	$1.6	$3.3	$9.8	$22.5	$30.4	$32.8	$34.1	$42.8
Population (in millions)	186	210	230.4	254	287.0	294.0	296.8	309.0
GDP (billion $)	$526.0	$1,039.0	$2,790.0	$5,803.0	$9,817.0	$11,712.5	$12,455.8	$16,170.5
General Inflation (index)	29.8	39.8	86.3	130.7	172.2	188.9	195.3	222.5
Healthcare Inflation (index)	22.6	36.7	77.6	162.8	260.8	310.1	323.2	388.5
NHE Percent of GDP	**5.2%**	**7.2%**	**9.1%**	**12.3%**	**13.8%**	**15.9%**	**16.0%**	**17.2%**

* projections
Note: All national health expenditures are in millions of dollars.
Sources: CMS (2007a, 2007b); U.S. Bureau of Labor Statistics (2007).

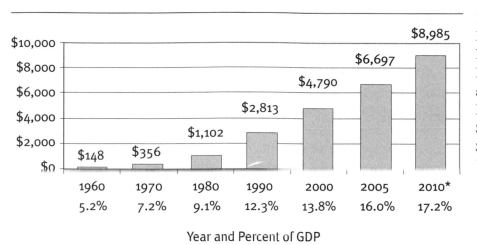

FIGURE 1.1
Per Capita
National Health
Expenditures
and Health
Expenditure's
Share of GDP:
Select Years,
1960–2010

* projected
Source: CMS (2007a, 2007b).

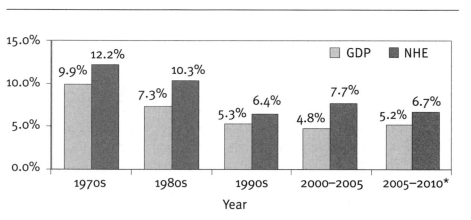

FIGURE 1.2
Growth Rates
for National
Health
Expenditures
and GDP: Select
Time Periods,
1960–2010

* projected
Note: NHE = national health expenditures.
Source: Computations by authors based on data from CMS (2007a, 2007b).

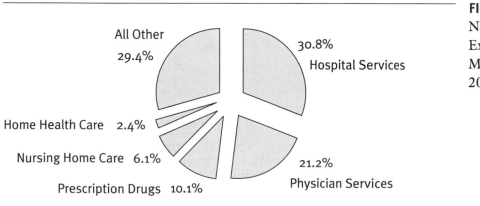

FIGURE 1.3
National Health
Expenditures by
Major Service,
2005

Source: CMS (2007a).

inflation increases accounted for 32.7 percent of overall health spending during this period.

• Of this remaining 4.5 percent per year, a substantial amount can be attributed to price increases for healthcare goods and services. The medical care component of consumer prices increased 4.3 percent during this period. This increase was 1.8 percent (4.3 percent–2.5 percent) more rapid than the overall inflation. Medical care price increases accounted for 1.8 percent per year of the remaining real per capita increase of 4.6 percent per year, or 23.1 percent of overall health spending increases.

• The remaining 2.7 percent per year (4.5 percent–1.8 percent) is a residual, but it can be aggregated as quantity and quality of services. After controlling for population, inflation, and relative prices of medical care goods and services, health spending increased by 2.7 percent per year (7.7 percent–0.7 percent–2.5 percent–1.8 percent). Quantity and quality increases accounted for 35.5 percent of overall health spending during the period.

Evidence-Based Management

Evidence-based medicine grew in the late 1990s (Clancy and Eisenberg 1998) and has become mainstream, as indicated by the publication of at least one on-line evidence-based medicine journal (Evidence-Based Medicine for Primary Care and Internal Medicine 2007). This decade has witnessed a corresponding increase in the emphasis on evidence-based management (Walshe and Rundall 2001; Pfeffer and Sutton 2006). While experience, judgment, intuition, and a good sense of the political environment are still critical skills, administrative decision making increasingly relies on information. Some may discount the value of information in the management process, stating that management is still more an art than a science. On the other end of the spectrum are the technocrats, who argue that management and information are inseparable and

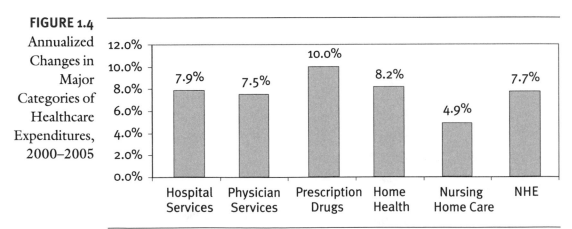

FIGURE 1.4
Annualized Changes in Major Categories of Healthcare Expenditures, 2000–2005

Note: NHE = national health expenditures.
Source: Computations by authors based on data from CMS (2007a).

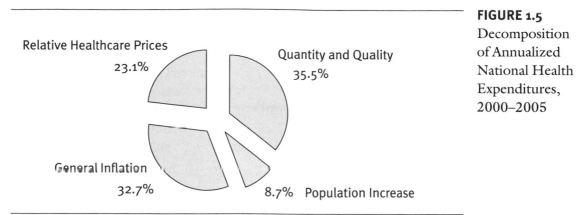

Relative Healthcare Prices
23.1%

Quantity and Quality
35.5%

General Inflation
32.7%

8.7% Population Increase

FIGURE 1.5
Decomposition
of Annualized
National Health
Expenditures,
2000–2005

Source: Computations by authors based on data from CMS (2007a, 2007b).

that all management decisions need to be completely rational and based entirely on an analysis of comprehensive information. The resulting revision in the method for making managerial decisions that relies more on information has now become part of the culture of healthcare organizations (Center for Organization, Leadership, and Management Research 2006). That new culture relies heavily upon organizational information systematically gathered, stored, analyzed, and reported by a wide array of health informatics professionals. The focus of this book lies between these two extreme views of the managerial world. The use of information is associated with both costs and benefits. These costs and benefits need to be assessed, and healthcare managers need to develop their skills in using information intelligently to support their organization's strategic and operational goals (Johnston, Pan, and Middleton 2002; Sidorov 2006).

Organizational Change

Healthcare markets continue to change as they face ongoing efforts to manage costs, quality, and access. As these markets—and the major delivery organizations within the markets—adapt, healthcare IM/IT will be required to accommodate these changing needs accordingly. Market-driven healthcare reform and efforts to increase market competition, initiated in the 1990s, have evolved but still cannot be fully judged as to their effectiveness. Wilensky (2006) and Ginsburg (2005) provide interesting historical perspectives on the changing healthcare landscape. They demonstrate that in the mid-1990s, nearly 75 percent of people with employment-based insurance had some form of managed care, and HMOs constituted the largest component. Insurance companies and hospitals poured into this market because of the potential for profits.

Managed care was designed to help contain costs by squeezing out inefficiency in the delivery system. However, much of the growth into managed care was not due to consumers choosing it as the preferred method of delivery. People selected managed care options to avoid paying higher premiums in alternative plans (Gilmer and Kronick 2005). Consumer backlash to managed care arose because of fear of restrictions on access to care. This sentiment was fueled by physicians who did not support managed care because its plans placed restrictions on the delivery of care and reduced physician reimbursement (Ginsburg 2005). HMOs in particular came under heavy criticism by consumers and physicians. The political battles over the "patient's bill of rights," which was developed in response to the managed care restrictions, is a reflection of these concerns.

Management improvements have made little progress in reducing the population of uninsured and underinsured citizens, and disease prevention remains an elusive goal in most health plans today. Gauthier and Serber (2005), in their report for the Commonwealth Fund, cite the U.S. Census Bureau statistic that nearly 46 million people in the United States are uninsured and expect that number to increase in the future. According to Davis and Rajkumar (2001), "lack of health insurance is a major barrier to care . . . and lack of high-quality, comprehensive insurance is a barrier to millions more." Gauthier and Serber (2005) report that disease prevention is often overlooked as well.

Future Healthcare Systems

The factors that drive healthcare change today—costs, evidence-based management, and organizational change—are in turn driven by the need to improve quality, control costs, and improve access. Responding with an evidence-based management approach, managed care and other delivery-of-care options and the expansion of coverage to the uninsured all increase the information needs of delivery organizations (hospitals and physician groups), insurance organizations, and consumers. Clinical and administrative data needed to assess and improve quality, identify potential cost savings, and make strategic decisions have become important as the pressure on healthcare rises.

Current trends in healthcare that will drive information technology priorities in the immediate future include the following:

- Concern about medical errors and overall quality of care
- Continued pressure for cost containment
- Consumer empowerment
- Growth in the use of evidence-based medicine
- Demand for protection of privacy and confidentiality of information

Medical Errors and Quality of Care

According to the IOM's (1999) landmark report, *To Err Is Human*, medical errors are a leading cause of adverse health consequences in hospitals. At least 44,000 and as many as 98,000 individuals die in hospitals per year as a result of preventable medical errors. They also result in greater direct and indirect costs borne by society as a whole. The report states that "the total national cost associated with adverse effects [of medical errors] was approximately 4 percent of national health expenditures in 1996" (IOM 1999, 41).

Conceptualizing quality of care in terms of medical errors, however, ignores more comprehensive aspects of quality. Davis and colleagues (2004) report on the measurement of six domains of quality just from the perspective of the patient. These include the following:

1. *Patient safety*—patient-reported medical error with serious health consequences
2. *Patient-centeredness*—patient assessment of quality of physician care, especially regarding involvement of patient in care decisions
3. *Timeliness*—patient-reported waiting time for hospitalizations, elective surgery, physician appointment
4. *Efficiency*—patient-reported coordination of care
5. *Effectiveness*—patient-reported ability to follow up on care ordered by physician
6. *Equity*—patient-reported influence of income on ability to receive care

This set of measurements gives an idea of the complexity of assessing quality. Davis et al. (2004) further report some of the problems with quality and the variability in the level of quality. They provide a sobering assessment of patient perspectives in the United States compared with patients in Australia, Canada, New Zealand, and the United Kingdom (Davis et al. 2004).

A widely cited report by Jencks, Huff, and Cuerdon (2003) indicated substantial differences in quality of care across states for Medicare patients as measured by a large number of quality indicators. Because of the perceived poor quality and the observed variability of quality measures, many organizations are seeking first to define quality and then report select aspects of healthcare quality to the public.

Cost Containment

As the cost analysis above suggests, healthcare expenditure growth will likely continue into the future; this trend is supported by federal government reports (see Figures 1.1 and 1.2). However, these analyses look backward and do not address the underlying socioeconomic factors that drive increases in spending in a more fundamental manner (Thorpe 2005). Among these factors are modifiable "population risk factors such as obesity and stress," although he points out that rising disease prevalence and new medical treatments account for much of the increase as well (Thorpe 2005, 1436). The analysis suggests that not all of the problem can be attributed to healthcare pricing or utilization, but both contribute substantially to it.

The trends in health spending increases, no matter how they are analyzed and decomposed, show no signs of abating and may threaten the quality of care for even the best-insured Americans. If 25 percent, 30 percent, or more of Americans lack meaningful access to basic care, the public health and emergency systems upon which all Americans rely will be strained to provide adequate care (Book 2005, 579). The real issue, however, is whether the growth per se genuinely constitutes a problem. Are we getting value for this investment in healthcare goods and services? Any review of the literature will demonstrate that identification and solutions to cost increases dominate the published articles; however, recent studies (e.g., Cutler, Rosen, and Vijan 2006) suggest that investments in healthcare have been relatively cost effective overall.

To demonstrate how vital information management is to the future, the ranking Democrat on the Senate Finance Committee as of this writing, Senator Max Baucus of Montana, suggests two basic reforms be implemented to improve the system (Baucus 2005). First, the way that providers are paid must be changed to a system that encourages value and efficient, effective, patient-centered care. Second, more spending on (i.e., investment in) information technology is needed.

Consumer Empowerment

Consumers have become increasingly sophisticated in their selection and use of healthcare. Empowered by the Internet, consumers are seeking medical information and joining together in support groups as they interact with physicians and other healthcare providers. Goldsmith states that "the patient is in charge of the process. . . . The Internet has enabled patients to aggregate their collective experiences across disease entities" (Reece 2000). Although providers express legitimate concerns about misuse and misunderstanding of information obtained from the Internet, the trend of its use by healthcare consumers is clear and irreversible. Oravec (2001) suggests that the healthcare system should help develop approaches that will empower consumers to use the Internet effectively as one part of a total healthcare strategy, rather than simply warn about the potential hazards of using inaccurate or misunderstood information.

More recently, Ellwood (2003) outlined a comprehensive set of recommendations that arose from a health reform meeting held in Jackson Hole, Wyoming, in 2002. The Jackson Hole Group looks for Congress to set up a "uniform, national information infrastructure and a process for its further development and implementation" (Ellwood 2003). The proposal calls for four infrastructure-related developments that include electronic health records; evidence-based clinical practices; public disclosure, analysis, and feedback of quality performance information; and giving patients genuine power and responsibility. The consumer empowerment movement is growing and is highly integrated with the need for information management in healthcare.

Evidence-Based Medicine

Landry and Sibbald (2001) define *evidence-based medicine* (EBM) as "an information management and learning strategy that seeks to integrate clinical expertise with the best evidence available to make effective clinical decisions that will ultimately improve patient care." It is a systematic approach to diagnosis and treatment that encourages the physician to formulate questions and seek answers from the best available published evidence. EBM is gaining momentum as an important mechanism for improving healthcare delivery. Some are suggesting that EBM will become the new paradigm for organizations to follow in providing care. To successfully incorporate EBM into healthcare, participants in healthcare organizations (i.e., physicians, patients, managers) must agree to follow the evidence wherever it applies (Ellwood 2001).

Information Privacy and Confidentiality

Protection of the privacy of health information is a major issue faced by all healthcare organizations. The Health Insurance Portability and Accountability Act of 1996 (HIPAA) allows individuals who change or lose jobs to maintain health insurance coverage for a period of time. The administrative simplification and privacy provisions of this law encourage electronic information exchange and establish standards and requirements for the electronic transmission of certain healthcare information. HIPAA also requires new safeguards to protect the security and confidentiality of that information, and it applies to any healthcare organization that provides or pays the cost of medical care under a variety of federal programs, including Medicare and Medicaid. HIPAA compliance was a major issue faced by healthcare organizations during the first part of this decade. The final rules for compliance took effect on April 14, 2001, and most organizations were required to comply by April 14, 2003 (U.S. Department of Health and Human Services 2001). More discussion of HIPAA is presented in Chapter 5.

To summarize the five healthcare trends that will likely drive information technology priorities in the future, managed care pioneer Paul Ellwood (2001) called for healthcare reform addressing many of the issues listed above using the acronym HEROIC:

H—health systems that emphasize the *health component* rather than the
   financial incentives
E—medical care organized around principles of *evidence-based medicine*
R—patients who assume greater *responsibility* for their own health and the
   cost of care they require
O—*outcomes* accountability and adoption of mistake prevention measures
I—use of *information technology* to hold the system together
C—*continuous commitment* to long-term relationships, including
   continuous health insurance coverage for everyone

Historical Overview of Information Systems

The first computer systems in healthcare date back to the early 1960s, when a small number of hospitals began to automate selected administrative operations, usually beginning with payroll and patient accounting functions. These systems were developed by analysts and computer programmers hired by the hospital and were run on large and expensive centralized computers referred to as "mainframes" (see Figure 1.6). Little attention was given to the development of clinical information systems to support patient care, and the paper medical record was the legal and clinical record of the treatment experience. A few systems were developed for the electronic storage and retrieval of abstracts of inpatient medical records, but these systems contained limited information and were operated on a postdischarge, retrospective basis.

Advances in technology during the 1970s expanded the use of information systems throughout industry, and hospitals were no exception. These systems eventually became part of other healthcare organizational settings such as clinics, physician office practices, and long-term care facilities. Computers became smaller and less expensive, and some vendors began to develop "applications software packages"—generalized computer programs that could be used by any hospital, clinic, or physician's office that purchased the system. Most of these early software packages supported administrative operations such as

FIGURE 1.6
Mainframe
Computer

Source: Courtesy of International Business Machines Corporation. Unauthorized use not permitted.

patient accounting, general accounting, materials management, scheduling, and practice management. Eventually, clinical systems were developed as well, particularly for hospital clinical laboratories, radiology departments, and pharmacies (for a description of current applications, see Chapter 8).

A virtual revolution in computing occurred in the 1980s with the development of powerful and inexpensive personal computers (PCs)—desktop devices with computing power and storage capacity that equaled or exceeded the large mainframe systems of the 1960s and 1970s (see Figure 1.7). A second major advance in this period was the development of electronic data networks, whereby PCs and larger systems could be linked together for the sharing of information on a decentralized basis. An increasing number of vendors entered the healthcare software business, and a much larger array of products became available for both administrative and clinical support functions. The use of PCs in physicians' offices, particularly for practice management, became commonplace. As demonstrated below, this ad hoc proliferation of systems and applications to meet specific clinical and administrative needs contributed to the integration challenges faced today.

The 1990s witnessed even more dramatic changes in the healthcare environment with the advent of market-driven healthcare reform and expansion of managed care. Much greater attention was given to the development of clinical information systems and strategic decision support systems to assist providers in achieving a critical balance between costs and quality in the delivery of care. These changes were supported by advances in technology through the use of laptop and, finally, notebook computers (Figures 1.8 and 1.9). This hardware expanded the ability of providers and others to take the data collection tool with them, access information from virtually anywhere, and communicate with others in the care team quickly.

At the same time, electronic data interchange and networking were used to link components of integrated healthcare delivery organizations and support enterprisewide information systems. Healthcare organizations now employ Internet technology to support internal communications and external connections with patients and business partners. Telemedicine applications

FIGURE 1.7
Personal
Computer,
Desktop

FIGURE 1.8
Laptop
Computer

FIGURE 1.9
Notebook and
Tablet
Computers

Source: Toshiba America Information Systems, Inc., Irvine, CA. http://www.toshibadirect
.com/td/b2c/pdet.to?seg=HHO&poid=362703. Used with permission.

now can link primary care providers at remote locations with clinical specialists
at centralized medical centers. These technologies provide potentially better
access to high-quality care at reasonable costs.

As an example, the Electronic Health Network (EHN), operated under
the direction of Dr. Glenn Hammack at the University of Texas Medical
Branch (UTMB) at Galveston, uses cutting-edge video, digital, audio, and
telecommunications technology to deliver care (Blanchet 2005). While this
major commitment to telemedicine has many components, the major activity
is EHN's Correctional Managed Care Program, which has provided "prison
health" to individuals incarcerated in Texas prisons since 1993. Today, the
program is a full risk-capitated delivery system. In 2004, it had $330 million

in revenue, covered 166,000 lives, and employed 3,700 workers. Texas is a large state geographically, and the technology enables UTMB to effectively connect clinical care in more than 100 locations for the Texas Department of Criminal Justice, Texas Youth Commission, Dallas County Jails, and Federal Board of Prisons in Beaumont.

The electronic medical record (EMR) used in the EHN is its key component. The EMR is a security encrypted, full-time Web-enabled record that gives the physician access to medical records regardless of patient location. It contains a pharmacy system for identifying drug interactions, and clinical laboratory and radiology services can input data and images directly into the system. UTMB finds that the expanded capacity to reliably, remotely deliver quality care for less cost makes sense for the organization.

Healthcare Information Priorities Today

Healthcare organizations operating in this environment of change are developing sophisticated information systems to support clinical operations and strategic management. Some of the major priorities for system development include the following:

- Protection of information security
- Development of clinical systems to support disease-management programs and reduce medical errors
- Interoperability
- Expanded use of the Internet and development of electronic health (e-health) applications
- Use of wireless devices to improve data entry and access
- Support for consumers through development of home applications

Information Security

HIPAA compliance was the top information technology priority listed by respondents to the 2002 annual leadership survey conducted by the Healthcare Information and Management Systems Society (HIMSS). Survey respondents included a cross section of senior managers, information technology managers, and other healthcare professionals (HIMSS 2002). According to Tabar (2001, 46), "the data security requirements under the Health Insurance Portability and Accountability Act are straightforward: Physical, administrative and technical security access controls and alarms must be in place. Penalties will be issued for breaches."

Information technology managers are organizing efforts to assess risks and identify gaps in existing information security processes and systems. Enterprisewide plans are needed that include privacy protection policies, control of access to information systems, contingency planning, and disaster-backup and recovery procedures. Technical safeguards must be combined with management control and educational programs to have a complete security system. Information security is discussed in more detail in Chapter 7.

Clinical Information Systems

Upgrading and improving clinical information systems was the highest priority item identified by respondents to the *Seventeenth Annual HIMSS Leadership Survey* (HIMSS 2006). Implementation of an EMR system was the stated priority of 61 percent of the respondents in 2006. Further, computerized practitioner order entry and enterprisewide clinical information sharing were listed as a priority by 52 percent and 49 percent of the respondents, respectively. According to the survey, 60 percent of organizations have installed an EMR system or have begun installation, and only 12 percent have not implemented, and have no plans to implement, such a system (HIMSS 2006).

Clinical information systems are essential for programs of disease management and evidence-based medicine. Disease management programs focus on prevention of crisis events among high-risk, high-cost patients (Baldwin 2001). The programs are rule based and automated. Systems supporting these programs must be able to measure outcomes and help establish conformity with best medical practices. They have expanded to become a supportive portion of healthcare delivery during this decade and have seen substantial growth into e-health and other newer technologies (Wiecha and Pollard 2004).

Clinical information systems are equally important in reducing medical errors. The Institute of Medicine (2001) followed up its landmark report on medical errors with *Crossing the Quality Chasm: A New Health System for the 21st Century*. This report calls for a complete upgrade of the information technology capabilities of healthcare delivery organizations throughout the United States. In addition, it calls for government funding of a program to provide investment for healthcare information technology, like what the Hill-Burton Program did for hospital facility construction since the late 1940s (Lovern 2001). Clinical information systems are discussed in more detail in Chapter 8.

Interoperability

The current movement to develop electronic health records (EHRs) to improve care delivery depends upon enabling systems to work together within and across organizations. This movement is vital for the development of standards. HIMSS (2005) adopted the following definition of *interoperability* from the perspective of the Nationwide Health Information Network initiative:

> Interoperability means the ability of health information systems to work together within and across organizational boundaries in order to advance the effective delivery of healthcare for individuals and communities.

The concept of interoperability has become complicated by the complex nature of information exchange needs. The Center for Information Technology Leadership uses four levels of healthcare data exchange to describe interoperability. These levels presume different technical requirements. This definition and the level of interoperability have been endorsed by the National Alliance for Health Information Technology (2007). The levels are as follows:

- *Level 1: Non-electronic data.* Examples include paper, mail, and phone calls.
- *Level 2: Machine-transportable data.* Examples include fax, email, and unindexed documents.
- *Level 3: Machine-organizable data* (structured messages, unstructured content). Examples include indexed (labeled) documents, images, and objects.
- *Level 4: Machine-interpretable data* (structured messages, standardized content). Examples include the automated transfer from an external lab of coded results into a provider's EHR. Data can be transmitted (or accessed without transmission) by health information technology systems without need for further semantic interpretation or translation. (Adapted from Walker et al. 2005)

Internet and E-Health Applications

Deployment of Internet technology was the second highest ranked priority of respondents to the 2002 HIMSS leadership survey. Development of Internet-based applications was listed as an immediate priority by 37 percent of the survey respondents. Ninety-four percent of the respondents' organizations had websites at the time of the survey, and the respondents claimed that their organizations' use of these sites for a variety of information-processing functions is growing. Promotion and marketing of services is the most widely used Internet application, followed by employee recruitment and provision of consumer health information (HIMSS 2002). The number and variety of e-health applications are expected to increase dramatically in the next few years. These applications are discussed in more detail in Chapter 8.

Wireless Technology

The deployment of wireless technology has been spectacular in the healthcare field. In the 2002 HIMSS leadership survey, wireless applications were highly "anticipated" technologies (HIMSS 2002) but not yet widely implemented. By the time of the 2006 HIMSS leadership survey, however, wireless technology was second on the list of technologies being used at respondent institutions (HIMSS 2006). At that time, 84 percent of institutions reported having some wireless implementations in place. That expansion will likely continue because, as reported in the 2006 survey, wireless technology was still sixth on the list of technologies being considered for implementation in the next two years. Stammer (2001, 50) states that "with wireless local area networks, clinicians can access patient data from their offices or patients' bedsides and file the data in the hospital information system or an electronic patient record." Patient monitoring via wireless telemetry is becoming commonplace. Handheld devices are being used for order entry, wireless dictation, and medical reporting.

Consumer Support Systems

As discussed previously, consumers have become increasingly sophisticated in their selection and use of healthcare. In response, healthcare organizations are developing support systems to attract and retain these empowered consumers to their health plans. Enhanced websites are being used in support of this goal. The 2006 HIMSS leadership survey reveals that the organizations represented in the survey are using websites for such purposes as marketing and promotion (91 percent), employee recruitment (91 percent), online provider directory posting (83 percent), and provision of consumer health information (74 percent). New to the 2006 survey in reporting Web use are remote employee access (53 percent), physician portal link (47 percent), and business-to-business transactions (29 percent) (HIMSS 2006).

Development of customer relationship management (CRM) systems will take on high priority for healthcare providers operating in highly competitive markets. A comprehensive CRM system includes sales, marketing, and customer service programs tailored to individual patients or health plan members. According to Joch (2001, 72), "a well-run CRM system can deliver a complete profile of the customer to anyone in an organization who needs it, whether it's a nurse checking medical records or a webmaster gathering statistics. The goal is to make the individual patient and the Web surfer both feel that they're getting information customized for their needs. Personal attention, in turn, brings customer loyalty and strength to the healthcare organization in a cutthroat market." Customer-oriented computer applications are discussed in more detail in Chapter 8.

Categories of Information Systems

Computerized information systems in healthcare fall into four categories: (1) clinical, (2) management, (3) strategic decision support, and (4) electronic networking and e-health applications.

Clinical information systems support patient care and provide information for use in strategic planning and management. Applications include computerized patient records systems; clinical department systems such as pharmacy, laboratory, and radiology; automated medical instrumentation; clinical decision support systems (computer-aided diagnosis and treatment planning); and information systems that support clinical research and education.

Operational management systems support non–patient-care activities in the healthcare organization. Examples include financial information systems, payroll, purchasing and inventory control, outpatient clinic scheduling, and office automation.

Strategic decision support systems assist the senior management team in strategic planning, managerial control, performance monitoring, and outcomes assessment. Strategic information systems must draw data from internal clinical and management systems in the organization as well as draw external data on community health, market-area demography, and activities of competitors. Consequently, information system integration—the ability of organizational information systems to communicate electronically with one another—becomes very important.

Healthcare organizations also engage in *electronic data interchange* with external organizations and business partners for such activities as insurance billing and claims processing, accessing clinical information from regional and national databases, communicating among providers in an integrated delivery system, and communicating with patients and health plan members. Many of these applications are Web-based, e-health applications.

Computer applications in healthcare organizations are described in detail in Part III of this book.

Summary

The management of healthcare organizations can be improved through the intelligent use of information. This requires systematic planning and management of information resources to develop information systems that support patient care, administrative operations, and strategic management.

Change is occurring rapidly in healthcare. Major forces of change that have a direct impact on the application of information technology include (1) concerns about medical errors, (2) continued pressure for cost containment, (3) consumer empowerment, (4) growth in the use of evidence-based medicine, and (5) demand for protection of privacy and confidentiality of information.

These environmental trends have resulted in a reordering of the information system priorities of healthcare organizations. These new priorities include (1) protection of information security, (2) development of clinical systems to support disease management programs and reduce medical errors, (3) interoperability, (4) expanded use of the Internet and development of e-health applications, (5) use of wireless devices to improve data entry and access, and (6) support for consumers through development of home applications.

Health information systems fall into four categories: clinical, management, strategic decision support, and e-health applications. Clinical information systems support patient care and provide information for strategic planning and management. Operational management systems support non–patient-care activities such as financial management, human resources management, materials management, scheduling, and office automation. Strategic decision support systems assist managers in planning, marketing, management control of operations, performance evaluation, and outcomes assessment. E-health network applications support electronic data interchange with external organizations and business partners, communication among providers in an integrated delivery system, and communication with patients and health plan members.

Web Resources

A number of websites provide useful information related to this chapter.

The Agency for Healthcare Research and Quality (http://www.ahrq.gov) is the health services research arm of the U.S. Department of Health and Human Services, complementing the biomedical research mission of its sister agency, the National Institutes of Health. It is home to research centers that specialize in major areas of healthcare research and is a major source of funding and technical assistance for health services research and research training at leading U.S. universities and other institutions.

The U.S. Bureau of Labor Statistics home page (http://www.bls.gov/cpi/) has many components that report varied data regarding the U.S. economy but particularly reports detailed information on consumer prices at a national and state level.

The Centers for Medicare & Medicaid Services home page (http://www.cms.hhs.gov/) contains access to a vast array of healthcare-related information regarding Medicare, Medicaid, research and statistics, regulations, and so forth.

The Disease Management Association of America (http://www.dmaa.org/research_documents.asp) has as its mission to promote population health improvement through disease and care management.

The Institute for Healthcare Improvement (IHI) (http://www.ihi.org/ihi) is a not-for-profit organization leading the improvement of healthcare throughout the world. IHI was founded in 1991 and is based in Cambridge, Massachusetts. IHI's work is funded primarily through fee-based program offerings and services and also through support from foundations, companies, and individuals.

The National Alliance for Health Information Technology (http://www.nahit.org) is a not-for-profit, member-based organization focused on demonstrating how healthcare information technology can and will improve healthcare outcomes. The Alliance is a unique forum in which senior leaders convene, speaking candidly about emerging issues in healthcare, and working collaboratively to create consensus-based solutions and action plans.

The National Association for Healthcare Quality (http://www.nahq .org/) empowers healthcare quality professionals from every specialty by providing vital research, education, networking, certification, professional practice resources, and a strong voice for healthcare quality.

The National Committee for Quality Assurance (NCQA) (http://web .ncqa.org/) is a private, 501(c)(3) not-for-profit organization dedicated to improving healthcare quality. NCQA has been a central figure in driving improvement throughout the healthcare system, helping to elevate the issue of healthcare quality to the top of the U.S. political agenda. Its mission is to improve the quality of healthcare with a vision to transform healthcare quality through measurement, transparency, and accountability.

Discussion Questions

1. Since most developers are not clinicians, and most clinicians are not developers, what measures are necessary to ensure the development of an effective health information system?
2. Why is it important for the information technology strategy to align with the organization's goals and objectives?
3. In what ways may improved healthcare information technology assist in continuity, communication, coordination, and accountability of patient care? Similarly, in what ways may improved management of health information assist in continuity, communication, coordination, and accountability of patient care? [Hint: Consider Goldsmith's discussion.]
4. How can information technology assist organizations in responding to the drivers of information technology changes?
5. Define and describe evidence-based medicine. Are there positive or negative aspects of this concept within the healthcare field?
6. Evaluate Ellwood's healthcare reform concept, HEROIC. Do you consider his points to be valid? Why or why not?
7. Why is the improvement of clinical information systems a high priority to most organizations?
8. Order the following types of systems from most important to least important within a healthcare organization, and discuss why you chose this order.
    Clinical
    Management
    Strategic decision support
    Electronic networking and e-health
    Consumer support
9. Of the professional organizations mentioned in this chapter, which organization's mission and goals are most consistent with your personal goals? Provide detailed reasons why you chose this organization.

References

Baldwin, F. D. 2001. "Putting Your Assets to Work." *Healthcare Informatics* 18 (4): 47–50, 52.

Baucus, M. 2005. "Looking at the U.S. Healthcare System in the Rear-View Mirror." *Health Affairs.* Web Exclusives, November 16, 544–45. [Online article; retrieved 12/28/07.] http://content.healthaffairs.org/cgi/content/abstract /hlthaff.w5.544v1

Blanchet, K. 2005. "Innovative Programs in Telemedicine." *Telemedicine and e-Health* 11 (2): 116–23.

Book, E. L. 2005. "Health Insurance Trends Are Contributing to Growing Healthcare Inequality." *Health Affair.* Web Exclusives, December 6, 577–79. [Online article; retrieved 12/28/07.] http://content.healthaffairs.org/cgi/content /abstract/hlthaff.w5.577v1

Center for Organization, Leadership, and Management Research. 2006. "A Paradigm Shift for Managers and Researchers: Evidence-Based Management." [Online article; retrieved 12/28/07.] http://www.colmr.research.va.gov/mgmt_ research_in_va/framework/evidence.cfm

Centers for Medicare & Medicaid Services (CMS). 2007a. "NHE Web Tables." [Online information; retrieved 2/1/08.] http://www.cms.hhs.gov/National HealthExpendData/Downloads/tables.pdf

———. 2007b. "NHE Projections 2007–2017." [Online information; retrieved 2/1/08.] http://www.cms.hhs.gov/NationalHealthExpendData/downloads /proj2006.pdf

Clancy, C., and J. Eisenberg. 1998. "Outcomes Research: Measuring the End Results of Healthcare." *Science* 282 (5387): 245–46.

Cutler, D. M., A. B. Rosen, and S. Vijan. 2006. "The Value of Medical Spending in the United States, 1960–2000." *New England Journal of Medicine* 355 (9): 920–927.

Davis, K., C. Schoen, S. Schoenbaum, A. M. Audet, M. Doty, and K. Tenney. 2004. *Mirror, Mirror on the Wall: Looking at the Quality of American Healthcare through the Patient's Lens.* Report no. 683 (January). New York: Commonwealth Fund.

Davis, W. S., and T. M. Rajkumar. 2001. *Operating Systems: A Systematic View,* 5th ed. Boston: Addison Wesley.

De Angelo, M. 2000. "Internet Solution Provides Important Component in Reducing Medical Errors." *Health Management Technology* 21 (2): 20–21.

Ellwood, P. M. 2003. "Crossing the Health Policy Chasm: Pathways to Healthy Outcomes." [Online article; retrieved 12/28/07.] www.ppionline.org/ppi_ci .cfm?knlgAreaID=111&subsecID=138&contentID=251324

———. 2001. "Does Managed Care Need to Be Replaced?" *Medscape General Medicine* 3 (5): 5.

Evidence-Based Medicine for Primary Care and Internal Medicine. 2007. Home page. [Online information; retrieved 12/28/07.] http://ebm.bmj.com/

Gauthier, A., and M. Serber. 2005. *A Need to Transform the U.S. Healthcare System: Improving Access, Quality, and Efficiency.* New York: Commonwealth Fund.

Gilmer, T., and R. Kronick. 2005. "It's the Premiums, Stupid: Projections of the Uninsured Through 2013." *Health Affairs*. Web Exclusives. [Online article; retrieved 1/4/08.] http://content.healthaffairs.org/cgi/reprint/hlthaff.w5 .143v1?maxtoshow=&HITS=10&hits=10&RESULTFORMAT=&author1= Gilmer&andorexactfulltext=and&searchid=1&FIRSTINDEX=0&resource type=HWCIT

Ginsburg, P. B. 2005. "Competition in Healthcare: Its Evolution Over the Past Decade." *Health Affairs (Millwood)* 24 (6): 1512–22.

Glaser, J., and D. Garets. 2005. "Where's the Beef? Part 1: Getting Value from Your IT Investments." In *The CEO-CIO Partnership: Harnessing the Value of Information Technology in Healthcare*, edited by D. Smaltz, J. Glaser, R. Skinner, and T. Cunningham III. Chicago: Healthcare Information and Management Systems Society.

Goldsmith, J. A. 1980. "The Healthcare Market: Can Hospitals Survive?" *Harvard Business Review* 58 (5): 100–112.

Healthcare Information Management Systems Society (HIMSS). 2006. *Seventeenth Annual HIMSS Leadership Survey: Final Report: Healthcare CIO*. Sponsored by ACS Healthcare Solutions. Chicago: HIMSS.

———. 2005. "Interoperability Definition and Background." [Online information; retrieved 12/28/07.] http://www.himss.org/content/files/interoperability _definition_background_060905.pdf

———. 2002. *Thirteenth Annual HIMSS Leadership Survey*. Sponsored by Superior Consultant. Chicago: HIMSS.

Institute of Medicine (IOM). 2001. *Crossing the Quality Chasm: A New Health System for the 21st Century*. Washington, DC: National Academies Press.

———. 1999. *To Err Is Human: Building a Safer Health System*. Washington, DC: National Academies Press.

Jencks, S. F., E. D. Huff, and T. Cuerdon. 2003. "Change in the Quality of Care Delivered to Medicare Beneficiaries. 1998–1999 to 2000–2001." *Journal of the American Medical Association* (289): 305–12.

Joch, A. 2001. "Customer Relationship Management." *Healthcare Informatics* 18 (2): 70, 72.

Johnston, D., E. Pan, and B. Middleton. 2002. *Finding the Value in Healthcare Information Technologies*. Boston: Center for Information Technology Leadership.

Kaushal, R., K. N. Barker, and D. W. Bates. 2001. "How Can Information Technology Improve Patient Safety and Reduce Medication Errors in Children's Healthcare?" *Archives of Pediatric Adolescent Medicine* 155 (9): 1002–7.

Landry, M. D., and W. J. Sibbald. 2001. "From Data to Evidence: Evaluative Methods in Evidence-Based Medicine." *Respiratory Care* 46 (11): 1226–35.

Lovern, E. 2001. "IOM Strikes Again." *Modern Healthcare*, March 5, 4–6.

National Alliance for Health Information Technology. 2007. "What Is Interoperability?" [Online article; retrieved 12/11/07.] http://www.nahit.org/cms/ index.php?option=com_content&task=view&id=186&Itemid=195

Oravec, J. A. 2001. "On the Proper Use of the Internet: Self-Help Medical Information and On-Line Healthcare." *Journal of Health and Social Policy* 14 (1): 37–60.

Pfeffer, J., and R. I. Sutton. 2006. "Evidence-Based Management." *Harvard Business Review* 84 (1): 62–74, 133.

Reece, R. L. 2000. "A New Industrial Order for Physicians: A Talk with Jeff C. Goldsmith, Ph.D." *Physician Executive* 26 (1): 16–19.

Sidorov, J. 2006. "It Ain't Necessarily So: The Electronic Health Record and the Unlikely Prospect of Reducing Healthcare Costs." *Health Affairs* 25 (4): 1079–85.

Smaltz, D., J. Glaser, R. Skinner, and T. Cunningham III (eds.). 2005. *The CEO-CIO Partnership: Harnessing the Value of Information Technology in Healthcare.* Chicago: Healthcare Information and Management Systems Society.

Stammer, L. 2001. "Wireless: As Technology Improves, New Applications Take Off." *Healthcare Informatics* 18 (2): 50, 52.

Tabar, P. 2001. "Data Security." *Healthcare Informatics* 18 (2): 46, 48.

Thorpe, K. 2005. "The Rise in Healthcare Spending and What to Do About It." *Health Affairs* 24 (6): 1436–45.

U.S. Bureau of Labor Statistics. 2007. "Price Index." [Online information; retrieved 12/28/07.] http://www.bls.gov/cpi/

U.S. Department of Health and Human Services. 2001. "Protecting the Privacy of Patients' Health Information." HHS Fact Sheet, May 9. Washington, DC: Department of Health and Human Services.

Walker, J., E. Pan, D. Johnston, J. Adler-Milstein, D. Bates, and B. Middleton. 2005. "The Value of Health Care Exchange and Interoperability." *Health Affairs.* Web Exclusive (W5–10-W5–18). [Online article; retrieved 2/1/08.] http://content.healthaffairs.org/cgi/content/full/hlthaff.w5.10/DC1

Walshe, K., and T. G. Rundall. 2001. "Evidence-Based Management: From Theory to Practice in Healthcare." *Milbank Quarterly* 79 (3): 429–457.

Wiecha, J., and T. Pollard. 2004. "The Interdisciplinary eHealth Team: Chronic Care for the Future." *Journal of Medical Internet Research* 6 (3): e22.

Wilensky, G. R. 2006. "Consumer-Driven Health Plans: Early Evidence and Potential Impact on Hospitals." *Health Affairs* 25 (1): 174–85.

LEADERSHIP: THE CASE OF THE HEALTHCARE ORGANIZATION CIO

Learning Objectives

1. List job duties and analyze functional responsibilities of senior healthcare leadership and the chief information officer (CIO).
2. Identify key knowledge, skills, and abilities of the CIO position.
3. Describe the alternative paths to leadership of healthcare information systems.
4. Prepare and assess an organizational chart for the information services area of a healthcare organization.
5. Illustrate future challenges faced by healthcare CIOs.

This chapter discusses the leadership, human resources, and management expertise required to make effective use of information and the information technology infrastructure in healthcare organizations. In the last edition of this book, this chapter was located in the "Conclusion and Future Directions" section. Moving the chapter to the front of the book for the new edition reflects both the increased complexity of information management in today's healthcare delivery environment and the important role that IM/IT leadership plays in managing that environment. Senior management of information systems departments must now plan for and implement systems to meet today's information needs; anticipate tomorrow's information needs for the organization; and ensure a smooth transition between today's systems and technology and those of tomorrow. While doing so, they confront rapidly evolving hardware and software capabilities and ever-changing government interventions that shift the rules influencing the collection, transmission, storage, retrieval, and dissemination of healthcare information.

Senior leadership cannot hope to master all or even most of these individual complex challenges. They must, however, understand these challenges in sufficient detail to effectively manage content experts. Consequently, this chapter details the current functional responsibilities of chief information officers (CIOs), including the organization, staffing, and budgeting of the IM/IT department and the organizational challenge of outsourcing or multisourcing information management/information technology (IM/IT) functions. It concludes with a brief examination of future trends in the role of the CIO and the leadership team of healthcare organizations.

Organizing for Healthcare Information Management

Determining what area of leadership is responsible for the management of information technology in the healthcare organization has always been a key responsibility of the chief executive officer (CEO) and the governing board. Historically, many healthcare organizations have assigned information management responsibility to the chief financial officer (CFO), reflecting the high priority assigned to fulfilling the need for accurate and timely financial information and, in particular, patient billing.

Because of the increasing importance of clinical information systems, the regulatory reporting requirements, and the use of information in strategic planning and decision support, often healthcare organizations now assign the responsibility for information management and communications to a separate executive-level position, the CIO. This shift has led to the publication of a host of books concentrating on the CIO and his or her evolving roles (e.g., Smaltz et al. 2005; Broadbent and Kitzis 2005).

The Senior Management Role Today

Discussions of the roles of senior IM/IT management begin with active engagement by senior executives in the organization. Weill and Ross (2004) studied organizations that successfully managed information technologies and identified 10 characteristics that these successful organizations had in common. Figure 2.1 summarizes these 10 items in a checklist.

Many features contribute to the success of organizational information technology endeavors, and this checklist reinforces the important role of the CIO and other senior leaders. The governance design (item 1) must focus on objectives and performance goals of the organization rather than simply on considerations of IM/IT's internal operations. Senior executives must design, lead, and regularly review the IM/IT governance functions. Similarly, in effective organizations, senior management must get involved in strategic decisions as well as technology decisions that have strategic implications (item 3). More than just involvement, good governance requires leaders to make choices (item 4). Conflicting goals in complex organizations are inevitable and, if not handled well, lead to problems.

At a more fundamental level, successful information technology must provide the right incentives and rewards (item 6) within the organization and assign ownership/accountability (item 7). Key to healthcare is the importance of incentives to foster synergy between and among operating units. Likewise, accountability for governance design, implementation, and performance must be firmly assigned at the CEO, CIO, or board committee level. Weill and Ross (2004) recommend that the board or CEO hold the CIO accountable for IM/IT governance, and clear success metrics must be part of the performance appraisal. With these considerations, the selection of the CIO leader is vital. Because information technology performance depends upon

---

1. Actively design governance
2. Know when to redesign
3. Involve senior managers
4. Make choices
5. Clarify the exception-handling process
6. Provide the right incentives
7. Assign ownership [of] and accountability for information technology governance
8. Design governance at multiple organizational levels
9. Provide transparency and education
10. Implement common mechanisms across the six key assets

FIGURE 2.1
Ten Features Common to Successful IM/IT Governance

Source: From *IT Governance: How Top Performers Manage IT Decision Rights for Superior Results* by Weill and Ross, Harvard Business School Press, 2004. Used with permission.

all organizational components, those accountable must possess a broad view of the organization (that is, no leader can protect his or her "turf"); other organizational leaders must be aware that they, too, contribute to information technology governance; and all must understand the symbiotic relation between IM/IT and the organization's strategic approach.

While they are considered relatively novel and were obtained from a variety of industries, the 10-item checklist of success indicators are not that far removed from those found historically in healthcare. Austin, Hornberger, and Shmerling (2000) report on management audits conducted by senior management at 10 healthcare organizations. The audits evaluated how well the following seven responsibilities for IM/IT management were carried out: (1) strategic information systems planning, (2) employment of a user focus in system development, (3) recruiting of competent personnel, (4) system integration, (5) protection of information security and confidentiality, (6) employment of effective project management in system development, and (7) postimplementation evaluation of systems. Virtually all of these responsibilities receive substantial direction from information systems governance.

To meet these responsibilities, a solid and mutually supportive relationship between the CEO and the CIO is essential. According to Charles Emory, CIO of Horizon Blue Cross Blue Shield of New Jersey, "Two-way communication, especially between CIOs and CEOs is particularly critical now . . . with use of the Internet making the results of senior management efforts visible to everyone, inside and outside the organization" (Hagland 2001, 19).

Functional Responsibilities of the CIO

Information systems can be useful to management, provided the process for planning, designing, installing, and operating such systems is itself well managed. The CEO and other senior managers of healthcare organizations must assume the responsibility for planning and controlling the development of effective information systems to serve their organizations, as observed above. These tasks cannot be delegated to technical personnel if information processes are to be truly supportive of high-quality patient care and managerial decision making. Information is essential in today's competitive environment for strategic planning, cost and productivity management, continuous quality improvement, and program evaluation purposes. Important senior management responsibilities are summarized in Figure 2.2.

The person assuming these responsibilities—increasingly known as the CIO—must have broad corporate and system understanding and also must have the ability to lead teams of technical experts responsible for complex information technology. Reporting directly to the CEO (or chief operating officer in some large organizations), the CIO serves two important functions: (1) to assist the senior management team and governing board in using information effectively to support strategic planning and management and (2) to provide management oversight and coordination of information processing and telecommunications systems throughout the organization.

The functions of the CIO are integral to any healthcare business, irrespective of size. In larger organizations, the CIO should be a full-time position. In smaller hospitals and clinics, these responsibilities may be assigned to another administrative officer. A small physician group practice must assign CIO functions or oversight to someone as well, often the group practice manager or one of the physicians in the practice who has an interest and some expertise in managing information technology. In short, even if an individual with the CIO title does not exist in the organization, someone must be responsible for making strategic and operational decisions regarding information technology for the organization.

The range and scope of specific CIO job responsibilities flow from the senior management responsibilities described above. The scope can be defined in a number of ways but generally includes the following:

- Enterprisewide planning
- Leadership
- Management oversight
- Human resources management
- Financial management

Figure 2.3 contains information synthesized from job descriptions and from leading healthcare search firms that describes the range and scope of responsibilities.

Notice that technical expertise is not mentioned as a separate responsibility. While the successful CIO cannot be ignorant of healthcare information systems and communication systems, he or she does not generally become directly involved in the details of software development or hardware design issues. At the same time, some degree of technical competence is crucial for the CIO to effectively manage an organization's IM/IT functions. Generally, the CIO must provide a vision for healthcare technology for the organization

FIGURE 2.2
Senior
Management
Responsibilities

- Management must insist on a careful planning process that precedes all major decisions related to the installation of computer equipment or the design of complex information systems. A master plan for information systems development should be created and updated at least once a year. The master plan should be linked to the strategic plan of the healthcare organization and should guide all specific implementation decisions.
- Management must employ a user-driven focus throughout the development process. Active involvement of personnel from all segments of the healthcare organization is essential. This participation should begin with a definition of information requirements before the organization considers acquisition of hardware and software. It should continue through all phases of analysis, design, system evaluation and selection, and implementation.
- Management must take the responsibility for recruiting competent personnel for the design and operation of information systems. Consideration should be given to recruitment of a CIO to serve as a member of the senior management team. When outsourcing is used, careful selection of vendors and contract negotiations with the assistance of legal counsel should precede the award of contracts for software, equipment, or services.
- Managers at the corporate level must establish policies and procedures to ensure integration of data files or interfacing among individual information systems for tracking patient flows, consolidating cost and financial data, monitoring quality of care, and evaluating individual products and services. Interoperability of data among systems is an absolute necessity in complex healthcare organizations, particularly those involving subsidiary units and central corporate management.
- Management personnel at all levels must adhere to legal and ethical obligations to maintain security of information systems and to protect the confidentiality of patients, human resources, and other sensitive information.
- The design of individual computer applications must be carried out by an interdisciplinary project team. Systems analysts and computer programmers will take the lead on technical analysis and design activities. Representatives of user departments should help guide the specification of system requirements and evaluate the technical design plans of the analysts. Management should be involved in all major design projects to ensure congruence with organizational goals and objectives, and it should insist on a user-driven system focus rather than a technology-driven focus.
- Once a project team has been organized, careful systems analysis should precede any implementation decisions. Shortcuts in the systems analysis phase will inevitably lead to problems later in the process.
- Managers must ensure that the preliminary design specifications for computer applications are in harmony with the master plan for information systems development.
- Detailed system specifications must be required before any implementation activities take place. These specifications should be reviewed formally and approved by all user departments and by management before proceeding with the next steps in system development.
- Throughout the analysis, design, and implementation phases of a project, management must require careful scheduling of all activities and should receive periodic progress reports as the project proceeds.

continued

FIGURE 2.2
Continued

- Managers must ensure thorough training of all personnel involved in the implementation phase of the new system.
- No computer application should be put into operation without first carrying out a comprehensive system test. The testing should cover all phases of system operation, including computer programs and procedures, personnel training, user satisfaction, ability of the system to meet original objectives, and accuracy of the initial cost estimates.
- Provisions must always be made for adequate maintenance after an application is operational. Maintenance procedures are essential to correct operational errors, to make system improvement, and to facilitate changes necessitated by changes in organizational needs.
- Management must make certain that information systems are periodically audited and that all systems are formally evaluated once they are installed and operating normally.

FIGURE 2.3
Major Duties
and
Responsibilities
of the CIO

The CIO provides leadership and a vision for developing and implementing information technology for the organization. Major duties and responsibilities include:
- Enterprisewide planning
- Information technology leadership
- Management and oversight
- Human resources management
- Financial management

Sources: Adapted from specific job descriptions and information provided on the websites of select search firms, including hrVillage.com, Community Clinics Initiative, Witt/Keifer, Healthcare Recruiters International, Heidrick & Struggles, Korn/Ferry International, and Tyler & Company.

and leadership for developing and implementing IM/IT initiatives. These initiatives increasingly range from the boardroom to the clinical suites. Many IM/IT initiatives are often designed to improve cost effectiveness of clinical and administrative functions, enhance the quality of healthcare service, and support business development. All initiatives assist the organization in navigating the constantly changing competitive marketplace.

The CIO will lead in planning and implementing enterprise information systems to support all aspects of both distributed and centralized clinical and business operations. Figure 2.4 provides a select list of knowledge, skills, and abilities of CIOs. Notice that a significant portion of the skill set and demonstrated abilities extends beyond the traditional IM/IT domain.

This discussion is not meant to imply that those with significant technical expertise cannot become the next CIO. There are many paths to this leadership position, and technical expertise provides as good a path as any other. However, moving to the C-suite, as the CIO title implies, does require a skill set beyond technical expertise.

- Collaboration
- Understanding the nature of the health system
- Formulation of IM/IT components of strategic plan
- IM/IT strategic business and market planning
- IM/IT needs analysis
- Organization's IM/IT situation
- IM/IT culture
- Assess state of industry
- Technology assessment
- Evaluation, adoption, and implementation standards
- IM/IT policy development

FIGURE 2.4
Select CIO
Required
Knowledge,
Skills, and
Abilities

Source: Waterloo Institute for Health Informatics Research (2007).

Characteristics of a Successful CIO

The CIO must possess a good understanding of the healthcare environment, be an experienced manager, and have sufficient understanding of information technology to ensure that information systems are properly planned and implemented. He or she must also assure that all IM/IT internal systems function properly. As a simple example, pharmacy systems, whether stand-alone or integrated, must operate continuously or the organization will be unable to control dangerous drugs (particularly narcotics), drug ordering and inventory control, control of drug distribution to patients, storage and retrieval of drug information, construction of patient drug profiles, maintenance of the organization's formulary, and generation of charges for billing (see Chapter 8). Success depends on many factors internal and external to the CIO areas of influence. In a recent article outlining the secrets of success, Kramer (2006) summarized the skills needed for success beyond those outlined above. Based on information from CIOs responding to a national survey, Kramer found that successful CIOs have skills in business, clinical processes, leadership, administration, and communication. These key items were listed in addition to "technical savvy."

Despite these findings, Healthcare Information and Management Systems Society (Scottsdale Institute and HIMSS Analytics 2005, Figure 20) survey data suggest that a key element of success for the CIO is a narrow focus on meeting budgets and timelines for projects. The broader goals of meeting financial or organizational business measurements are recognized but are less important. Further, nearly two in three respondents to that survey indicated that success depends in part on the active role that the CEO plays in supporting IM/IT projects. The CEO does not set the vision or direction of IM/IT in most cases but must actively support the CIO's initiatives.

Interestingly, factors beyond the specific characteristics of the CIO do matter as well. The Scottsdale Institute and HIMSS Analytics (2005, Figure 19) survey findings suggest that executive ownership and accountability in

IM/IT projects as well as the alignment of IM/IT process to the business goals of the organization are critical factors for IM/IT success. However, governance per se was given as a critical success factor by few respondents.

More important than specific training, the successful CIO must have work experience in healthcare. The same Scottsdale Institute and HIMSS Analytics (2005, Figure 8) survey indicates that most CIOs and directors of information systems come from a healthcare IM/IT experience. Fewer than one in eight current CIOs got their start in other industries. Nearly a quarter of respondents indicated that they had formal management education specific to information systems, and an equal percentage had technical IM/IT training. More than one-third (38 percent) of respondents had business training. Relatively few had clinical origins. In the future, as IM/IT supports care delivery, it will be important for CIOs to have a clinical as well as a healthcare management background. Alternatively, the CIO may need a medical information officer as part of his or her organization to serve as a liaison to clinical healthcare delivery.

Organization of the Information Systems Department

The organizational structure for the information systems department should be guided by the institution's strategic objectives and information systems plan (see Chapter 3). Thus, the CIO must be aware of where he or she fits into the broader organizational framework and how best to structure the internal operating responsibilities. With respect to reporting relations, the pervasive nature of the management of information in healthcare organizations and the key role information management plays in achieving the organization's strategic initiatives suggest that the CIO should report to the CEO. Despite this seeming necessity, the most recent data from Scottsdale Institute and HIMSS Analytics (2005, Figure 2) suggest that only a little more than a third (37 percent) of CIOs report to their CEO. An almost equal percentage (38 percent) report to the head of finance or the CFO. The remainder of the CIOs responding to the 2005 survey report to a chief operating officer, a chief medical officer, or another senior executive.

As mentioned above, the CIO oversees a broad range of functions, so the organizational chart must be sufficiently complex to fully capture that scope of responsibility. Organizations have not standardized that range of services reporting to the CIO. Consequently, organizational charts look different across institutions. The size and complexity of tasks to be carried out by a central information systems department in a healthcare organization are affected by a number of factors, including the following:

- Degree of centralization or distribution of computer systems throughout the organization
- Use of in-house developed systems

- Use of packaged software or contracts with application service providers
- Extent to which functions/tasks are outsourced to contractors

Despite this variety in organizational approaches, a fairly typical information systems organizational structure for a single hospital or medical center can be derived (see Figure 2.5). In this scenario, the information systems department manager reports to the CIO, along with the director of management engineering, the director of telecommunications, and the director of health information management. In large healthcare organizations and systems, these directors often have substantial staffs, whereas in midsize organizations, a single person might occupy several of these functional boxes and even have other job responsibilities. In small organizations, a single person might be responsible for all of these functions. In any case, the functions will exist.

Looking in more detail at the organization of the IM/IT department reveals that beyond the first level of reporting relations to the CIO, the organizational structure is even more variable. Figure 2.6 depicts the configuration for an IM/IT operations division. Such a division often consists of four major components: systems development, software evaluation, user support, and operations. Professional staff members in systems development are responsible for system design and implementation. This subdepartment is itself organized into three main sections: programming, systems analysis, and system maintenance. The software evaluation subdepartments are responsible for evaluation of software systems in the health applications area. They must also review and approve all hardware and software acquisitions proposed by user departments and provide technical support on software utilization. The user support staff often will operate a "help desk" that users can contact for hardware and software assistance. Finally, the operations subdepartment includes network maintenance, data preparation and editing, and computer operations.

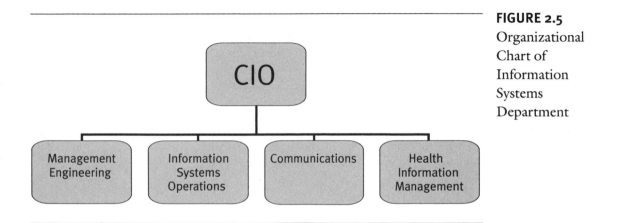

FIGURE 2.5

Organizational Chart of Information Systems Department

FIGURE 2.6
Organizational
Chart of the
Systems
Operations
Division

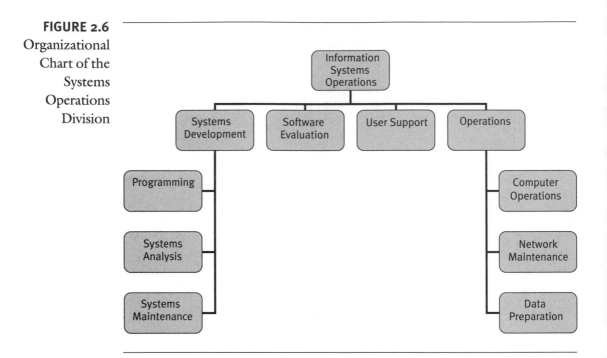

The general organizational structure may vary, but data are available to support the specific structure as presented here. Scottsdale Institute and HIMSS Analytics (2005, Figure 7) survey data, for example, indicate that 71 percent of IM/IT departments had telecommunications, 18 percent had health information management, and 9 percent had biomedical engineering staff reporting to them. For larger organizations, it is more likely that the CIO will have only a narrowly defined IM/IT function.

Beyond this typical organizational structure, two other characteristics are important to note:

1. Most organizations (85 percent) report having an IM/IT steering committee. The role of this committee is to provide strategic direction for information systems decisions. The IM/IT steering committees tend to provide strategic approval (90 percent) for IM/IT decisions, have involvement in budgetary decisions (63 percent), and play a role in vendor selection (33 percent). These committees are generally viewed as improving IM/IT operational and strategic effectiveness and link the IM/IT department to potential and actual end users. Smaller organizations are less likely to have this linkage function.

2. In many organizations, some information systems staff report to directors in departments outside of information systems and do not report directly to the CIO. For example, while 40 percent of survey respondents indicated that none of their staff reported outside of information systems, 40 percent indicated that they had staff reporting to laboratory

departments, 35 percent had staff reporting to the radiology department, and 25 percent had staff reporting to the pharmacy department. This complexity necessitates a leadership and governance model to promote coordination, standards, and efficiency (Scottsdale Institute and HIMSS Analytics 2005).

Staffing of the IM/IT Department

Given the organizational structure defined in the prior section, IM/IT departments and sections must be populated. Selecting the individuals with the necessary skills and expertise is the next responsibility of the CIO. The best organizational structure of IM/IT will not be successful without optimal staffing. Naturally, from the CIO's perspective, matching the skills and expertise of his or her direct reports with their areas of responsibility is most important, but staff selection and assignment is essential throughout IM/IT. Staffing decisions should follow from the organizational design of the unit. Generally, the directors reporting to the CIO should have more technical and operational knowledge, experience, and expertise in their assigned areas than the CIO. Leadership must be able to count on these individuals to plan, design, and implement the best technology solutions in their area. For example, health information management should be headed by an experienced and certified registered health information administrator with broad knowledge of information flow and electronic health record knowledge.

As a rule, three levels of personnel must be recruited for staffing an information systems department: professional, technical, and clerical. Professional staff include systems analysts and computer programmers. Although finding talented persons who can fill both roles is possible, care must be exercised in not equating the two. Systems analysis requires broad-based skills that computer programmers often do not possess. It is a highly creative process requiring someone with both technical knowledge of analytical and design techniques and a broad organizational focus. Because most systems are complex and involve substantial human-machine interaction, the systems analyst must be able to deal effectively with people and must understand how the organization carries out its mission. Programmers often have a more narrow orientation and are skilled in the technical tasks of software development and maintenance. Programming requirements are changing. As healthcare organizations move toward the implementation of client/server architecture, network programmers are largely replacing those who used to write and maintain large programs for mainframe computers.

An experienced technical manager, reporting to the CIO, should head information systems operations. He or she must have up-to-date knowledge of the technical aspects of systems analysis, computer programming, hardware and software, networks, and telecommunications systems. The manager must be willing to spend the time and effort necessary to stay abreast of the latest technical knowledge in a rapidly changing field. In addition, the manager must be an experienced financial manager and must be skilled in interpersonal relations.

Technician-level personnel operate the computers and maintain the communications network. Skilled network managers are highly trained and are often in short supply. The operations supervisor must be both a skilled technician and an effective manager. Equipment maintenance is usually handled by contracting with vendors who supply periodic preventive maintenance and emergency repairs on call (see the section on outsourcing).

The approach to organizing and staffing the IM/IT department depends upon the level of complexity of the organization. For example, an integrated delivery system composed of multiple facilities is usually much more complex than that of a single facility, resulting in a more complex IM/IT function. Further, as a matter of culture, some systems are highly centralized, with all software development carried out by a corporate information technology staff. In other, less complex systems, more responsibility may be delegated to operational units. Whatever the approach, the organizational structure must facilitate electronic information exchange across the enterprise (DeFord and Porter 2005).

Staffing for IM/IT has grown rapidly in recent years and appears to be continuing upward. Most respondents in the HIMSS (2006) CIO survey indicated staffing would grow in the future. Of the types of staff most in demand, network and architecture support has the greatest identified need (27 percent), although that need is less than in past years. Other growth areas include clinical informaticists (24 percent), process/workflow designers (24 percent) and application support/development staff (22 percent). In total, only 1 in 12 respondents indicated no current IM/IT staffing needs.

Budgeting the IM/IT Department

Budgets for IM/IT in healthcare organizations are increasing, but they remain low both in absolute terms and relative to similar spending in other industries (Salkever 2004). Fully 54 percent of respondents indicated that their organization spent 2.5 percent or less of their operating budget on IM/IT, and only 14 percent indicated that they spent more than 3.5 percent on IM/IT (HIMSS 2006). More than 70 percent of CIOs indicated that IM/IT spending will increase in the coming year, which corresponds closely to survey responses in the last several years. Of this total, an increase was expected in the future by 45 percent of the respondents, and only 1 in 16 indicated that budgets would decrease. More than half of respondents (54 percent) noted that, regardless of an increase or a decrease in dollars budgeted, the percentage of their organizations' operating budget that is presently spent on IM/IT will remain within the same budget range in 2006. Reasons for the increase in spending are growth in the number of systems and technologies (80 percent), alignment with the long-term IM/IT or organizational strategic plan (48 percent), and an overall budget increase (41 percent). For those expecting a decrease, nearly half of the respondents (46 percent) attributed this decrease to overall budget decreases at their organization.

The budget increases for healthcare IM/IT are likely to continue as labor shortages continue to drive labor costs up and as technology advancements lead to more opportunities for expanded and enhanced services. Despite the emphasis on hardware and software, however, labor costs continue to be the key driver of IM/IT costs. Starting with the CIO, Table 2.1 presents the average, median, and quartile ranges of salaries for CIOs overall, for CIOs in various work settings, and for select numbers of IM/IT staff. As can be seen, the "average" CIO in all settings made $151,000 in 2006, with 25 percent making more than $180,000 and 25 percent making less than $115,000. Project managers on average made $86,800, and 25 percent earned more than $97,500.

Outsourcing and Multisourcing

Many healthcare organizations are considering outsourcing portions of their information systems functions as an alternative to in-house staffing. The decision to outsource entails purchasing the services from an external vendor or contractor (buy) rather than hiring the staff and producing the service in-house (make). This make-buy decision must be seriously considered as the complexity of healthcare IM/IT increases. Traditionally, the term *outsourcing* has been associated with a contract for facilities management. More recently, however, the term is used in a broader context to denote contracting with

TABLE 2.1 Salary Information for CIO and Select IM/IT Staff, 2006

Title	Average	Median	75% Earn More Than	25% Earn More Than
CIO	$151,319	$145,000	$115,000	$180,000
CIO—Multihospital/IDN	$172,096	$170,000	$140,000	$208,000
CIO—Stand-Alone Hospital	$140,354	$130,000	$106,000	$166,000
CIO—Other Facility	$125,233	$116,500	$80,000	$182,500
CIO—Consulting Firm	$170,214	$176,000	$135,000	$185,000
CIO—Physician Office	$139,400	$142,500	$100,000	$185,000
Director of Information Service	$103,570	$101,000	$84,000	$117,000
Management Engineer	$87,360	$87,000	$70,000	$110,000
Software Developer/Engineer	$79,802	$85,000	$69,616	$110,000
Security Officer	$111,149	$97,347	$93,600	$133,900
Project Manager	$86,859	$85,000	$72,000	$97,500
Systems Analyst	$63,306	$61,000	$55,000	$76,000
Medical Records Director	$79,626	$76,760	$59,000	$107,000
Help Desk Operator	$46,216	$40,000	$27,040	$95,000

Note: IDN = Integrated Delivery Network
Source: HIMSS and HIMSS Analytics (2006). Used with permission.

the best-qualified company to meet a specific information systems objective. This may involve multisourcing to a number of different vendors as well as the conventional outsourcing to a single vendor.

Some of the major potential benefits of outsourcing include the following:

1. Reduction of in-house staffing requirements
2. Smaller investment in capital equipment
3. More flexibility in meeting changing requirements and adopting new technology
4. Reduction in the time required to implement new applications
5. More predictable cost structure, particularly if fixed-price contracting is employed

Outsourcing is not without potential danger and risks to the organization and to the CIO leading the outsourcing initiatives and come with the following pitfalls:

1. Too much dependence on vendors, with the possibility that a critical contractor might go bankrupt or change business direction
2. High costs associated with vendor fees and profit structure
3. Employment of contractors who do not understand the operation and culture of healthcare organizations

Hensley (1997) describes some of the principles to follow in outsourcing. He emphasizes the importance of weighing the cultural fit with the vendor; suggests that outsourcing be part of a long-term strategy (not just a quick fix); and recommends good reference checking, looking for staying power among vendors being considered. Further, Hensley states that healthcare organizations should not contract out the things they do best, should not become obsessed with short-term savings, and should not negotiate such favorable terms in a contract that a business partner is put out of business.

Waymack (2000) offers the following four suggestions for selecting outsourcing firms:

1. Seek long-term commitments, because the costs of switching vendors can be substantial.
2. Require relevant experience with the specific service to be outsourced.
3. Develop performance measures for selection based on the services to be outsourced.
4. Do not base evaluation solely on the lowest bid.

From the broader business perspective, many back-office functions are commonly outsourced. For example, Hali (2007) reports that more than two of three firms engage in some form of business process outsourcing. His study examines accounts receivable specifically and finds five key arguments for outsourcing:

1. *Bottom line*—Contrary to the general expectation, outsourcing does not reduce costs but may generate increased recoveries. This is the primary reason firms outsource accounts receivable.
2. *Expertise*—Because you outsource to a firm whose core business is the outsourced function, the firm's staff have greater expertise in the function and you achieve excellence.
3. *Technology*—Similarly, the firm you work with employs the most current technology. That often leads to better outcomes. Because this technology often requires substantial investment, the firm has technology-based cost advantages.
4. *Consistency*—A dedicated staff in the outsourcing firm ensures that invoices are followed up on in a timely and professional manner.
5. *Core business focus*—By outsourcing an important but noncore business, you are free to concentrate on your core business.

Similarly, Menachemi and colleagues (2005) report systematically on the nature and extent of outsourcing by urban/rural status, ownership (not-for-profit/for-profit), hospital size, system affiliation, CIO reporting relationship, and information technology strategy value. They also report outsourcing rates for a number of specific IM/IT functions in six broad categories. The categories, with examples of function and reported outsourcing rates, include the following:

1. *Development/integration*—applications development, 11.3 percent
2. *Staffing*—CIO, 14.4 percent
3. *Operations/management*—personal computer support, 15.5 percent
4. *Employee support and training*—help desk, 6.2 percent
5. *Applications and services*—transcriptions, 51.5 percent
6. *Web-related*—e-business, 4.1 percent

Many examples of outsourcing can be found, all with direct application to a particular type of information technology. For instance, Jefferson Regional Medical Center in the Pittsburgh area worked with Siemens Medical Solutions to fulfill the strategic goal of bringing "medical excellence closer to home" (Siemens Medical Solutions 2005, 1). For Jefferson, this goal meant reducing costs and enhancing its quality reputation. Information technology was targeted as the vehicle to implement the goal, and the decision to outsource IM/IT was integral to achieving it. Jefferson employed a CIO to manage the Siemens outsourcing relationship. Their joint vision was that IM/IT should always deliver appropriate technology and resources to meet the hospital's strategic goals.

This outsourcing collaboration was reported to result in many positive effects; some of the key results included the following:

- The decision support and managed care recovery unit recovered $1 million in revenue in 16 months through the use of Siemens' Contract Management System.
- This unit recovered an additional $400,000 in charges in 16 months by correcting clinical documentation issues concerning comorbidity conditions prior to patient discharge.
- Jefferson's accounting department worked with IM/IT to automate employee time reporting and management to reduce payroll department staff by half while improving manager online reporting capacity.

The successful outsourcing experience appears to be leading to other joint efforts. Jefferson and Siemens are currently collaborating to provide personal digital assistants (PDAs) for physicians. Using fingerprint identification technology for security, physicians will be able to access patient information from their PDAs throughout the hospital. In the future, this collaboration and outsourcing will invest in technology to tackle picture archiving and communications system integration, critical care, and electronic medical records (EMRs).

Results of the CIO portion of the *Seventeenth Annual HIMSS Leadership Survey* (HIMSS 2006) indicated that 38 percent of the organizations responding to the survey outsourced the development and maintenance of their websites, 33 percent outsourced dictation and transcription services, 19 percent outsourced applications development, 19 percent outsourced project management, 18 percent outsourced both the help desk function and database management, and 17 percent outsourced telecommunications. Interestingly, these numbers were similar to prior years, except that outsourcing personal computer support, network operations support, and technical support did not make the 2006 list, and dictation and transcription was new to the outsourcing list in 2006. Twenty-nine percent of respondents indicated that they did not outsource any IM/IT functions.

Evolving Role of the Senior IM/IT Executive

Looking into the future of IM/IT and the role of the IM/IT executive is an exercise filled with uncertainty. A number of analysts have carefully considered the role that advancements in IM/IT are likely to have on the organization of health delivery entities. Brynjolfsson and Hitt (2000) and Oliner and Sichel (2000), among others, examine the relationship of technology and productivity growth. They find that organizational change is needed to capture the potential to which computers and other technology offer support. Without fundamental changes in the ability of managers to "invent new processes, procedures and organizational structures that leverage this capability" (Brynjolfsson and Hitt 2000, 24), the gains from increased IM/IT spending may not be realized. The CIO is at the center of the changing role of IM/IT and its potential impact on healthcare delivery system. However, the future-looking findings from the HIMSS Analytics (2005) *Annual Report of the US Hospital IT Market* reveal the nature of that future:

- *Hospitals continue to underinvest in IM/IT spending* as represented in the low percentages of installed EMR and clinical applications. Hospitals have done a better job of purchasing and implementing applications such as revenue cycle management, financial management, and health information management; even these are legacy applications that may not be able to address the future of ever more complex billing requirements.
- *Replacement technologies and applications* are emerging in the EMR environment. Leaders must constantly look for emerging technologies that have known application advantages but are currently cost prohibitive. Price decreases in the future may make them financially attractive as well. For example, radio-frequency identification (RFID) is beginning to replace current bar-coding applications as RFID becomes more cost effective.
- *Interoperability concerns,* driven by increasing implementation of EMRs, are affecting ancillary and clinical departmental applications. National guidelines for interoperability will eventually standardize the applications in pharmacy, radiology, laboratories, and ambulatory settings, but until they are fully applicable, interoperability is a major concern for the CIO.
- *Ambulatory application environments* still need to fully adopt EMR beyond the current low rate.
- *Healthcare executives must support increased IM/IT budgets* and establish business unit accountability for achieving value from IM/IT-enabled business and clinical initiatives.

Specific business issues faced by senior executives in healthcare IM/IT have remained essentially the same from year to year in recent years. HIMSS (2006) indicates that customer satisfaction, Medicare cutbacks, reducing medical errors, and cost pressures are the four top business priorities, all of which were at or near the top in 2005. New to the 2006 survey, interoperability was the fifth leading business concern.

Senior Leadership's Role

In discussing the changing role of healthcare CIOs, Wood (2000, 81) states, "in the past, chief information officers were responsible for nothing else but assuring a constant flow of information. Today, they are being asked to do a great deal more. From E-business to E-health strategy, the chief information officer is the focal point of an organization's ability to leverage new technology." The CIO role has expanded since Wood made this statement, with the explosion of concern about healthcare quality, cost pressure, efficiency concerns due to labor shortages, and other constraints. CIOs have emphasized their strategic role rather than their technical management role (Morrissey 1996). The complicating and often unmentioned point is that the CIO position is usually not the first job that person holds out of college. Most CIOs started their career in intermediate-level positions and, if successful, rose to the CIO position. The initial jobs can be in the information systems/information technology areas or can be outside of this domain entirely. CIOs of the future may come from medicine, nursing, or other clinical/administrative areas. The prior jobs, especially in information systems/information technology, require the candidate for CIO to have technical or data management skills to be successful. In other words, CIOs do not need the technical skills once they become a CIO but may need those skills to get there.

One way of looking at this new role is to realize that the CIO no longer just manages one of many operating units within a healthcare organization. He or she must now look beyond IM/IT and engage in significant strategic thinking on behalf of his or her unit as well as the entire organization. The broad classifications of CIO activities encompass the following three distinct interest groups:

1. *Up*—The CEO and/or the board rely upon the CIO to assist in strategic and operational planning for the organization as a whole by supporting enterprisewide planning. This is a future-looking role, which is, by nature, strategic. However, they also require the CIO to effectively manage data quality and integrity to comply with government regulations such as the Sarbanes-Oxley Act of 2002.
2. *Horizontal*—Executive leaders throughout the hospital, such as the CFO, chief medical officer, and chief nursing officer, also rely upon and work closely with the CIO to improve data collection, storage, analysis, and reporting.
3. *Internal*—The CIO must still be able to effectively manage the information technology business unit.

A Scottsdale Institute and HIMSS Analytics (2005) report suggests that less than half of respondents to a survey indicate that the CIO is facilitating IM/IT-related discussions with the board. More often, the CEO or other senior executive has responsibility for board discussions. This trend is not consistent with the growing responsibility of the CIO position. Partly as a result of this incongruity, the future of the CIO is uncertain. For example, the Sarbanes-Oxley reporting requirements may have shifted the responsibility of data integrity away from the CIO and back to the CFO. With that responsibility, CFOs want to control the data warehousing and data management functions more closely. Schwartz (2005) suggests that the CIO as a title will disappear. Functions in the CIO's domain may in the future report through the CFO.

In the future, greater board involvement is likely. Currently, 56 percent of healthcare organization boards approve budgets, and only 39 percent approve specific systems projects (Scottsdale Institute and HIMSS Analytics 2005). Given the central role of IM/IT systems in influencing healthcare quality and organizational competitiveness, boards will likely be more involved in IM/IT decisions in the future.

Priorities for Application Development

Reduction of medical errors and enhancement of patient safety will continue to be "hot issues" among government agencies and private consumer organizations. The Leapfrog Group, a consortium of major purchasers of healthcare, announced early in the 2000s that it was expanding to hospitals its efforts to reduce preventable medical mistakes (Leapfrog Group 2002). Chapter 8 addresses computerized physician order entry as a technique to reduce medication errors in hospitals. Emphasis on the development of computer-based records will continue and will likely be placed on records systems that can support evidence-based medicine and disease management programs.

Communications between patients and providers, facilitated by the Internet, will expand in the next 10 years. Armed with information obtained online, patients will participate more fully in decisions about their care. Home-based monitoring systems will become more common and will help to reduce the need for repeated outpatient visits and to delay or defer the need for institutional care.

Reemphasis on the use of IM/IT for strategic decision support is likely in the next few years. This topic received considerable attention in the early 1990s but was sidetracked by data conversion concerns in anticipation of the year 2000 and then further put off as components of the Health Insurance Portability and Accountability Act were implemented.

System Communications and Interfaces

Developing efficient communications among and between computer applications on an enterprisewide basis continues to be problematic for many healthcare organizations. As reported earlier in this chapter, management audits conducted by senior managers in 10 major healthcare organizations revealed that "most organizations reported concern about this issue [system integration] and stated that they were working toward a solution" (Austin, Hornberger, and Shmerling 2000, 235).

Some organizations continue to have problems in obtaining meaningful data from transaction processing systems to use in decision support and management studies. More emphasis on process reengineering during systems analysis and selection could help to improve the situation. This ongoing problem has now been clearly identified and labeled *interoperability*. As seen in Chapter 1, to improve, care delivery systems must work together within and across organizations. HIMSS Analytics (2005) adopted a definition of interoperability as the ability of health information systems to work together within and across organizational boundaries to advance the effective delivery of healthcare for individuals and communities. Naturally, this is complex in concept and application. The National Alliance for Health Information Technology (2007) endorsed four levels of interoperability with different technical specifications and containing varied organizational implications as defined by Walker and colleagues (2005):

1. *Nonelectronic data*—Sharing information does not include any use of information technology and thus relies on conventional phone service.
2. *Machine-transportable data*—Sharing information with generally available information technology, but that information has not necessarily been standardized and thus cannot be manipulated. This transmission relies on fax transmission or sharing of portable document format files only.
3. *Machine-organizable data*—Sharing information via electronic information technology, but the messages are generally not fully standardized. Data received must be modified by programs (interfaces) that help the receiver to understand its meaning. This transmission might consist of sharing of files stored in incompatible formats.
4. *Machine-interpretable data*—Sharing information via electronic information technology, but the information has been fully standardized in terms of format and vocabulary. This transmission might include coded information from a lab to the receiver's EMR.

Because of this interest, investigators are looking to assess the value of information exchange, which depends upon interoperability. The Center for Information Technology Leadership assessed the expected net value of electronic data transactions using the New York State health information exchange model. It concentrated on measuring the value from clinical encounters among hospitals, medical group practices, and other providers and among major payers, laboratories, pharmacies, and other key stakeholders. The model assumes a full transition to computer-linked data exchange of standardized information, and the measurement was conducted over a 10-year implementation period. The center estimated a net value of electronic data transactions of 3.3 percent of total health expenditures in the state in 2003, or about $4.54 billion (Hook et al. 2006).

Technology

Technology will continue to improve and will offer new opportunities for healthcare organizations during the next 10 years. The most frequently identified technologies cited by respondents to a HIMSS Analytics (2005) survey planned for implementation in the next two years were sign-on/identity management technology, bar-coding technology, speech recognition, and PDAs. This list will likely grow as new applications emerge and become commonplace. For the CIO and other healthcare information technology leaders, the prospect of mastering existing technologies, much less forecasting the next innovation, is overwhelming. Successful leaders will need to maintain a high level of awareness, be flexible to adapt and adopt, and become continuous learners.

Other Challenges

The evolving role of the CIO will face myriad challenges in the future. In addition to those discussed above, survey information suggests the following key priorities to consider (HIMSS Analytics 2005):

- *Security concerns.* Internal breaches of security continue to be the primary security concern identified by healthcare IM/IT executives.
- *Regional health information organizations (RHIOs).* Only 14 percent of respondents report that their organization participates in a RHIO, and nearly three-quarters of respondents report that their organization has not yet begun to plan to participate in a RHIO. This will be a vocabulary item for all CIOs in the future, and the prevalence of RHIOs will rise immediately after interoperability is resolved.
- *Website use.* Few (14 percent) CIOs report that scheduling is currently available on the Web, but many indicate they are moving in that direction.
- *IM/IT outsourcing.* The trend to greater outsourcing, reported above, will continue and may even accelerate in the future.

Summary

This chapter discussed the leadership, human resources, and management expertise required to make effective use of information and information technology infrastructure in healthcare organizations. The organizational position of the CIO has evolved over the years and is now a separate, executive-level role. This elevation is due to the growing importance of clinical systems, regulatory reporting requirements, and the use of information in strategic planning and decision support.

Today, the CIO generally reports directly to the CEO, primarily assists the senior leadership team in using information effectively, and provides management of information processing and telecommunications in the organization. The required skills of the CIO include enterprisewide planning, leadership, management oversight, human resource management, and financial management.

The IM/IT department's organization has also evolved over the years. Generally, managers in management engineering, information systems operations, communications, and health information management report directly to the CIO. It is noted, however, that this department varies widely by size and complexity of the organization. Most IM/IT departments have an information systems steering committee to assist in providing strategic direction. One added complexity of the CIO role is that many organizations have information systems staff who report to operational units outside of information technology.

The evolving role of IM/IT will force the CIO to work "up" to the CEO and board, work horizontally with other hospital leaders, and work internally to manage the IM/IT business unit. Key priorities for the coming years include application development, systems communications, technology adoption, security concerns, RHIOs, website use, and IM/IT outsourcing.

Web Resources

A number of trade and professional organizations support the work of information professionals in the healthcare field, and their websites provide a significant amount of information.

American College of Healthcare Information Administrators (ACHIA). A subunit of the American Academy of Medical Administrators, ACHIA is a personal membership organization for information managers with special focus on continuing education and research in healthcare information administration. For more information, visit www.aameda.org/Specialtygroups/ACHIA/healthcare.html.

American Health Information Management Association (AHIMA). AHIMA is a personal membership organization of information professionals who specialize in the utilization and management of clinical information. For more information, visit www.ahima.org.

American Medical Informatics Association (AMIA). The term *medical informatics* is used to describe the science of storage, retrieval, and optimal use of biomedical information for problem solving and medical decision making. AMIA is a personal membership organization of professionals interested in computer applications in biomedicine. For more information, visit www.amia.org.

College of Healthcare Information Management Executives (CHIME). CHIME is a personal membership organization of CIOs in the healthcare field. CHIME provides professional development and networking opportunities for its members. For more information, visit www .cio-chime.org.

Healthcare Information and Management Systems Society (HIMSS). HIMSS is a personal membership organization representing professionals in clinical systems, information systems, management engineering, and telecommunications. HIMSS provides professional development opportunities to its members through publications and educational programs. For more information, visit www.himss.org.

Waterloo Institute for Health Informatics Research. This comprehensive site details the competencies necessary for CIOs and other IM/IT leadership. At this site, you can view the challenge faced by the CIO or other leader, a detail of the micro roles necessary to meet that challenge, an assessment of the importance of this challenge/role, and even suggestions for how to gain the experience necessary for the role. For more information, visit http://learningspace.uwaterloo.ca/hi/index.php.

Discussion Questions

1. Why is healthcare/clinical experience more important for healthcare CIOs today than in past years?
2. What other factors can increase the size and complexity of the information systems structure, besides those factors already listed?
3. Information systems steering committees are used in most healthcare organizations to make strategic and budgetary decisions. Do you consider the information systems steering committees to be a good design? Why or why not?
4. Why is demand increasing for healthcare IM/IT staffing?
5. Compare the roles/functions and the average salary of a CIO with that of other IM/IT personnel. Are the roles complementary or substitutes? Can you justify salary differences?
6. Do the benefits of outsourcing outweigh the risks? Order the highly ranked outsourced services for riskiest to least risky and explain your rationale for the decision.
7. Based on the changing roles of CIOs, do you agree or disagree with Schwartz (2005) that the role of CIO will disappear?
8. Why is system integration such an important topic in healthcare information technology?
9. Several priorities were given in the chapter for application development. Can healthcare IM/IT assist in any other important priorities?
10. Conduct research regarding the concept of RHIOs and explain a RHIO's importance to a CIO.

References

Austin, C. J., K. D. Hornberger, and J. E. Shmerling. 2000. "Managing Information Resources: A Study of Ten Healthcare Organizations." *Journal of Healthcare Management* 45 (4): 229–39.

Broadbent, M., and E. Kitzis. 2005. *The New CIO Leader: Setting the Agenda and Delivering Results.* Boston: Harvard Business School Press.

Brynjolfsson, E., and L. Hitt. 2000. "Beyond Computation: Information Technology, Organizational Transformation and Business Performance." *Journal of Economic Perspectives* 14 (4): 23–48.

DeFord, D., and D. Porter. 2005. "To Centralize or Decentralize? That Is the Question." In *The CEO-CIO Partnership: Harnessing the Value of Information Technology in Healthcare*, edited by D. Smaltz, J. Glaser, R. Skinner, and T. Cunningham III. Chicago: Healthcare Information and Management Systems Society.

Hagland, M. 2001. "CIO of the Year." *Healthcare Informatics* 18 (4): 18–19.

Hali, M. 2007. "A/R Outsourcing—Coming of Age in the New Millennium." [Online article; retrieved 9/20/07.] www.lowdso.com/Articles1.html

Healthcare Information and Management Systems Society (HIMSS). 2006. *Seventeenth Annual HIMSS Leadership Survey. Final Report: Healthcare CIO*. Sponsored by ACS Healthcare Solutions. Chicago: HIMSS.

Hensley, S. 1997. "Outsourcing Moves Into New Territory." *Modern Healthcare* 27 (2): 39–43.

HIMSS and HIMSS Analytics. 2006. *2006 HIMSS Compensation Survey Results.* [Online information; retrieved 12/6/07.] http://www.himss.org/surveys/compensation/ ASP/memberIndex.asp

HIMSS Analytics. 2005. *Annual Report of the US Hospital IT Market*. Chicago: Healthcare Information and Management Systems Society.

Hook, J., E. Pan, J. Adler-Milstein, D. Bu, and J. Walker. 2006. "The Value of Healthcare Information Exchange and Interoperability in New York State." *AMIA Annual Symposium Proceedings*. 953. [Online article; retrieved 12/31/07.] www.pubmedcentral.nih.gov/articlerender.fcgi?tool=pubmed&pubmedid=17238572

Kramer, S. 2006. "The Secrets of Successful CIOs. Top CIOs Talk About What It Takes to Lead So Others Want to Follow." *Healthcare Informatics* 23 (10): 24–30.

Leapfrog Group. 2002. "The Leapfrog Group Expands Patient Safety Improvement Initiative Into 12 New Regions." Press release, April 22.

Menachemi, N., D. Burke, M. Diana, and R. Brooks. 2005. "Characteristics of Hospitals That Outsource Information System Functions." *Journal of Healthcare Information Management* 191 (1): 63–69.

Morrissey, J. 1996. "CIO Pay Averages $110,000 a Year." *Modern Healthcare* 26 (10): 122–124.

National Alliance for Health Information Technology. 2007. "What Is Interoperability?" Work Products, National Alliance for Health Information Technology. [Online article; retrieved 12/11/07.] http://www.nahit.org/cms/index.php?option=com_content&task=view&id=220&Itemid=115

Oliner, S. D., and D. E. Sichel. 2000. "The Resurgence of Growth in the Late 1990s: Is Information Technology the Story?" *Journal of Economic Perspectives* 14 (4): 3–22.

Salkever, A. 2004. "A Paperless Health-Care System?" *Business Week*, July 7. [Online article; retrieved 12/31/07.] www.businessweek.com/technology/content/jul2004/tc2004077_8164_tc_171.htm

Schwartz, E. 2005. "The End of the CIO? Reality Check." [Online article; retrieved 12/14/07.] http://www.infoworld.com/article/05/10/18/ 43OPreality_1.html

Scottsdale Institute and HIMSS Analytics. 2005. *Healthcare Leaders Report: The Changing Landscape of Healthcare IT Management and Governance.* Chicago: HIMSS Analytics.

Siemens Medical Solutions. 2005. "Proven Outcomes: Jefferson Regional Medical Center Case Study." [Online article; retrieved 11/5/06.] http://www.out sourcing-requests.com/common/sponsors/70899/Proven_Outcomes.pdf

Smaltz, D., J. Glaser, R. Skinner, and T. Cunningham III (eds.). 2005. *The CEO-CIO Partnership: Harnessing the Value of Information Technology in Healthcare.* Chicago: Healthcare Information and Management Systems Society.

Walker, J., E. Pan, D. Johnston, J. Adler-Milstein, D. Bates, and B. Middleton. 2005. "The Value of Health Care Information Exchange and Interoperability." *Health Affairs.* Web Exclusive, January 19. [Online article; retrieved 2/2/08.] http://content.healthaffairs.org/cgi/content/full/hlthaff.w5.10/DC1

Waterloo Institute for Health Informatics Research. 2007. [Online information; retrieved 2/8/08.] http://learningspace.uwaterloo.ca/hi/index.php

Waymack, P. 2000. "Four Tips for Selecting Outsourcing Firms." *Health Management Technology* 22 (8): 19.

Weill, P., and J. Ross. 2004. *IT Governance: How Top Performers Manage IT Decision Rights for Superior Results.* Boston: Harvard Business School Press.

Wood, G. M. 2000. "The Changing Role of the Healthcare Chief Information Officer." *Managed Care Interface* 13 (9): 81–83.

IM/IT GOVERNANCE AND DECISION RIGHTS

Learning Objectives

1. Explain why strategic planning has become more important for healthcare organizations.
2. Summarize the five major components of information management/ information technology (IM/IT) governance.
3. Describe the major elements of a healthcare organization's planning elements.
4. Assess the major elements of a healthcare IM/IT strategic plan.
5. Describe systems theory and explain why it is vital to healthcare IM/IT governance and planning.

The competitive advantage that successful information management/ information technology (IM/IT) governance may bestow has become the center of much discussion and even some debate. Smaltz, Carpenter, and Saltz (2007) and others (Broadbent and Kitzis 2005; Glaser 2002; Weill and Ross 2004) conclude that effective governance and expanding decision rights, inherent in IM/IT leadership, are essential for organizational success. The discussion of what *governance* and *decision rights* mean and how these concepts have evolved in healthcare organizations is a major portion of this chapter. Such emphasis on governance does not imply that the more traditional strategic information systems planning is either unimportant or out of date. Planning is still vital and is an important part of IM/IT governance.

Today, more than in the past, successful IM/IT governance and planning must address challenges from outside IM/IT operations. Broad questions that need to be addressed include: What is IM/IT governance? How does the governance model differ from historical strategic information systems planning? What changes must be made in organizations to transform IM/IT functions to a corporate asset?

This chapter presents an overview of IM/IT governance and strategic planning in healthcare organizations from the perspective of an integrated governance model. Topics covered include the background of governance and planning, the purposes of planning, the importance of system integration, organizing the IM/IT strategic planning effort, a brief introduction to systems theory, and management control and decision support systems.

Background of IM/IT Governance and Strategic Planning

Historically, information systems in many healthcare organizations evolved piecemeal, rather than resulting from a carefully controlled planning process. Specific requirements for capturing, storing, and retrieving data when needed were developed on an ad hoc basis as new programs and services were added. As a result, the same data were captured repetitively, files were duplicated, and information was not always available when needed. Analysts recognized that if an IM/IT planning process was not in place, priorities for development of individual computer applications were often established by the exigencies of the moment.

Recently, IM/IT priorities have changed to focus on integration of systems across multiple facilities, automation of patient records, and improved decision support for clinicians and managers. Achieving these complex objectives requires a careful planning process to develop a functional, scalable, and flexible information architecture that facilitates data exchange and provides users real-time access to information remotely from all locations.

Strategic information systems planning is the process of identifying and assigning priorities to the applications of information technology that will assist an organization in executing its business plans and achieving its strategic goals and objectives. This historical definition, which might have been seen as many as 10 years ago, does not sound much different from that of IM/IT governance above. Despite the similarities between the two definitions, there are subtle differences with regard to the importance of the external focus of healthcare IM/IT orientation. Many have analyzed IM/IT governance issues from theoretical perspectives to applied perspectives. While much conceptual work has been done, a useful conceptualization was developed recently that led to a Conceptual Framework for IT Governance (Brown and Grant 2005). The Conceptual Framework provided a logical structure for assessing the work of others by classifying prior efforts to understand IM/IT decision making as either related to governance (centralized versus decentralized decision framework) or a form of contingency analysis (why and how decisions are made in an organization). Menning and Carpenter (2005) provide a comprehensive review of current healthcare IM/IT governance alternatives in place, summarize the roles of governance, describe what works in healthcare, and list some potential impediments or pitfalls to avoid. This was done from the perspective of the experienced healthcare IM/IT leader. One of the few empirical investigations examines in detail how two very different organizations built and sustained an effective governance structure (Smaltz, Carpenter, and Saltz 2007). They conclude that governance effectiveness may depend in part upon attaining five domains of governance (strategic alignment, risk management, resource management, performance management, and value delivery). Finally, Weill and Ross (2004) developed characteristics of successful IM/IT governance that was presented as a component of healthcare IM/IT leadership in Chapter 2.

The importance of information systems planning has increased as healthcare organizations have grown in size and complexity and as information technology has become increasingly sophisticated. More than assigning management to coordinate an orderly planning process, healthcare IM/IT governance now requires managers to expand beyond IM/IT operations to ensure that information technology is used to effectively support the strategic priorities of the organization (Weill and Ross 2004; Menning and Carpenter 2005).

Discussions today with chief information officers (CIOs) often center on topics such as mergers, acquisitions and divestitures, and other strategic options for the organization, as opposed to internal operational issues and new technology. The *Sixteenth Annual HIMSS Leadership Survey* (HIMSS 2005a, Figures 8 and 9) revealed that reducing medical errors was the top priority identified by CIOs in the current period and was second only to implementing the electronic medical record as a priority in the next two years. This is just one example of how challenges outside of formal IM/IT operations occupy the attention of CIOs today.

Early in this decade, Gabler (2001) pointed out that governing boards and senior managers of healthcare organizations are increasingly concerned about the business value of investments in information technology and want assurances that information systems will deliver strategic benefits to the enterprise. Strategic IM/IT planning has assumed higher priority as a result.

Purpose of Strategic Governance and IM/IT Planning

IM/IT governance helps the organization make business decisions more accurately and in a timelier manner. With that benefit in mind, many have attempted to define the purpose and scope of IM/IT governance (Sambamurthy and Zmud 1999; Weill and Ross 2004; Broadbent and Kitzis 2005; Lutchen and Collins 2005). Although they reached no strict agreement, differences among these analysts are mostly nuance. Menning and Carpenter (2005) provide general guidelines, which, with some modification, appear in Figure 3.1 as the five primary components of successful healthcare IM/IT governance. Each component is discussed in more detail in the following sections.

Developing a Consistent IM/IT Strategy

Information systems should support the strategic goals, objectives, and priorities of the organization they serve. As healthcare organizations have become more sophisticated, they use information more effectively in strategic positioning within the environment in which they operate (Austin, Trimm, and Sobczak 1995, 27).

FIGURE 3.1
Components
of IM/IT
Governance

1. Developing a consistent IM/IT strategy
2. Aligning IM/IT with organizational strategy
3. Developing IM/IT infrastructure, architecture, and policies
4. Setting IM/IT project priorities, and overseeing investments in IM/IT infrastructure
5. Using IM/IT benefits assessment to enhance accountability

As mentioned above, hospitals and other healthcare organizations historically employed information technology to support day-to-day operations. Increasingly, healthcare managers are recognizing the role of information systems in increasing market share, supporting quality assessment and improvement, and adding value to the organization. To accomplish these strategic objectives, the IM/IT plan must be consistently applied across the multiple operating units with an organization. Creating consistent applications in an environment that has grown piecemeal and that consists of employees often not reporting directly to the CIO presents a challenge.

To demonstrate how this trend has evolved, the following information shows the growth and change in IM/IT planning. In 1996, 35 percent of the respondents to the Healthcare Information and Management Systems Society (HIMSS) annual leadership survey indicated that their organizations did not have a strategic IM/IT plan (HIMSS 1996). By contrast, in January 2002, only 8 percent of the responding organizations indicated that they did not have such a plan in place (HIMSS 2002). By 2005, the question of having a strategic IM/IT plan in place was not posed in the survey. It was replaced by a question asking whether the plan is an integrated component of the entire organization's plan (46 percent responded yes) or is integrated in content but a separate plan (44 percent responded yes) (Scottsdale Institute and HIMSS Analytics 2005).

Aligning IM/IT with Organizational Strategy

The IM/IT plan must be closely aligned with the strategic plans of the organization. The issue of alignment has been an integral part of the IM/IT planning mantra for years (Wilson 1989; Ward and Griffiths 1996). Aligning IM/IT strategy with overall organizational strategy requires, first, a consistent IM/IT plan and, second, a view by IM/IT leadership that recognizes the importance of the interrelationships among IM/IT, the rest of the organization, and the external environment. Moreover, Stacey and Skinner (2005) argue that alignment involves three essential elements for success. First, an alignment of purpose must be in place. IM/IT leadership and organizational leadership must agree that they are trying to achieve the same ends. Second, they must agree to work to develop goals and tactics jointly to meet those ends. Third, these two groups must share the responsibility and accountability to achieve the ends. In the words of Stacey and Skinner (2005, 41), "we're in this together."

Because business objectives change over time, the information technology plan should be reviewed frequently to ensure it remains in alignment with current organizational strategy. Implementing an aligned plan is much more difficult than stating the need for alignment. To assist leaders in achieving strategic alignment, the following six questions must be addressed by the CIO and organizational leadership together from the perspective of the organization:

1. What does the organization do?
2. Who does the organization do it to or for?
3. Where does the organization do it?
4. When does the organization do it?
5. Why does the organization do it?
6. How does the organization do it?

Developing IM/IT Infrastructure, Architecture, and Policies

Healthcare organizations must make choices and set priorities for their information systems. The plan should identify the major types of information required to support strategic objectives and establish priorities for installation of specific computer applications, the architecture upon which the systems function, and the detailed rules that drive IM/IT operations.

To meet strategic objectives and develop high-priority applications, the healthcare organization must develop blueprints for its information technology infrastructure. This involves decisions about hardware configuration (architecture), network communications, degree of centralization or decentralization of computing facilities, and types of computer software required to support the network.

HIMSS has attempted to determine current and future information technology use and adoption through its annual leadership survey. It has found that use has not varied much during the first decade of the twentieth century. The 2005 annual leadership survey (HIMSS 2005a) identified the same four information technologies in current use as reported in the 2002 survey:

1. High-speed networks
2. Intranets
3. Wireless information systems
4. Client/server systems

After the infrastructure and architecture are developed as described above, the IM/IT steering committee (see discussion later in this chapter) should oversee the development of a set of enterprisewide policies that govern the design, acquisition, and operation of information systems throughout the organization. Important policies needed by every organization include data security policies; data definition standards; policies governing the acquisition of hardware, software, and telecommunications network equipment; and policies on use of the Internet.

Data Standardization   As discussed previously, system integration is an important element of strategic IM/IT planning in healthcare organizations. Most computer applications must include the ability to share information with other systems. For example, a laboratory results-reporting system must be able to transfer information for storage in the computerized medical records system operated by the organization.

Electronic data exchange cannot occur without some level of standardization of data structures used in computer applications. For this reason, healthcare organizations should consider developing a data dictionary that specifies the format of each data element and the coding system (if any) associated with that element. For example, the data element "date of birth" might be defined as follows in the organization's data dictionary:

Date of birth—Eight-digit numeric field with three subfields:
   Month—two digits ranging from 01 to 12
   Day—two digits ranging from 01 to 31
   Year—four digits ranging from 1850 to 2100

Notice that the range of the subfield for year in this example is designed to accommodate historical records of patients with birth dates back to the mid-nineteenth century and accommodate future records through the end of the twenty-first century.

In addition to data compatibility among information systems within the organization, there is a growing need to facilitate extra organizational exchange of information among health systems, government and private insurance companies, medical supply and equipment vendors, and other entities. A number of projects have been initiated to develop voluntary, industrywide standards for electronic data interchange in the healthcare field. Examples of these projects include the following:

- The American National Standards Institute (ANSI) (www.ansi.org/) X.12 Group is working on specifications for transactions involving the processing of health insurance claims.
- The Health Industry Bar Code Supplier Labeling Standard (www.hibcc.org/about.htm) is working to provide common coding of supplies, materials, and equipment.
- Health Level Seven (HL7) (version 3) (www.hl7.org/) is a standard for healthcare electronic data transmission.

- The Healthcare Information Technology Standards Panel (HITSP) was awarded a contract from the U.S. Department of Health and Human Services to support a new collaborative effort to harmonize healthcare information technology standards.

The HL7 project was initiated in 1987. It is a voluntary effort of health-care providers, hardware and software vendors, payers, consultants, government groups, and professional organizations with the goal of developing a cost-effective approach to system connectivity. It is aimed at the development of standards for clinical and administrative data. As with other standard-developing organizations certified by ANSI, HL7 develops messaging specifications that enable organizations to exchange clinical and administrative data. It has been working on improvements to these specifications since 1987; version 3 of HL7 embodies a new approach that addresses many of the weaknesses of earlier versions and encompasses messaging, component specifications, structured document architecture, and more. Even earlier versions provided a coherent set of standards for messages, component interfaces, and documents that all users can embrace (Beeler 2001).

The federal government has continued to support the creation and adoption of HL7 and other data exchange standards. As a part of the presidential initiative on consolidated health informatics, the departments of Health and Human Services, Defense, and Veterans Affairs announced the adoption of HL7 messaging standards along with prescription drug, imaging, and other standards in 2003 (Presidential Initiatives 2006). These standards enable the federal agencies to share information and improve coordination of care. Similarly, in the following year five additional standards related to information exchange were announced (Presidential Initiatives 2006).

In addition to these *voluntary* efforts at industrywide data standardization, the Health Insurance Portability and Accountability Act of 1996 (HIPAA) established *mandatory* electronic data standards and standard transaction formats for claims processing. Providers are required to follow these standards to receive reimbursement from Medicare, Medicaid, and other health insurers. As a means of addressing growing mandatory standards, HITSP will bring together a wide range of stakeholders to identify, select, and harmonize standards for communicating data throughout the healthcare spectrum. Under a contract from the United States Department of Health and Human Services and the sponsorship of ANSI, HIMSS, the Advanced Technology Institute, and Booz Allen Hamilton (a strategic partner), HITSP will attempt to accelerate the adoption of health information technology and the secure portability of health information across the United States (HIMSS 2005b).

The purpose of HITSP is to develop a generally accepted set of standards specifically to enable and support "widespread interoperability, accurate use, access, privacy and security of shared health information" (HIMSS

2005b). HITSP is designed to function with public and private partnerships that have the potential to access much of the healthcare community. If successful in getting healthcare software developers and users to adopt these standards, it will buoy the Nationwide Health Information Network initiative for the United States called for by President George W. Bush by Executive Order #13335, which established the National Information Technology Coordinator.

As part of the strategic information systems planning process, the information systems steering committee should study requirements for data interchange, including HIPAA mandates, and should develop a policy on data standardization for the organization. For example, many hospitals and integrated delivery systems (IDSs) are specifying that all software purchased from vendors must meet an industry standard protocol such as HL7.

Hardware and Software Standards   A number of technical policies related to information systems need to be developed by healthcare organizations. Most of these are highly technical and should be developed by the CIO or director of information systems. However, the information systems steering committee should oversee the development of a broad set of policies related to the acquisition of computer hardware, software, and network communications equipment for the organization.

The committee must determine whether the organization will require central review and approval of all computer hardware and software purchases. As the costs of personal computers and related software packages have come down, their purchase has moved to fall within the budgetary authority of individual organizational units. However, some compelling reasons exist for requiring central review and approval, regardless of cost, including the following:

1. Central review helps ensure compatibility with enterprisewide data standards such as HL7 (see above).
2. Central review of personal computer purchases can ensure that data terminals and workstations use a common operating system, such as Windows.
3. Central review and purchasing of generalized software provides cost advantages through the acquisition of site licenses for multiple users of common packages (word processing, spreadsheets, database-management systems, etc.).
4. Central review ensures that hardware and software will be of a type that can receive technical support and maintenance from the information systems staff.
5. Central review can help prevent illegal use of unlicensed software within the organization.

The information systems steering committee should also approve the network communications plan for the enterprise. A variety of network configurations is possible, and the network plan must be compatible with the overall information systems development plan for the organization.

Setting IM/IT Project Priorities and Overseeing Investments in IM/IT Infrastructure

The IM/IT function must also effectively oversee the purchase and implementation of IM/IT infrastructure consistent with the needs of the organization. The specialized knowledge and skills of IM/IT staff and the growing complexity of the underlying technology make this role vital to the success of IM/IT operations. While the use of technology has made information available and accessible to clinical and administrative staff across the organization, the infrastructure upon which software and other applications operate in the systems through which data are transmitted remains in the domain of IM/IT. While end users are vital considerations in the priority-setting process, governance of IM/IT requires organizational IM/IT leadership to effectively manage the priorities among alternative investment options (Menning and Carpenter 2005). This management includes items directly from the IM/IT strategic plan such as an example, outlined by Stacy and Skinner (2005, 44), in which a hospital had to change all of its human resources, finance, patient accounting, and other support services information systems to enable integration with the rest of the health system and investments that arise episodically (a good example was Y2K considerations; see Wilson and McPherson [2002]).

Using IM/IT Benefits Assessment to Enhance Accountability

The final purpose of strategic IM/IT planning is to provide data to estimate the budget and resources required to meet the objectives and priorities established through the planning process. Planning will provide the basis for development of operating and capital budgets for information technology in the organization. The importance of this purpose has increased as CIOs report the growth in importance of the drive to obtain value from IM/IT (Glaser and Garets 2005). Turisco (2000, 13) called for value management in justifying information technology investments: "There is a growing demand for ensuring that healthcare [information technology] IM/IT investment practices and processes not only justify the large cash outlays, but track and realize the value. . . . Values can only be realized through measurable business changes supported by the business units." More recently, the Center for Information Technology Leadership has published a number of articles arguing that greater documentation of IM/IT value is essential (e.g., Johnston, Pan, and Middleton 2002). This "call to the field" identified three dimensions from which to derive healthcare IM/IT value: financial, clinical, and organizational. The *financial* dimension is the most obvious source of value. It consists of cost reductions, revenue enhancements, and productivity gains. *Clinical* enhancements would seek evidence of IM/IT's impact on service delivery (adherence to protocols) and clinical outcome indicators. *Organizational* enhancements include such items as stakeholder satisfaction improvements and risk reduction. In all cases, Johnston, Pan, and Middleton's fundamental point is that healthcare executives currently must rely on "anecdote, inference, and opinion to make critical IM/IT decisions" (2002, 1).

Organization of the Planning Effort

The development of information systems in a modern healthcare organization is a complex task involving major capital expenditures and significant staff commitments if the systems are to function properly. Development of a consistent, integrated master plan for information systems development is essential. To exclude this critical planning activity would be analogous to beginning a trip from New York to out West without knowing precisely where you are going (San Francisco? Seattle?), how you plan to travel (air, car, train, bus), what route you plan to take (northern, middle, southern), in what time frame you must get there, or how much money you have for the trip. While we would not do this as individuals, organizations continue to move directly into the acquisition of computer systems without any kind of master plan. The following sections provide guidelines for those organizations that have yet to implement an information systems strategic plan.

General Approach

The chief executive officer (CEO) should take direct responsibility for organizing the planning effort. As discussed above, appropriate governance creates an environment in which the board of trustees assigns responsibility, authority, and accountability to the CEO; thus the impetus for action rests with the CEO. Many structures have been proposed for this planning effort, ranging from highly centralized to informal discussions between the CEO and the CIO (Menning and Carpenter 2005). Naturally, the level of sophistication of this structure depends on the size and complexity of the organization and the nature of the environment in which it operates.

Generally, because the CEO often does not have the expertise or time to develop this plan, an information systems steering committee should be formed with representatives from major elements of the organization contributing to and benefiting from IM/IT functions. This committee should include representatives from the medical, nursing, financial management, human resources management, planning and marketing, facilities management, clinical support services, and information technology staff. The committee should be directed by a senior manager, preferably the CIO if such a position has been established. Strategic information planning is primarily a managerial function, not a technical one. A suggested organizational chart for the planning effort is shown in Figure 3.2. The IM/IT steering committee will usually have subcommittees to better manage discrete aspects of the steering committee's responsibilities. Specific subcommittees may differ as local needs dictate, but the following three components need to be specifically addressed:

1. *New and replacement IM/IT priorities.* The identification and planning for new and, importantly, replacement applications will serve to determine the scope of user needs.
2. *Infrastructure specifications.* Technology infrastructure specifications must include the most technically proficient members of your committee.
3. *Capital and operating budget.* The budget group is essential to keeping the scale and scope of technology needs under control.

Committee composition includes senior staff in IM/IT as well as representatives from the key constituencies across the organization. Additional personnel from the organization and technical consultants can be appointed members of specific subcommittees as needed. The chairs of the subcommittees usually come from the steering committee.

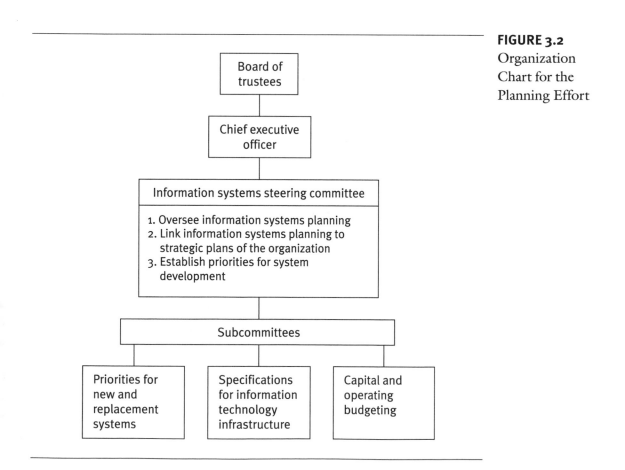

FIGURE 3.2

Organization Chart for the Planning Effort

Consideration also should be given to use of outside consultants if additional technical expertise is needed in the planning process. Except for the largest, most organizations cannot employ all of the specialized technical expertise necessary to make quality, informed decision about information technology. Consequently, hiring these experts is a necessity, but consultants should be chosen carefully. They should possess technical knowledge of systems analysis and computer systems and should be well informed about healthcare organizations. Consultants must be independent practitioners not associated with any equipment manufacturer or firm that sells software. When hiring independent consultants, executives must be sure that the consultants have no bias or stand to benefit from the decisions made, especially in cases when the organization lacks the in-house expertise to validate consultants' recommendations. Finally, consultants should be familiar with the latest technological developments but must be able to resist the temptation to push for applications that are too close to the leading edge.

Lohman (1996) suggests that the following factors be considered in selecting an information systems consultant (the advice is still valid more than 10 years after publication):

1. *Independence and objectivity.* The consultant should exclusively focus on the interests of the client.
2. *Healthcare expertise.* The consultant should have an understanding of healthcare business and clinical issues.
3. *Resources.* The consultant should have sufficient breadth and depth of resources to complete the assignment without "on-the-job training."
4. *Effective personality.* The consultant should have an appropriate mix of character traits and skills.

Consultants should be used as sources of technical information and as facilitators of the planning process. They should not be employed to do the planning; this must be the responsibility of knowledgeable managers and users of information within the organization itself. Consultants can be of the most assistance by advising those on the steering committee of the functionality specifications of the technology or systems being considered and the system-level consequences of an action or decision. Before using a consultant's "off the shelf" planning product, ensure that the planning methodology is compatible with the organization's culture and strategic priorities.

Boyd (2005) presents an interesting set of reasons for and against outsourcing IM/IT. Although his discussion is more in the context of outsourcing fundamental IM/IT functions, the reasoning applies in the case of hiring consultants to advise the steering committee. Simply put, organizations should outsource to take advantage of the capacity and expertise of the external resource and reduce the fixed costs of having added expertise in-house.

The CEO should ensure that staff members participating on the steering committee are provided sufficient "release time" from their normal duties so that they can participate fully in the planning efforts. Release time estimates should be drawn up in advance, and formal written notification of this time should be provided to all involved. The administration and board of trustees should be prepared to spend a significant amount of the institution's human resources on carrying out this important task.

As stated above, the organization's CIO should chair the steering committee, if the CIO position has been established. Reporting directly to the CEO or chief operating officer, the CIO serves two important functions: (1) assisting the senior management team and governing board in using information to support strategic planning and management and (2) providing management oversight and coordination of information systems and telecommunications throughout the organization. See Chapter 2 for a full description of the role of CIO.

Elements of a Strategic Information Systems Plan

Figure 3.3 lists seven major elements that should be included in the strategic IM/IT plan, each of which is discussed in detail below.

Corporate Goals and Objectives

The strategic IM/IT plan should begin with a review and concise statement of major organizational goals and objectives for the three- to five-year planning period. IM/IT goals and objectives should be aligned with the strategic objectives of the organization as mentioned above. For example, if reduction of medical errors is a major priority, then this goal should be reflected in the priorities for IM/IT development, paying particular attention to medical records, clinical protocols, clinical decision support systems, and incident reporting. If diversification and expansion of the market service base are strategic objectives, then information systems should focus on utilization analysis and forecasting, analysis of changes in the demographic profile of the service market, and analysis of resource requirements for new service development. If an urban medical center has placed priority on expansion of ambulatory care services, but IM/IT priorities continue to focus on inpatient services, then the organization has a serious problem of goal displacement.

Critical success factors are often used in defining information requirements and IM/IT goals during the planning process (Rockart 1979; Ward and Griffiths 1996). More recently, variations on the approach have been adopted. Kuperman and colleagues (2006) use a "requirements-driven" approach for quality improvement. They identified data warehousing and clinical encounter documentation as the critical factors that would lead to improved patient quality. Similarly, Johnson (2005) used a continuous cycle of assessment, prioritization, and scheduling to optimally allocate scarce information technology resources. Senior management needs to define these

FIGURE 3.3
Elements of the
Information
Systems
Strategic Plan

1. Statement of corporate/institutional goals and objectives
2. Statement of information systems goals and objectives
   a. Management information needs
   b. Critical success factors
   c. Information priorities
3. Priorities for the applications portfolio
   a. Clinical
   b. Management/administrative
   c. Electronic networking and e-health
   d. Strategic decision support
4. Specification of overall systems architecture and infrastructure
   a. Level of distribution
   b. Network architecture
   c. Data location (central data warehouse to total data distribution)
   d. Integration via Internet
   e. Database security and control requirements
5. Software development plan
   a. Commercial packages
   b. In-house development
   c. Contract software development
   d. Application services providers
   e. Combinations of the above
6. Information systems management and staffing plan
   a. Central information systems staffing and control
   b. Limited central staffing in support of department-level information systems staff
   c. Outsourcing
   d. Combinations of the above
7. Statement of resource requirements
   a. Capital budget (hardware, software, network communication equipment)
   b. Operating budget (personnel, supplies, consultants, training, etc.)

requirements for IM/IT, but that level of management in healthcare organizations often has difficulty specifying its needs for management information. By specifying those critical areas where things must go right for the organization to flourish, managers assist the IM/IT planning team in determining information requirements and setting priorities for system development. Effectively communicating goals among these levels of the organization is critical to success.

Information Systems Goals and Objectives   Objectives should be as specific as possible and should flow from a review of strategic priorities and an analysis of deficiencies and gaps in current information processes. It is suggested that the CIO and other members of the steering committee consult a good text or "how to" book on strategic planning at this stage so that goals and objectives are well specified (Swayne, Duncan, and Ginter 2005). Avoid general statements of objectives such as "information systems for Metropolitan Health System should be designed to improve the quality of care and increase the efficiency of system operations." Such statements are self-evident and nonfunctional as far as planning is concerned. Rather, a detailed list of objectives should be established that will provide specific targets against which future progress can be measured and systems can be evaluated. Examples of specific objectives might include the following:

• Information systems for the health plan should be designed such that all records from the master patient index file are available online to all physicians in the plan.
• Information systems for the clinic should be designed such that all diagnostic test results are available online within two hours after the tests have been completed.
• Information systems should be designed such that information on inpatient and outpatient activity by major diagnostic categories is reported to corporate management on a monthly basis, with reports indicating the health system's share of the total services provided in the market area.
• Disease-management protocols for the ten highest-volume chronic conditions should be available online and should be used to provide automatic reminders to all physicians practicing in the hospital.
• If the organization is a university affiliated health system, expand the university's current information infrastructure to optimally meet the ongoing needs of the institution in the areas of research, education, patient care, and community service.
• Support the institution's information technology users through the formation of a service center.

These goals and objectives then provide the pool from which the organization must derive its set of key priorities.

Healthcare organizations will not be able to acquire all the systems they need in any given year. The statements of corporate and IM/IT objectives will aid the steering committee in preparing a priority list of individual computer applications to be acquired. The applications priority list, in turn, will be essential in planning how limited resources can be used to have the greatest impact on strategic priorities. Chapter 8 provides a comprehensive presentation and discussion of application opportunities.

Applications Priority List

The applications list should consider the needs of all major functional areas of the healthcare organization for financial, human resources, resource utilization and scheduling, materials management, facilities and project management, and office automation information systems. Both new and replacement systems should be considered, and the need for major changes to existing systems should be reviewed as well. Applications should be rank ordered in the recommended sequence for implementation, and items on the applications priority list should be linked to specific organizational strategies. If an information systems steering committee determines that financial control is the most pressing organizational problem, the development of a new financial information system might assume highest priority.

Many healthcare organizations have initiated programs of business process reengineering to achieve operational efficiency through dramatic improvement in core processes used in the organization. The pay-for-performance movement sponsored by government and business has raised the urgency of process improvement (Rosenthal et al. 2006). This broad movement makes clear not only the importance of IM/IT but also the involvement of all components of the delivery systems (Petersen et al. 2006). Many of these reengineering projects involve development of new information systems, and these should be considered by the information systems steering committee in developing the applications priority list.

After the priority list has been completed, the steering committee should report preliminary results back to the CEO and board of trustees. The statement of objectives and priority list should be carefully reviewed and modified as necessary to make sure that together they reflect the positions of senior management and the board.

Systems Architecture and Infrastructure Specification of overall systems architecture is a critical task in the planning process. Chapter 6 provides an overview of healthcare IM/IT system architecture and infrastructure. In short, the plan must specify an overall system architecture and infrastructure to include the following:

1. *The degree to which computing will be centralized or decentralized throughout the organization.* Opinions differ about the degree to which computing should be centralized or decentralized in healthcare organizations (DeFord and Porter 2005). Carr (2003) argues that IM/IT no longer matters for obtaining competitive advantage in healthcare organizations. The notion is that information technology is such an integral part of all aspects of the healthcare delivery system that no one organization benefits relative to its competition from having extensive information technology. DeFord and Porter (2005) argue convincingly that information technology infrastructure as one part of overall IM/IT is still valuable and benefits from centralization. In their opinion, centralized information technology does the following:
   - Reduces variability
   - Improves security
   - Reduces human resource requirements
   - Enhances flexibility
   - Reduces procurement costs
   - Reduces total cost of ownership

- Improves end-user satisfaction
- More effectively and efficiently aligns IM/IT to business needs

Proponents of decentralization argue that this approach places control of information systems back where it belongs—in the hands of users. Decentralization fosters innovation in system design and develops increased user interest and support. Local flexibility is maintained, and the frustrations of lengthy programming and processing backlogs at a central facility are avoided.

2. *The network architecture that specifies how computers and workstations will be linked together through communication lines and network servers.* Chapter 6 includes a detailed description of alternative network architecture configurations, including the following:
   - Central mainframe architecture
   - Client/server architecture
   - File/server architecture
   - Distributed processing architecture

   Data distribution plans will help determine which type of network architecture should be employed by the healthcare organization. Alternatives range from creation of large, centralized (enterprisewide) "data warehouses" to complete distribution of data in which each organizational unit on the network maintains its own database.

3. *The manner in which data will be stored and distributed throughout the organization, including database security and control requirements.* Many healthcare organizations, particularly IDSs, are moving toward a combination of approaches to data distribution. For example, the IDS might develop a centralized data warehouse containing a master patient index and computerized records for all patients in the system. Individual organizational units (hospitals, ambulatory care centers, etc.) might maintain their own data files for patient appointments, employee records, inventory control, budgeting, and financial management. The telecommunications network supporting the system will be designed to facilitate electronic exchange of information so that patient records are accessible at all treatment sites and financial information can be transmitted to corporate offices on a periodic basis. In addition to describing the network architecture, the plan should specify how the infrastructure will support related activities such as audio, video, and wireless communications; document imaging; and radiographic imaging.

4. *The manner by which individual applications will be linked so that they can exchange information.* The subject of interoperability is discussed more fully in Chapter 2. This is a key strategic consideration that affects all clinical and administrative components of the delivery system.

Regardless of the approach followed for data distribution and system integration, data standards will be required. This topic is discussed in detail later in this chapter. Data security and protection of information confidentiality is discussed in Chapter 5.

The subcommittee that reviews systems architecture must include competent technical staff and/or consultants working closely with representatives of management, the medical staff, and other major system users.

Software Development Plan

The information systems plan should also specify procedures for software development. In the early days of healthcare computing (1960s to 1980s), most hospitals and other healthcare organizations employed a staff of computer analysts and programmers to develop computer applications in-house. Today, most healthcare organizations rely primarily on software packages purchased from commercial vendors. A wide array of software products is available; see, for example, the annual resource guide published by *Health Management Technology* magazine, which is available online at www.healthmgttech.com. This source presents a vast listing of companies, including a brief description of the company, its product categories, and contact information.

Use of applications service providers (ASPs) is another alternative for software acquisition that is growing in popularity among healthcare organizations. An ASP is an organization that contracts with a healthcare provider to provide access to and use of applications on an off-site server on a subscription basis (Monohan 2001). Many large healthcare organizations and IDSs use combinations of these software development options. Commercial software may be combined with tailor-made programs developed by in-house staff, particularly programs that support database management and electronic communications across the network. ASPs may be used for selected applications by smaller units affiliated with the enterprise.

Information Systems Management and Staffing Plan

The IM/IT strategic plan should specify the management structure for information systems. Most healthcare organizations still employ an in-house staff for system operation and management, even if all or most software is purchased from commercial vendors or leased from ASPs.

Decisions must be made on the extent to which technical staff will be centralized or distributed among the major user departments of the organization. An increasing number of organizations are outsourcing all or some of their information-processing functions to contractors who provide on-site system implementation and management services.

Centralized staffing offers the advantages of economies of scale and reduction in the number of technical personnel to be employed. Decentralized staffing brings systems management closer to the user and offers the potential for increased support and user involvement in system development and operation.

Outsourcing of information systems functions allows the healthcare organization to get out of the information technology business through contracting with experts in the field. However, the costs of outsourcing may be high and may tend to generate too much distance between users and technical systems specialists.

The final element of the information systems plan specifies resources required to carry it out. The capital budget should include five- to ten-year projections for the cost of computer hardware, network and telecommunications equipment, and software. The operating budget includes costs for personnel, supplies and materials, consultants, training programs, and other recurring expenses. Both budgets should be updated annually, and the timing for their preparation should be coordinated with the overall organizational budget cycle. *Statement of Resource Requirements*

Although the information technology budgets for healthcare organizations lag behind those of other information-intensive industries, the *Seventeenth Annual HIMSS Leadership Survey* reports that budgets are increasing in an attempt to keep pace with developing technology. Seventy-two percent of the survey respondents indicated that their budgets would increase in the current year, and only 6 percent expected their budgets to decrease (HIMSS 2006).

The planning process is the subject of many other books, but for completeness of the discussion here, a "generic" planning methodology adapted from Glaser (2002) is provided in Figure 3.4. This plan starts with the necessary gathering of information to review existing organizational strategies with senior management and middle management. The goal is to identify information systems needs by contrasting existing resources with the requirements that will meet users' expressed needs. Glaser suggests that much of the information gathering is done by external consultants.

Once the gap between needs and capabilities is determined, the next step is to delineate information systems alternatives. These alternatives will require key implementation steps to be specified, followed by estimates of resource requirements and timelines for implementation. Finally, the full plan with recommendations is presented to management.

Review and Approval of the Information Systems Plan

The IM/IT plan should specify an overall schedule and set of target dates for implementation. Although cost estimates and target dates will be preliminary at this point, they will assist management and board members in evaluating the magnitude of organizational commitments required to implement the recommended set of alternatives.

After the IM/IT steering committee has approved the plan, it should be presented to executive management and the governing board for their review and approval prior to implementation. The written plan should be submitted to management in advance of a formal presentation and discussion session.

FIGURE 3.4

Generic IM/IT
Strategic
Planning
Methodology

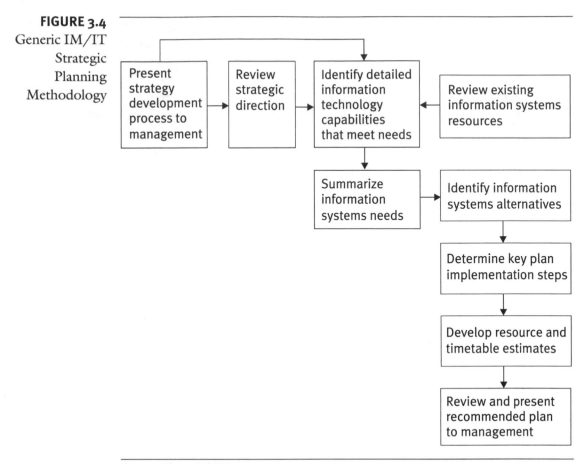

Source: Glaser (2002).

As with any plan, the strategic IM/IT plan must be a dynamic instrument that is reviewed periodically and regularly updated. At least once a year, the information systems steering committee should review progress in meeting the original criteria set forth in the plan, and the plan should be changed as necessary. This review process is essential for the steering committee to monitor progress toward meeting goals and report that progress to IM/IT leadership. It may also put forward a suggestion that the organization change strategic direction should the environment change dramatically.

End-User Computing

A problem that many healthcare organizations face is what to do about dissatisfaction among organizational units whose information systems needs are not identified as priorities in the strategic information systems plan. End-user computing strategies offer one potential solution to this problem.

Many employees have become sophisticated in computer use. Powerful personal computer systems with user-friendly software and user-oriented programming tools have helped to facilitate end-user computing that does not require the services or resources of the central information systems department.

End-user computing most often involves use of departmental software packages purchased from vendors (e.g., laboratory, pharmacy, radiology systems) or leased from an application service provider. In some cases, computer-literate users may write programs to meet specialized needs in their departments. An example would be end users at an outpatient clinic in a large medical center creating and maintaining a database of companies that provide medical supplies for the clinic.

End-user computing offers the potential to expand the base of IM/IT development and overcome issues that arise when a low priority is assigned to certain applications that are nevertheless viewed as important to units within the organization. End-user computing must be approached cautiously, however. Most activities in healthcare organizations are interrelated, and computer applications must be able to exchange information for efficient operations (see the next section on standards and policies). If a departmental system can stand alone, management might authorize acquisition, provided that department funds are available and the system is developed in accordance with the strategic IM/IT plan and enterprisewide standards and policies. If the system will need to exchange information with other units of the organization, central control and planning is needed before the end-user department is authorized to acquire the system. *Data compatibility*—use of common codes and data definitions for electronic information exchange across the organization—should be mandatory (see the following section).

Strategic Information Systems Planning for IDSs

IDSs must consider the need for integration of information systems across institutions as well as within individual organizational units. Such integration is particularly critical in vertically integrated organizations where patients may progress and seek treatment at various organizational components, including clinics, surgical centers, acute care hospitals, substance abuse centers, and skilled nursing facilities. Information systems must be patient centered to aggregate data from the various medical care units and track patients throughout the system. At the same time, corporate system management must recognize that different types of facilities within the organization (hospitals, ambulatory care centers and clinics, nursing homes, home health agencies) have their own distinct information requirements. Corporate policy must provide mechanisms for specialized information systems to meet the needs of individual units in the system.

Information systems for an IDS must also be able to provide comparative financial data for management to efficiently allocate resources to individual units. Such a capability is especially critical when healthcare costs are paid on a capitation basis. Corporate management will need to carefully monitor how patient care dollars are being spent across system units for actuarial risk analysis. The IDS also will have special information needs for market research and analysis of competitor services. Physician performance in various components of the system must be monitored as well.

At the technical level, information systems for an IDS may require standardization of coding and data definition for all organizational units—for example, a common chart of accounts for financial reporting. If such an approach is not feasible, then complex data conversion tables will be required to facilitate electronic data exchange. To serve corporate management information needs and operational support requirements of each medical care unit, IDSs need to strike a balance between centralized data management and local control of data processing.

In recent years, hospitals have merged to form corporate systems, medical centers have acquired community hospitals and brought them into their organizations, and some corporate systems have sold or divested some of their existing facilities. These mergers and changes in ownership can create special problems with respect to information systems at the individual facilities.

If the corporate system has highly centralized information processing through a corporate data center and a new facility is acquired, special planning will be required to bring the new unit into the central system while allowing it to continue to use its current hardware and software to support ongoing operations. If computing within the corporate system is decentralized at the facility level, the newly acquired facility may not have compatible hardware and/or software with other units of the enterprise. Conversion programs may be required to convert data from these legacy systems to meet corporate reporting requirements. Unique information-processing problems usually result from these mergers, acquisitions, and joint ventures. Management at both the corporate and institutional levels must be prepared to address these problems as the plans for organizational change are developed.

Transition

Many health systems are developing data warehouses to serve the needs of facilities within their systems. Breen and Rodrigues (2001, 87) present a case study on development of a data warehouse and conclude, "Successful implementation of a data warehouse involves a corporate treasure hunt— identifying and cataloging data. It involves data ownership, data integrity, and business process analysis to determine what the data are, who owns them, how reliable they are, and how they are processed."

The Cleveland Clinic, Cleveland, Ohio, has extended its efforts to report quality indicators by using its administrative and clinical data repository of patient data to aggregate and report physician indicators of quality. In its settings, advanced practice nurses (APNs) provide primary care to patients in the ambulatory setting, but their data are traditionally linked to the primary care provider and not to the nurse. The extension is to link patient information assembled via its electronic health record to the APN managing the patient.

In this way, quality outcomes can be reported for this vital provider group, demonstrating APNs' contribution to patient care (Kapoor et al. 2006).

Even the federal government has developed the data warehouse concept for collection, storage, and dissemination of the vast quantity of healthcare data it manages (see the website for the National Center for Health Statistics, part of the Centers for Disease Control and Prevention, at http://www.cdc.gov/nchs/datawh.htm or the Environmental Protection Agency website at http://www.epa.gov/enviro/ for examples).

Importance of System Integration: What

Certain background concepts are important to an understanding of the effective application of information technology in healthcare organizations. These concepts include a review of general systems theory, key principles of management related to the development and operation of information systems, and the need for change management in adapting systems to the organizational culture.

Systems Theory

Systems theory provides the conceptual foundation on which the development of information systems is based. Healthcare managers should have a general understanding of this theory to determine how information systems function in their organizations, particularly in using information for management control. Scientists have completed considerable research on systems and how they function in all phases of our society. Interest in *general systems theory* developed in the post–World War II period. Initial research efforts were focused primarily on the physical sciences, with the study of strategic military weapons systems, systems for space exploration, and automated systems of all kinds to reduce manual labor and improve the overall quality of life.

In the 1960s, attention shifted to the application of systems theory to the social sciences, including organizational theory and management. Although much of this work is highly theoretical and of interest to those involved primarily in research, some general discussion of systems theory is a useful background for understanding management control systems in healthcare delivery and for setting forth principles of information systems analysis and design.

The systems approach is important because it concentrates on examining a process in its entirety, rather than focusing on the parts, and relates the parts to each other to achieve total system goals. Management control requires that performance be compared against expectations and that feedback be used to adjust the system when performance goals are not being met.

Systems analysis is a fundamental tool for the design and development of information systems. It is the process of studying organizational operations and determining information systems requirements for a given application.

Systems analysis employs concepts from general systems theory in analyzing inputs, processes, outputs, and feedback in defining requirements for an information system. The remainder of this section presents a general overview of systems theory and its application in healthcare organizations.

A variety of systems comprise the functioning of healthcare organizations. These systems can be categorized into three groups: mechanical systems, human systems, and human-machine systems. *Mechanical systems* are an integral part of the physical plant, serving such purposes as heating and cooling; monitoring temperature, pressure, and humidity; and supplying chilled and heated water.

Most of the essential functions of a healthcare organization are carried out through *human systems*—organized relationships among patients, physicians, employees, family members of patients, and others. Many of these systems are formally defined. For example, nursing care is provided in accordance with a scheduled set of predetermined protocols and procedures, and nursing service personnel are trained and supervised in the proper execution of this "system of care." Many things also happen through informal relationships, which often become well defined and known to those in the organization. Thus, certain activities get accomplished by "knowing the right person" or sending informal signals to key individuals about actions that need to be taken.

With the development of modern information technology, many systems fall into the third category, *human-machine systems.* These are formally defined systems in which human effort is assisted by various kinds of automated equipment. For example, computer systems have been developed to continuously monitor the vital signs of critically ill patients in intensive care units of medical centers.

Information systems in healthcare organizations fall into the second and third categories of this simple taxonomy; that is, information systems will be either human systems or human-machine systems designed to support operations. Information systems that operate without any type of machine processing of data are referred to as *manual* systems. Although much of this book deals with computer-aided information processing, most of the principles set forth here, particularly those dealing with systems analysis and design, apply equally to the development of manual systems for processing information.

Healthcare organizations also can be described in a broader context. Figure 3.5 is a systems diagram for a healthcare organization that shows the relationships among various inputs and environmental factors as these factors influence the provision of services to the community. In this context, mechanical, human, and human-machine systems would constitute elements, or subsystems, of the conversion process.

Systems Characteristics

Certain basic concepts are central to a general understanding of systems and how they function. These are presented in the following paragraphs.

FIGURE 3.5
The Healthcare Organization as a System

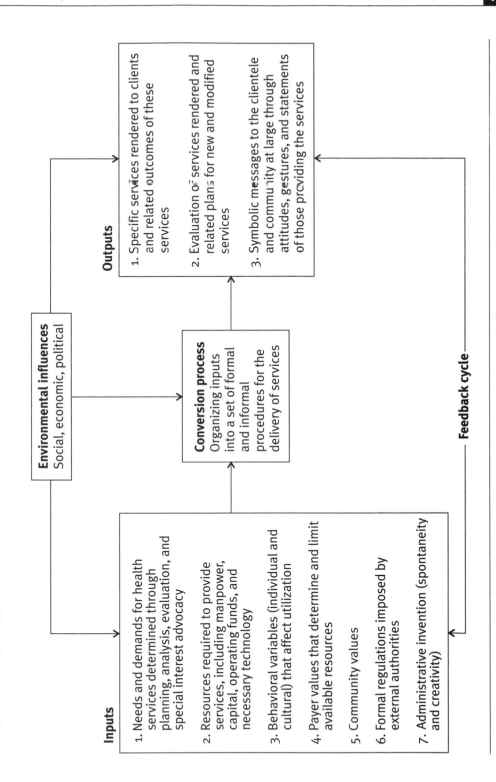

A system must have unity or integrity. A system must be something that can be viewed as an entity in its own right, with unity of purpose in the accomplishment of some goal or function. A system must have an identity and must have describable boundaries that allow it to be defined without reference to external events or objects.

Systems at work in healthcare organizations are, for the most part, very complex. The intricate web of complex relationships that constitute most social systems often makes it difficult to describe simple cause-and-effect relationships among individual components of the system. The phenomenon of system complexity is often described by stating that a system is more than the sum of its parts.

Complex systems are further defined by their hierarchical structure: Large systems in healthcare organizations can be divided into several subsystems, and these subsystems in turn are subject to further subdivision in a nested format. For example, the patient care component of an integrated delivery system is composed of several subsystems—a diagnostic subsystem, a therapeutic subsystem, a rehabilitative subsystem, and so forth. Each of these subsystems in turn can be further described by a series of smaller systems. The entire network of systems and subsystems nests together in a structured way to describe the patient care system of the organization (see Figure 3.6).

FIGURE 3.6
Healthcare
Organization
Systems
Network

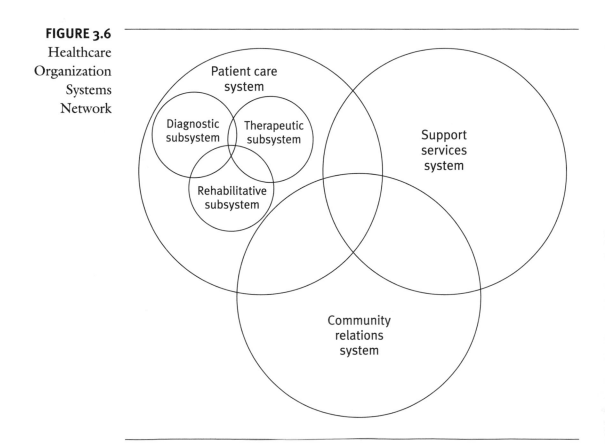

Although most organizational systems are dynamic and subject to frequent change, they nonetheless must possess some stability and equilibrium. The system must continue to function in the face of changing requirements and changes in the external environment in which it operates. To accomplish this, procedures must be sufficiently generalized to accommodate a variety of situations that can be expected to develop. Complex systems must be self-adapting and must include control functions that are continuous and automatic. When the system can no longer adapt to changing requirements or major changes in the external environment, it no longer functions as a system and breakdown has occurred.

Systems can be either deterministic or probabilistic. In a deterministic system, the component parts function according to completely predictable or definable relationships. Most mechanical systems are deterministic. On the other hand, human systems or human-machine systems (including information systems) are probabilistic because all relationships cannot be perfectly predicted. In healthcare organizations, for example, most clinical systems are subject to fairly extreme fluctuations in the quantity and nature of the demand for patient services. Systems theory, then, provides a perspective—a way of viewing not just the parts, not just the whole, but the spectrum of relationships of the parts viewed in the context of the unitary purposes of the system as a whole.

The simplest of all systems consists of three essential components: one or more inputs, a conversion process, and one or more outputs (see Figure 3.7). Consider, for example, the appointment-scheduling process of an ambulatory care center as a simple system. *Inputs* to the system consist of appointment requests from patients; physician schedules; and clinic resources, including personnel, treatment rooms, and supporting materials. The *conversion process* includes a set of actions: the scheduling clerks collect information from patients, match patient requirements to available time slots, and make appointments. *Output* of this simple system consists of patients scheduled for service in the clinic. Note that the output of this system becomes the input for several other functional systems of the clinic—medical records, patient accounting, and others.

Most systems also involve feedback. Feedback is a process by which one or more items of output information "feeds back" and influences future inputs (see Figure 3.8). In the example just cited, feedback will occur in the form of adjusted information on the number of time slots available as patients are scheduled for the clinic. Each time an appointment is made, input data on times available are revised and updated.

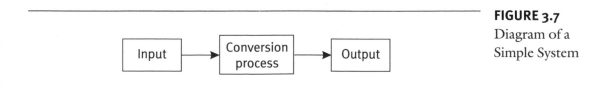

FIGURE 3.7
Diagram of a
Simple System

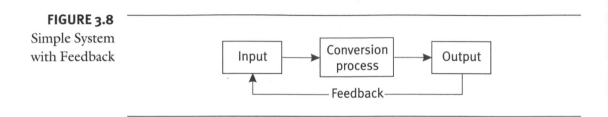

Systems are either open or closed. A *closed system* is completely self-contained and is not influenced by external events. In an *open system*, the components of the system exchange materials, energies, or information with their environment (see Figure 3.9); that is, they influence and are influenced by the environment in which they operate. All closed systems eventually die (cease to function as a system). Only open systems that adjust to the environment can survive as systems over time.

Environmental Factors in Open Systems

Healthcare systems, with the exception of certain purely mechanical systems in the physical plant, fall into the category of open systems. Human or human-machine systems in healthcare organizations are influenced by a variety of environmental factors (sometimes referred to as *exogenous factors* or variables) that are important to consider in understanding how a system functions. These environmental factors fall into four broad categories: social, economic, political, and physical environment.

Healthcare systems are influenced by *social factors*—characteristics of individuals and groups of people involved in the transactions that organizations undertake. Social factors affect patient behavior and patterns of utilization of services. Informal patterns of behavior develop among employees, and these have definite effects on the way operating systems function. The organizational roles played by physicians and other health professionals interact with the formal functioning of healthcare systems. Social factors are important determinants of system functioning, and systems analysts need to be well versed in the art of human-factors engineering when designing systems.

A second major category of environmental factors is *economic* in nature. Systems are directly dependent on the availability of resources, and fluctuations in the local and national economy will influence both demand and resources. It is well known, for example, that elective procedures are often deferred by patients during times of economic recession.

Healthcare systems are also affected by *political factors*. A variety of special interest groups place competing demands on healthcare organizations, and systems are influenced both by community politics and by organizational politics. These political realities must be considered in the analysis and design of systems for the institution.

The *physical environment* constitutes the final category of environmental factors affecting organizational systems. The amount of space available and the way in which system components relate physically to each other will influence the effectiveness of a system.

To summarize briefly, healthcare systems are open systems influenced by a variety of social, economic, and political factors and by the physical environment within which they function.

Cybernetic System

The final concept to be introduced in this brief review of general systems theory is the concept of a cybernetic, or self-regulating, system (Weiner 1954). Feedback in a cybernetic system is controlled to adjust the future functioning of the system within a predetermined set of standards. The following components are added to the general system components to provide this automatic control:

1. A *sensor* element continuously gathers data on system outputs.
2. Data from the sensor are fed into a *monitor* for continuous matching of the quantity or quality, or both, of performance against *standards*—predetermined expectations of system performance.
3. Error signals from the monitor are sent to a *control unit,* whose purpose is to generate correctional signals that automatically modify inputs and conversion processes to bring the functioning of the system back into control.

The most often cited example of a cybernetic system is a thermostatic control system for the automatic heating and cooling of a building. The sensor unit continuously measures ambient temperature and sends signals to the monitor, which compares the current temperature to preset standards. Through the control process, automatic correction signals are sent back to the

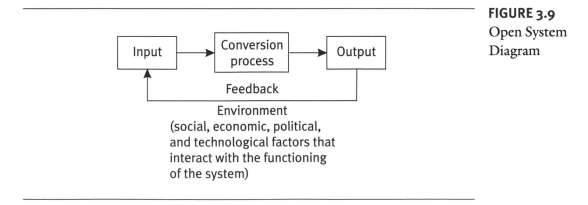

FIGURE 3.9
Open System
Diagram

heating/cooling units of the system to keep the temperature within control limits.

Management Control and Decision Support Systems

Organized systems in healthcare organizations should be designed as cybernetic systems with formal management controls built in as an integral part of the design. The inputs to this generalized system include the demand for services by patients and those who represent them and the resources required to provide services such as labor, materials, capital, and technology. The conversion process consists of actions taken by employees of the healthcare organization aided by formalized procedures, informal patterns of functioning, and supporting equipment. System outputs include the services rendered to patients and the specific patient and community outcomes related to these services.

Management control is introduced in cybernetic components of the system (see Figure 3.10). The sensor component continuously gathers data on the quantity of services rendered, the quality and other characteristics of these services, and the resources consumed in their provision. Data from the sensor (management reports) are monitored against the standards, established in advance, of quantity (production and service goals), quality of care, efficiency of the service process, and patient outcomes. When standards are not met, a control process is activated to initiate necessary changes and improvements. The control process contains several components, including education and training of personnel, community education programs, reengineering of the process of care, personnel changes to improve service, utilization of employee incentives, initiation of disciplinary action, and many others.

A key component in the establishment of management control systems is the establishment of standards for performance and quality control. The task of developing standards is not an easy one and requires considerable effort and thoughtful planning among managers and professional personnel practicing in or employed by the healthcare organization. Standards can be developed in a number of ways. They may be established by administrative or medical authority in the institution. In some cases, they may be developed through negotiation and subsequent agreement between employees and supervisors. Empirical studies of previous performance, using industrial engineering techniques, offer another approach to standards setting. In certain areas of operation, standards are mandated by external regulations, legal requirements, or accrediting agencies.

Whatever the approach to the development of standards for healthcare systems, standards are essential to avoid management control that operates on an ad hoc basis. Standards require careful management planning, continual review and revision, and frequent reinforcement through incorporation into the formal reward system. They are essential to effective management control.

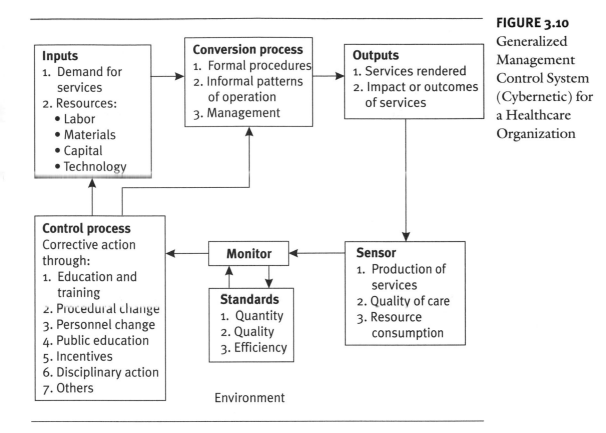

FIGURE 3.10

Generalized Management Control System (Cybernetic) for a Healthcare Organization

As an example of these concepts, the operation of a centralized clinical laboratory in an integrated delivery system can be described as a cybernetic system with planned controls built into the system for quality assurance and performance-control purposes. Figure 3.11 is a schematic diagram describing the functioning of the laboratory in system terms.

System inputs include scheduled demand (laboratory tests planned, ordered, and scheduled in advance) and unscheduled demand (tests required to be processed on an emergency, or stat, basis). Resource inputs include technical personnel in the laboratory, materials and equipment used in the testing process, and related technology. The conversion process consists of those formal and informal organizational actions related to collecting specimens; conducting laboratory tests; and reporting results to appropriate points in the hospitals, outpatient clinics, and other service units of the IDS. System outputs include the test reports sent back to clinicians ordering the tests, charges for services transmitted to the patient accounting department for billing purposes, and various statistical reports.

Cybernetic components for management control are also included. The sensor component is the management reporting system of the laboratory by which data on the number of tests conducted by various categories, quality control data, and records of resources consumed (including personnel time

FIGURE 3.11

Clinical
Laboratory as a
Cybernetic
System

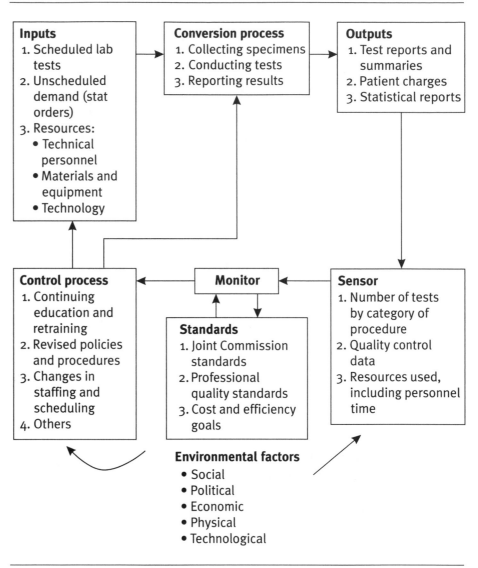

Inputs
1. Scheduled lab tests
2. Unscheduled demand (stat orders)
3. Resources:
   • Technical personnel
   • Materials and equipment
   • Technology

Conversion process
1. Collecting specimens
2. Conducting tests
3. Reporting results

Outputs
1. Test reports and summaries
2. Patient charges
3. Statistical reports

Control process
1. Continuing education and retraining
2. Revised policies and procedures
3. Changes in staffing and scheduling
4. Others

Monitor

Sensor
1. Number of tests by category of procedure
2. Quality control data
3. Resources used, including personnel time

Standards
1. Joint Commission standards
2. Professional quality standards
3. Cost and efficiency goals

Environmental factors
• Social
• Political
• Economic
• Physical
• Technological

of laboratory technicians) are collected and recorded. These data are used by laboratory managers who monitor actual performance against predetermined standards, including those established by The Joint Commission, professional standards of quality established by the chief pathologist and medical staff, and cost and efficiency (productivity) goals established jointly by the administrative and medical personnel in the organization. When standards are not met, corrective actions are initiated, including activation of continuing education and retraining; revision of operating policies and procedures, including recalibration of test equipment if necessary; change in staffing patterns and scheduling; and the like. The laboratory operates overall as an open system influenced by several contextual or environmental factors, including the physical environment of the laboratory facility, current economic conditions of the IDS, social and political factors related to interaction of personnel in the laboratory, and the advancement of technology.

Information for Management Control

Any management control system is information dependent. Information requirements permeate the system diagrams presented in the preceding parts of this chapter. For health programs to be properly managed, information is needed about each of the major system components previously described.

Input information must be collected to monitor demand continuously, both scheduled and unscheduled, as well as the resources consumed in the provision of services. Operational procedures must be constantly observed through information on exceptions, error rates, system malfunctions, and similar performance measures on a management-by-exception basis. Output information on the quantity and quality of services rendered must be matched with information on related outcomes of the provision of specific services. In addition, the effective manager must keep in close contact with the environment in which his or her department or institution functions. Environmental information—such as demographic characteristics of the service population, previous utilization patterns, services offered by other organizations, and recent changes in community values—is essential to this task. An effective information system will be designed with these kinds of management information needs in mind.

What, then, are the attributes of information useful for management control in the delivery of healthcare? Some of the more important characteristics of effective management information are listed in Figure 3.12 and discussed below.

Characteristics of Useful Information

The first, and perhaps most essential, characteristic is that information, to be useful, must contain *information, not just raw data*. Data must be intelligently processed in accordance with predesigned plans before it becomes information useful to management or operating personnel.

- Information—not data
- Relevant
- Sensitive
- Unbiased
- Comprehensive
- Timely
- Action oriented
- Uniform (for comparative purposes)
- Performance targeted
- Cost effective

FIGURE 3.12
Characteristics of Useful Management Information

Health information must be *relevant* to the purposes for which it is to be used. It must be sufficiently *sensitive* to provide discrimination and meaningful comparisons for operating managers. Many information systems provide data that are so aggregated that they provide no meaningful indicators for management planning or control purposes. Overall hospital cost per patient day is a good example. By contrast, separating costs into fixed and variable components and allocating variable costs by diagnostic groupings and level of care provide more useful information to management.

Useful information must be *unbiased* and not collected or analyzed in such a way that it meets self-fulfilling prophecies. Information should be *comprehensive* so that all elements or components of a system are visible to those responsible for administering that system.

Information must be *timely*, presented to users in advance of the time when decisions or actions are required. Many information systems produce beautiful reports that are completely useless because of failure to meet operational time requirements. Information should be *action oriented*, designed to aid the manager directly in the decision process rather than just to present passive facts about current operations. For example, information from an inventory control and materials management system should include direct indicators of when specific items need to be reordered rather than just give data on current numbers in stock.

Information systems should have as their goal the production of *uniform* reports so that performance indicators can be compared over time both internally against previous performance and externally against the experience of other comparable organizations. Good information will also be *performance targeted*, designed and collected in reference to predetermined goals and objectives of the institution. Finally, information should be *cost effective*. The anticipated benefits to be obtained from having the information available should be worth the costs of collecting and processing that same information.

Importance of Systems Integration: Why

System integration is one of the most important objectives of strategic IM/IT planning. Healthcare delivery generally involves a wide range of providers. While much of that care provision used to occur primarily in a hospital or in a physician's office, today, care is provided in many settings by many providers. Getting these diverse groups to coordinate care has been a challenge because of geographic and organizational separation. For optimum care, these organizations must become more highly interconnected.

The first challenge is for units of the organization to communicate with one another and share clinical information. Clinicians need information that is generated by several different departments (radiology, pathology, etc.) to make diagnostic and treatment decisions. Mixing of clinical and financial information is essential for effective management and strategic decision support.

Internal communication and sharing of information is only half the battle. The concept of system integration has expanded from the need for connecting within an organizational entity to connectivity across organizations (Markle Foundation 2004). Healthcare organizations need to be connected externally for both business and regulatory reasons. The federal government's mandate for interoperability has raised the urgency for system integration and has led to the establishment of the Certification Commission for Healthcare Information Technology (CCHIT). This commission is charged with creating standards by which healthcare organizations can communicate information. It is thought that government standards will force vendors to develop software that meets interoperability requirements. In addition, the connectivity must include business partners for healthcare organizations and all other providers in an integrated delivery network. For example, Figure 3.13 represents a schematic diagram of the information requirements for a truly integrated delivery system (Markle Foundation 2004).

Oas (2001) states that system integration has been slow in coming to healthcare. Information systems developed in the 1980s focused on billing and business office functions. Most of these systems contained limited clinical information. In the 1990s, emphasis shifted to automation of clinical processes and provision of access to clinical data to individuals across the enterprise. Seamless integration and information sharing is essential in today's environment. However, much has yet to be done to achieve this. CCHIT Chair Mark Leavitt indicated that providers in the healthcare field still have limited ability for any two member entities to exchange information (Robeznieks 2006).

Achieving system integration requires careful front-end planning prior to the selection and acquisition of computer hardware and software. Some of the technical aspects of data and software integration are discussed elsewhere in the book. The planning processes described in the remainder of this chapter are essential to help ensure that systems are connected for information sharing across the organization.

The business case for integration stems from the vital role that comprehensive information has on clinical and administrative decision making. The potential for computerized physician order entry (CPOE) to reduce medical errors rests firmly on IM/IT capacity and integrated medical, nursing, and pharmacy systems (see Hillestad et al. 2005 and Johnston et al. 2003 for general discussions and findings regarding CPOE). Strategic growth through fully utilizing the joint inpatient, ambulatory, and physician practices relies upon seamless information flows among and between these entities. Finally, the new movement to regional health information networks (RHIOs) will require access to and sharing of clinical and financial information among organizations. Investing in the capacity of organizations to share clinical and financial information is occurring in an era of significant cost constraints for healthcare and IM/IT.

FIGURE 3.13

Information Requirements for an Interconnected Network

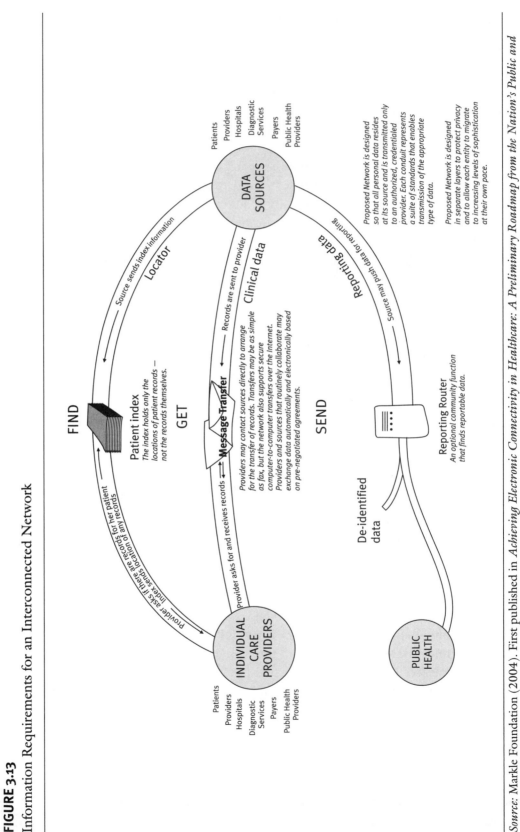

Source: Markle Foundation (2004). First published in *Achieving Electronic Connectivity in Healthcare: A Preliminary Roadmap from the Nation's Public and Private-Sector Healthcare Leaders.* Used with permission.

Summary

IM/IT governance has expanded in scope and importance along with the growing integrative role of health information in healthcare organizations. Healthcare organizations that successfully implement IM/IT must have a governance structure that effectively (1) develops a consistent IM/IT strategy; (2) aligns IM/IT with organizational strategy; (3) develops IM/IT infrastructure, architecture, and policies; (4) sets IM/IT project priorities and oversees investments in IM/IT infrastructure; and (5) uses IM/IT benefits assessment to enhance accountability.

To attain that success, organizational leadership must formulate an IM/IT plan that is linked to the strategic plan of the organization. The plan should include (1) a statement of information systems goals and objectives aligned with organizational goals and priorities; (2) a list of priorities for the computer applications portfolio (clinical, management/administrative, electronic networking and e-health, and strategic decision support); (3) specification of overall system architecture and infrastructure; (4) a software development plan; (5) an information resources management plan; (6) a statement of resource requirements, including projected capital and operating budgets; and (7) schedules and target dates for implementation of various elements of the plan.

The planning process should be guided by an enterprisewide information systems steering committee with membership from senior management, medical staff, nursing staff, financial management, human resources management, planning and marketing, facilities management, and clinical support services. The CIO should chair the committee if the healthcare organization has established such a position.

System integration—that is, the ability of information systems to communicate with one another and share information—is essential. Integration can be achieved through a number of alternative information network architecture configurations, including a central mainframe approach, client/server architecture, file/server architecture, and distributed processing.

The planning process should include development of major institutional policies related to information systems. The information systems steering committee should oversee policies related to data security, privacy, and confidentiality; data standardization; acquisition of hardware, software, and telecommunications network equipment throughout the enterprise; and policies on use of the Internet.

An understanding of general systems theory is useful for healthcare managers in designing and developing management control systems and in obtaining the kinds of information that are required to enable such systems to function effectively. Healthcare systems are characterized as "open systems." These are influenced by the environment in which they function, and they exchange information with that environment. Key environmental factors include political, social, and economic variables that influence system performance as well as the physical environment in which the system functions. Healthcare systems are also considered "cybernetic systems" if they include formally planned components that introduce automatic control into the systems. Cybernetic components include sensors to gather data on current system functioning; monitors to compare these data against predetermined standards; and control elements to change inputs or process, or both, when system functioning is out of control. Management control systems in healthcare organizations can be designed according to principles of cybernetic system theory.

Healthcare delivery viewed in a systems context is information dependent. Effective information for management control purposes has several important characteristics, including relevance, sensitivity, objectivity, comprehensiveness, timeliness, action orientation, uniformity, performance targeting, and cost effectiveness. Good information systems are developed with these characteristics constantly on the minds of those charged with design and implementation.

Web Resources

Government sources for data warehousing include the National Center for Health Statistics, part of the Centers for Disease Control and Prevention, http://www.cdc.gov/nchs/datawh.htm, and the Environmental Protection Agency, http://www.epa.gov/enviro/.

For diverse examples of hospital and healthcare organization information technology strategic plans, including guidelines and templates available from associations and vendors, see the following:

- The Joint Commission provides a detailed template for information management planning and broader strategic planning at http://www.olcsoft.com/IM_Strategic_Plans_for_JCAHO.htm.
- Stanford University Medical Center has made available details of its IM/IT strategic plan and planning process at http://medstrategicplan.stanford.edu/retreat03/IRT.ppt.
- Consulting firm jjwild provides a case study involving many of their clients, including Johnson Medical Center, at http://www.jjwild.com/resources-casestudies.html.
- Strategic Plan for the University of Medicine and Dentistry of New Jersey, http://informatics.umdnj.edu/iaims/pdf/Strategic_Plan_20.PDF.
- University of Texas Health Sciences Center at Tyler, http://www.uthct.edu/files/pdf/rtts_strategicplanirm_fy2004–2007.pdf.
- Indiana University School of Medicine Information Systems Strategic Plan, http://technology.iusm.iu.edu/strategicplan/bground.pdf.

For more information on the HL7 project, go to www.hl7.org.

The American National Standards Institute (ANSI) (www.ansi.org) X.12 Group is working on specifications for transactions involving the processing of health insurance claims.

The resource guide published by *Health Management Technology* magazine (available online at www.healthmgttech.com) contains a vast array of vendors organized by function.

Discussion Questions

1. With the change in the definition of IM/IT governance, why is the external focus of healthcare IM/IT orientation important?
2. What factors should be considered when developing a consistent IM/IT strategy?
3. Should the IM/IT strategy be developed with the IM/IT department in mind and then aligned with the organization, or should the IM/IT strategy be developed with the organizational strategy in mind?
4. Why is data standardization becoming increasingly important in healthcare?
5. Several reasons for central review of software and hardware standards were presented. What other ways would central review assist the organization?
6. The need for a master plan for information systems development was discussed. What factors/concepts should be included in this plan?
7. What would be the functions of the individuals in the steering committee, such as medical, nursing, financial management, human resources management, facilities management, and clinical support services staff? Why is it important to have all these areas represented on the steering committee?
8. There are several reasons to prefer centralized computing over decentralized computing, and vice versa. Which would you prefer, and why?
9. What are your opinions on end-user computing? What are the advantages and disadvantages?
10. What is the importance of data warehouses/clinical data repositories?
11. Give five different examples of simple systems and include the input(s), conversion process, and output(s). Ensure that there is some feedback between your examples.
12. Why do closed systems eventually die, while open systems may continue to be upgraded and modified?
13. Find examples of the use of cybernetic systems in healthcare, other than the examples provided.
14. What other challenges exist with systems integration between/among healthcare organizations? What are the solutions to these problems?

15. Find two RHIOs currently in existence. Provide an overview of each RHIO and then determine the differences between them.

16. What governance challenges do RHIOs pose for healthcare organizations in general and specifically for healthcare IM/IT?

References

Austin, C. J., J. M. Trimm, and P. M. Sobczak. 1995. "Information Systems and Strategic Management." *Health Care Management Review* 20 (3): 26–33.

Beeler, G. W. 2001. "The Crucial Role of Standards." *Healthcare Informatics* 18 (2): 98–104.

Boyd, J. 2005. "The Grass Is Greener? Outsourcing and the Merits of Marriage." In *The CEO-CIO Partnership: Harnessing the Value of Information Technology in Healthcare*, edited by D. Smaltz, J. Glaser, R. Skinner, and T. Cunningham III. Chicago: Healthcare Information and Management Systems Society.

Breen, C., and L. M. Rodrigues. 2001. "Implementing a Data Warehouse at Inglis Innovative Services." *Journal of Healthcare Information Management* 15 (2): 87–97.

Broadbent, M., and E. Kitzis. 2005. *The New CIO Leader: Setting the Agenda and Delivering Results*. Boston: Harvard Business School Press.

Brown, A., and G. Grant. 2005. "Framing the Frameworks: A Review of IT Governance Research." *Communication of the Association for Information Systems* 15: 696–712.

Carr, N. 2003. "It Doesn't Matter." *Harvard Business Review* 81 (5): 41–49.

DeFord, D., and D. Porter. 2005. "To Centralize or Decentralize? That Is the Question." In *The CEO-CIO Partnership: Harnessing the Value of Information Technology in Healthcare*, edited by D. Smaltz, J. Glaser, R. Skinner, and T. Cunningham III. Chicago: Healthcare Information and Management Systems Society.

Gabler, J. M. 2001. "Linking Business Values to IT Investments." *Health Management Technology* 22 (2): 76–77.

Glaser, J. 2002. *The Strategic Application of Information Technology in Health Care Organizations*, 2nd ed. San Francisco: Jossey-Bass.

Glaser, J., and D. Garets. 2005. "Where's the Beef? Part 1: Getting Value from Your IT Investments." In *The CEO-CIO Partnership: Harnessing the Value of Information Technology in Healthcare*, edited by D. Smaltz, J. Glaser, R. Skinner, and T. Cunningham III. Chicago: Healthcare Information and Management Systems Society.

Healthcare Information and Management Systems Society (HIMSS). 2006. *Seventeenth Annual HIMSS Leadership Survey: Final Report: Healthcare CIO*. Sponsored by ACS Healthcare Solutions. Chicago: HIMSS.

———. 2005a. *Sixteenth Annual HIMSS Leadership Survey*. Sponsored by Superior Consultant. Chicago: HIMSS.

———. 2005b. "New Healthcare Information Technology Standards Panel Formed under Contract by DHHS." October 6. [Online press release; retrieved 12/1/06.] www.himss.org/ASP/ContentRedirector.asp?ContentID=65351

———. 2002. *Thirteenth Annual HIMSS Leadership Survey*. Chicago: HIMSS.

————. 1996. *Seventh Annual HIMSS Leadership Survey*. Chicago: HIMSS.

Hillestad, R., J. Bigelow, A. Bower, F. Girosi, R. Meili, R. Scoville, and R. Taylor. 2005. "Can Electronic Medical Record Systems Transform Health Care? Potential Health Benefits, Savings, and Costs." *Health Affairs* 24 (5): 1103–17.

Johnson, W. 2005 "The Planning Cycle." *Journal of Healthcare Information Management* 19 (3): 56–64.

Johnston, D., E. Pan, and B. Middleton. 2002. *Finding the Value in Healthcare Information Technologies*. Boston: Center for Information Technology Leadership.

Johnston, D., E. Pan, B. Middleton, J. Walker, and D. Bates. 2003. "The Value of Computerized Provider Order Entry in Ambulatory Settings." [Online article; retrieved 9/1/06.] http://citl.org/research/ACPOE_Executive_Preview.pdf

Kapoor, R., J. Fuchs, C. Lutz, and A. Jain. 2006. "A Model for Extending Physician-Specific Process Measures to the Advanced Practice Nurses." *AMIA Annual Symposium Proceedings*. 975.

Kuperman, G., A. Boyer, C. Cole, B. Forman, P. Stetson, and M. Cooper. 2006. "Using IT to Improve Quality at New York-Presbyterian Hospital: A Requirement-Driven Strategic Planning Process." *AMIA Annual Symposium Proceedings*. 449–53.

Lohman, P. 1996. "Measure Consultant's Objectivity and Character Before Contracting." *Health Management Technology* (July): 31.

Lutchen, M., and A. Collins. 2005. "IT Governance in Healthcare Setting: Reinventing the Healthcare Industry." *Journal of Healthcare Compliance* 7 (6): 27–30.

Markle Foundation. 2004. *Achieving Electronic Connectivity in Healthcare: A Preliminary Roadmap from the Nation's Public and Private-Sector Healthcare Leaders*. [Online report; retrieved 12/31/07.] http://www.connectingforhealth.org/resources/cfh_aech_roadmap_072004.pdf

Menning, W., and R. Carpenter. 2005. "Who's Minding the Store? Effective IT Governance." In *The CEO-CIO Partnership: Harnessing the Value of Information Technology in Healthcare*, edited by D. Smaltz, J. Glaser, R. Skinner, and T. Cunningham III. Chicago: Healthcare Information and Management Systems Society.

Monohan, T. 2001. "And an ASP Is . . . ?" *Healthcare Informatics* 18 (2): 54–56.

Oas, B. 2001. "Integration: Organizations Streamline the Business of Healthcare by Joining Disparate Systems." *Healthcare Informatics* 18 (2): 58–60.

Petersen, L. A., L. D. Woodard, T. Urech, C. Daw, and S. Sookanan. 2006. "Does Pay-for-Performance Improve the Quality of Health Care?" *Annals of Internal Medicine* 145 (4): 265–72.

Presidential Initiatives. 2006. "Consolidated Health Informatics." [Online information; retrieved 1/1/07.] http://www.whitehouse.gov/omb/egov/c-3-6-chi.html

Rosenthal, M., B. Landon, S. L. Normand, R. Frank, and A. Epstein. 2006. "Pay for Performance in Commercial HMOs." *New England Journal of Medicine* 355: 1895–1902.

Robeznieks, A. 2006. "Leavitt Surveys Road to Interoperability." *Modern Healthcare*, October 30. [Online article; retrieved 7/1/07.] www.modernhealthcare.com/apps/pbcs.dll/article?AID=/20061030/FREE/61030014/1029/newsletter02

Rockart, J. F. 1979. "Chief Executives Define Their Own Data Needs." *Harvard Business Review* 57 (2): 81–84.

Sambamurthy, V., and R. Zmud. 1999. "Arrangements for Information Technology Governance: A Theory of Multiple Contingencies." *MIS Quarterly* 23 (2): 261–90.

Scottsdale Institute and HIMSS Analytics. 2005. *Healthcare Leaders Report: The Changing Landscape of Healthcare It Management and Governance.* Chicago: HIMSS Analytics.

Smaltz, D., R. Carpenter, and J. Saltz. 2007. "Effective IT Governance in Healthcare Organisations: A Tale of Two Organisations." *International Journal of Healthcare Technology and Management* 8 (1–2): 20–41.

Stacey, R., and R. Skinner. 2005. "Crystal Balls: The Elusive Art of Business and IT Strategic Alignment." In *The CEO-CIO Partnership: Harnessing the Value of Information Technology in Healthcare,* edited by D. Smaltz, J. Glaser, R. Skinner, and T. Cunningham III. Chicago: Healthcare Information and Management Systems Society.

Swayne, L. E., W. J. Duncan, and P. M. Ginter. 2005. *Strategic Management of Health Care Organizations,* 5th ed. Malden, MA: Blackwell Publishing.

Turisco, F. 2000. "How to Justify the Investment: Principles for Effective IT Value Management." *Health Management Technology* 21 (3): 12–13.

Ward, J., and P. Griffiths. 1996. *Strategic Planning for Information Systems,* 2nd ed. New York: John Wiley and Sons.

Weill, P., and J. Ross. 2004. *IT Governance: How Top Performers Manage IT Decision Rights for Superior Results.* Boston: Harvard Business School Press.

Weiner, N. 1954. *The Human Use of Human Beings: Cybernetics and Society.* Garden City, NY: Doubleday Anchor.

Wilson, T. D. 1989. "The Implementation of Information Systems Strategies in UK Companies: Aims and Barriers to Success." *International Journal of Information Management* 9 (4): 245–58.

Wilson, K. J., and C. E. McPherson. 2002. "It's 2002: How HIPAA-Ready Are You?" *Health Management Technology* 23 (1): 14–15, 20.

THE IM/IT PORTFOLIO MANAGEMENT OFFICE

Learning Objectives

1. Identify some of the primary causes of information management/ information technology (IM/IT) project failures.
2. Describe the main differences between IM/IT project management, IM/IT program management, and IM/IT portfolio management.
3. Describe the five key processes of project management.
4. Understand how project metrics and portfolio dashboards can facilitate IM/IT governance.
5. Describe the major roles and functions of the portfolio management office.
6. Identify the actions/changes that are necessary within an organization to reach the synchronized stage discussed by Jeffery and Leliveld (2004).

Healthcare in the United States now consumes more than 15 percent of gross domestic product, yet U.S. residents generally do not live longer, nor are they healthier, than those in other developed nations that spend less than half that amount on healthcare (Goldman and McGlynn 2005). The reality of these statistics, along with the Institute of Medicine's (IOM 1999) report on preventable deaths in the United States, has energized the federal and state governments in ways that will continue to put pressure on healthcare organizations. For example, plans for reduced reimbursement rates will put a crimp on the increasing bottom-line pressures to ensure that any investments in capital gain the envisioned returns. Clearly, just by their sheer size, seven-, eight-, or even nine-figure expenditures on electronic health record (EHR) projects (depending on the size of the organization) should automatically create a heightened need for due diligence among healthcare executives—nothing can get an executive fired faster than spending $50 million with nothing to show for it.

In their 2006 presentation "IT Disasters: The Worst IT Debacles and the Lessons Learned from Them" at the American College of Healthcare Executives Congress on Healthcare Leadership, Hunter and Ciotti provide ample evidence that risks are associated with large-scale information management/information technology (IM/IT) projects. While inadequate planning and foresight are problematic in such projects, the single greatest cause of project failure is poor execution (Bossidy and Charan 2002; Hunter and Ciotti 2006). Furthermore, some of the literature has suggested that IM/IT systems may even cause, rather than reduce, medical errors (Han et al. 2005; Koppel et al. 2005; Ash et al. 2007). However, a careful reading of the original academic articles shows obvious design and implementation problems indicating that medical errors are caused by human error, not the IM/IT itself.

Figure 4.1 depicts the results of a recent Standish Group study that found only 29 percent of IM/IT projects achieved anticipated benefits (Hayes 2004). Organizations that fall into the category of the 71 percent who fail to achieve benefits often rely on the collected experience of the individuals who have previously implemented IM/IT at the organization but typically do not employ disciplined project management methodologies such as those suggested by the Project Management Institute (www.pmi.org; discussed in more detail below). Healthcare delivery is a complex business with incredibly multifaceted, interdependent workflows, yet the field as a whole has been inexplicably slow to adopt professional project management methodologies. Organizations that fall into this category typically "go live" only to find that large stakeholder groups or key workflows have been overlooked. These organizations must then scramble, after implementation, to reengineer processes that easily could have been proactively addressed had the organization followed disciplined project management methodologies.

This chapter provides an overview of healthcare IM/IT project management and encourages healthcare organizations to improve their project success rate by establishing an IM/IT portfolio management office (PMO).

What Is an IM/IT Portfolio Management Office?

The following set of definitions is used in the chapter to refer to terms related to portfolio management:

- A *project* is a temporary effort to create a unique product, service, or result (PMI 2004).
- *Project management* is the planning, organizing, directing, and controlling of company resources for a relatively short-term objective that has been established to complete specific goals and objectives (Kerzner 2003).
- A *program* is a group of related, often interdependent projects.
- A *portfolio* is a collection of programs and projects.
- *Portfolio management* encompasses managing the collections of programs and projects in a portfolio. This includes weighing the value of each project, or potential project, against desired organizational strategic business and clinical objectives. It also encompasses monitoring active projects for adherence to specified objectives and desired outcomes, balancing the portfolio among the other investments of the organization, ensuring the efficient use of resources, and balancing return on investment with risk (Kaplan 2005).

FIGURE 4.1
IM/IT Project
Success Rate

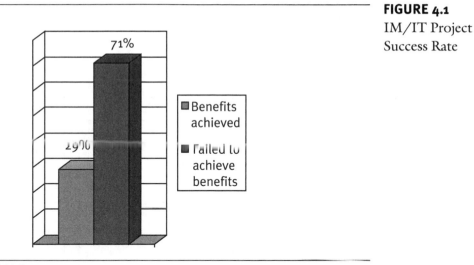

Source: Hayes (2004).

- A *portfolio management office* is a centralized organization dedicated to improving the practice and outcomes of projects via holistic management of all projects. Often the terms *project management office*, *program management office*, and *portfolio management office* are used interchangeably in the business press. All three imply the professional management and oversight of an organization's entire collection of projects. But the term *portfolio management office* specifically refers to the activity of providing investment decision support capabilities to an organization's overall IM/IT governance structure and processes. If the term *project management office* or *program management office* is used, it does not necessarily mean that these investment decision support capabilities are in place, but organizations that use the term *portfolio management office* use that term intentionally to more accurately reflect that it has IM/IT portfolio investment decision support capabilities (Jeffery and Leliveld 2004).

Figure 4.2 illustrates how projects, and programs of projects, might interrelate within a typical healthcare IM/IT portfolio.

Individual projects, such as a new inpatient EHR or a new pharmacy system, are grouped into a program of clinical applications projects. Ideally, clinical application projects are led or championed by an influential stakeholder from within the clinical leadership of an organization. Likewise, upgrades of an existing financial budgeting system and implementation of a new human resource system are grouped into a program of business applications. Business application projects are ideally led or championed by an influential business stakeholder. Purely infrastructure-type projects, like a network upgrade or implementing wireless technology, are grouped into a program of infrastructure projects that are championed or led by the chief information officer

FIGURE 4.2

IM/IT
Portfolio

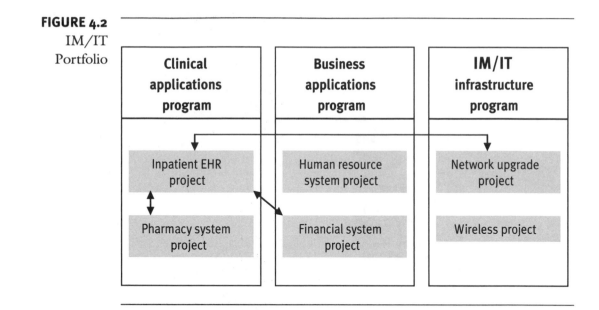

(CIO) or one of the CIO's key directors. All of the projects in all of the program groupings then make up the entire IM/IT portfolio of projects in the organization that can be professionally managed via formal IM/IT portfolio management structures and practices—an IM/IT PMO.

Why Is a PMO Essential?

As indicated at the beginning of this chapter, more than 70 percent of IM/IT projects fail to achieve anticipated benefits (Hayes 2004). One of the primary causes of failed IM/IT projects, particularly in healthcare, stems from a "silo" IM/IT project management mentality, which occurs when projects are initiated, planned, and fully executed without effectively considering their impact on other, preexisting systems or other projects being planned and executed in a parallel approach. As indicated in Figure 4.2, contemporary healthcare applications have significant interdependencies that, if not explicitly and deliberately addressed, can have unintended consequences. Table 4.1 provides some real-world examples of unintended consequences of IM/IT projects that were planned and executed in relative isolation.

While the examples described in Table 4.1 may seem like obvious, common-sense mistakes, in reality healthcare delivery organizations have literally thousands of cross-departmental interrelated workflows that must be considered when embarking on a new IM/IT project. Figure 4.3 depicts the high-level application interfaces that are in place currently at a typical academic medical center and is representative of any medium- to large-size integrated delivery system. The graphic conveys an incredibly complex web that relies heavily on interfacing applications wherever possible. The sheer volume of

IM/IT Project	Project Outcome
New pharmacy system: The pharmacy director sponsored a new "best of breed" pharmacy system project	The pharmacy system project was expertly managed and implemented on time and within budget. However, only after the system was implemented did the pharmacist realize that this new proprietary best-of-breed system could not be reliably interfaced with the hospital's preexisting EHR system, which had a built-in computer physician order entry capability. As such, when a provider entered an order for a pharmaceutical into the EHR system, that order must be printed out in the pharmacy and then reentered into the new pharmacy system. From a pure project management standpoint, the project was successful, but from an enterprise portfolio standpoint, an inefficient, labor-intensive workflow was created to overcome the lack of integration that this silo-based project management approach created.
Voice over Internet protocol (VoIP) project: A telecommunications director sponsored a switch to digital phone service	The telecommunications director of a large metropolitan hospital system wanted to save millions of dollars annually by switching from a traditional telephone service model to a VoIP model, whereby the hospital system's existing computer network would be used to provide digital phone service. However, the project did not consider the robustness of the existing computer network, which had single points of failure in many of its buildings. The digital phone service was implemented, and soon thereafter, anytime a network outage occurred to one of the buildings, all phone service for the building was affected. More than an inconvenience, these outages eroded consumer trust and market appeal. Using contingency funds, the hospital system scrambled to redesign its computer network to provide the level of redundancy and reliability needed to ensure digital phone service. Had a portfolio management approach been taken for this project, computer network inadequacies could have been identified up front and computer network upgrades could have been built into the project plan.

TABLE 4.1
Examples of IM/IT Projects that Did Not Follow an IM/IT Portfolio Management Approach

interdependencies reflected in this figure clearly makes a case that individual projects or programs of applications should not be managed in silos but rather in a professional PMO focused on successfully achieving envisioned benefits of particular projects.

In many ways, allowing informal, silo-based project management to occur in a healthcare organization is somewhat like attempting to minimize collisions at an airport without the benefit of a flight control tower. Not incidentally, Figure 4.3 resembles a typical major airline hub city with flights

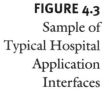

FIGURE 4.3
Sample of
Typical Hospital
Application
Interfaces

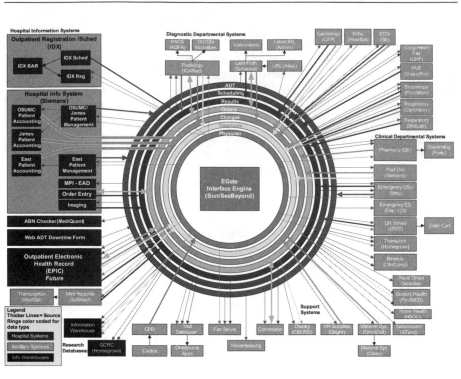

coming and going from all of the points on the compass. Yet it depicts a real organization's current applications and how each is interfaced and interrelated. The level of interrelatedness depicted in Figure 4.3 strongly suggests the need for a professional "control tower" approach to managing IM/IT projects at healthcare organizations. In fact, Gartner Research suggests that "three out of four successful $500,000-plus projects will be planned and tracked with project office support; while three out of four failed projects will not" (Light et al. 2005, 4). An organization's ability to successfully and efficiently implement large IM/IT projects increases as its project management maturity moves from no professionally managed projects to simple project management up through program management and ultimately to portfolio management.

Typically as an organization's maturity with respect to IM/IT project management increases, its overall cost of IM/IT projects decreases significantly, and the success rate of IM/IT projects increases substantially. Also, a nonintuitive overall time savings occurs: One would suspect it would actually take more time to accomplish the additional work of identifying and tracking interdependencies with other projects across the portfolio of projects. However, Kendall and Rollins (2003) suggest that this additional expense of planning time, which is marginal, actually reduces the number of surprises and "gotchas" that occur when unforeseen interdependencies invariably crop up in projects that are run in a more informal, silo approach—overall project time is reduced. Additionally, one of the main causes of time delays in projects is when "scope creep" occurs—when the original agreed-upon requirements for a system are continually expanded by the sponsors of the project. With project management methodologies in place, these attempts to add new requirements are collected as requirements for a future version of the system so that the original system scope can be implemented within the established time frames.

The next section provides information on project management methodologies. Thereafter, managing collections of projects is discussed and the suggestion is reiterated that a PMO is a logical organizational response to the increasing IM/IT complexity in healthcare organizations.

Project Management

Project management entails the following five key processes (PMI 2004):

1. *Project initiation:* defining and authorizing a project
2. *Project planning:* defining the objectives, scope, and plan of action to achieve the desired outcomes
3. *Project execution:* actions to complete the work that was defined in the project planning process
4. *Project monitoring and controlling:* measurements designed to assess how well a project is being executed to budget and deliverables as well as to alert project managers to potential corrective actions that might be necessary from time to time
5. *Project closing:* actions to formally terminate all activities associated with the project either by delivering a finished product or by ceasing effort on a canceled project

Professionalizing project management at a healthcare delivery organization means that each IM/IT project should follow these five key processes. While project management frameworks are important, hiring professionally trained and ideally credentialed project managers is equally important. A number of project management credentialing organizations exist, including the Project Management Institute (PMI), which offers both the Project Management Professional (PMP) certification and the Program Management Professional certification.

The PMP certification ensures that an individual has mastered a requisite body of knowledge on project management (outlined in Table 4.2) and has at least 60 months of project management experience.

Furthermore, survey data (Taylor 2004; Lee 2006) suggest that increasing the number of individuals within the organization with these professional project management skills and experience and following an explicit IM/IT project management process framework increases the likelihood of IM/IT project success, as depicted in Figure 4.4.

Project Management Knowledge Areas	Individuals Must Know How To:
Initiation and integration	Develop project charter
	Develop scope statement
	Develop project plan
	Direct and manage execution
	Monitor and control project work
	Direct integrated change control
	Close project
Scope management	Enact scope planning
	Develop scope definition
	Create work breakdown structure
	Verify scope
	Control scope
Time management	Define activity
	Sequence activity
	Estimate activity resources
	Estimate activity duration
	Develop schedule
	Control schedule
Cost management	Estimate costs
	Budget costs
	Control costs
Quality management	Develop quality plan
	Assure quality
	Control quality
Human resources management	Develop human resources plan
	Acquire project team
	Develop project team
	Manage project team
Communications management	Develop communications plan
	Distribute information
	Report on performance
	Manage stakeholders
Risk management	Develop risk management plan
	Identify risks
	Complete qualitative risk analysis
	Complete quantitative risk analysis
	Develop risk response plan
	Control and monitor risk
Procurement management	Plan purchase/acquisition
	Plan contracting
	Request seller response (requests for proposals)
	Select seller
	Contract administration
	Close contract

Source: PMI (2004).

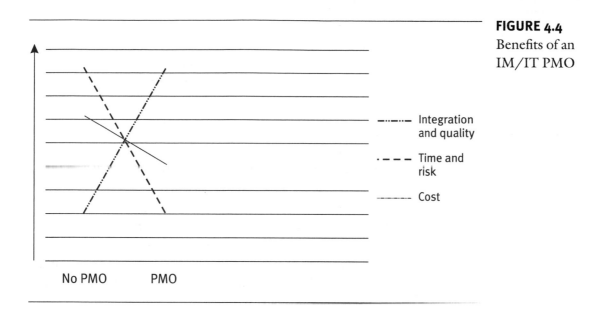

FIGURE 4.4
Benefits of an
IM/IT PMO

Project Management Tools

A number of project management applications are available that provide the automated support to more professionally manage projects. While not intended to be an exhaustive list, the following are applications that can provide the automation to support the five key project management processes outlined previously. Additionally, many of these applications carry the higher level program/portfolio management capabilities discussed later in this chapter. These applications include but are not limited to:

- Clarity (Computer Associates)
- Changepoint (Compuware)
- Project (Microsoft)
- Rational Portfolio Manager (IBM)
- Project Portfolio Management (Planview)
- Project Management (Mercury)
- P6 (Primavera)

Standardizing IM/IT operations on a set of project and portfolio management tools provides a common way to establish the processes and business rules that an organization uses for managing projects. For instance, if a healthcare organization's applications group uses one tool while the infrastructure group uses a different tool, and the informatics and analytics group uses no tool at all, it becomes incredibly difficult to put in place the standardization of project management processes that is a prerequisite for managing interdependencies between projects and thus to achieve program or portfolio management capabilities.

While entire textbooks have been written on project management and the tools that are available to support it, for illustrative purposes, project plans and Gantt charts are discussed as examples of key artifacts that are easily developed from within most of the above project management/portfolio management tools.

Project Plans All project management applications should have the ability to create a project
and Gantt plan and display it in a way that easily shows task interdependencies. Figure
Charts 4.5 shows a simple example of some of the tasks in an infrastructure project for a hospital system. This list of tasks is known as a "work breakdown structure" in project management parlance. Note how the interdependencies are clearly visible by the linking arrows that show which tasks must be fully completed before its successor task can begin. Other tasks without these interdependencies can be accomplished in parallel (i.e., they have no interdependencies but must nevertheless be accomplished to complete the project). Project management applications also have the useful ability to collapse these tasks into the critical path of a project—these are all of the tasks that have predecessor (tasks that must be completed before the next task can be started) or successor (tasks that cannot begin until a certain task or tasks have been completed) interdependencies. The reason that critical path analysis is important is that it provides a forecast of the shortest possible time in which the overall project can be completed.

Program Management

As noted earlier, organizations that put in place program management capabilities have moved beyond simply managing individual projects to managing the interrelationships between projects and/or preexisting applications and systems. While managing this level of complexity takes slightly longer to plan up front, the extra time expended is recovered during the execution phase of the project in reduced surprises and cost overruns associated with unforeseen interdependencies. In essence, the critical dependency analysis and management depicted in Figures 4.5 and 4.6 are simply extended beyond a single project to interdependencies that exist within a particular program of projects or even across programs of projects as depicted in Figure 4.2.

Portfolio Management

Along with the professional project management expertise described in the previous sections, organizations that employ a portfolio management approach also have tightly coupled IM/IT governance (essentially the decisions about which information technology to invest in and which not to invest in) with its portfolio management office (Smaltz, Carpenter, and Saltz 2007). In other words, one can think of project and/or program management as ensuring that things are done right within a particular project, whereas portfolio

FIGURE 4.5

Project Plan in Gantt Chart Format

	Task Name	Duration	Start	Finish
1	⊟ **Infrastructure Upgrades**	**240 days?**	**Tue 2/28/06**	**Mon 1/29/07**
2	⊟ **Novell Client Removal**	**180 days?**	**Tue 2/28/06**	**Mon 11/6/06**
3	PC Domain Migration	60 days	Tue 2/28/06	Mon 5/22/06
4	SAN Expansion	15 days?	Tue 2/28/06	Mon 3/20/06
5	⊟ **Build File & Print Architecture**	**135 days**	**Tue 3/21/06**	**Mon 9/25/06**
6	Build File Servers	30 days	Tue 3/21/06	Mon 5/11/06
7	Test/Trial Migration	15 days	Tue 5/2/06	Mon 5/22/06
8	Migrate File Data	90 days	Tue 5/23/06	Mon 9/25/06
9	Build Print Servers	30 days	Tue 3/21/06	Mon 5/11/06
10	Test/Trial Migration	15 days	Tue 5/2/06	Mon 5/22/06
11	Migrate Print Data	10 days	Tue 5/23/06	Mon 6/5/06
12	Build New Image	15 days	Tue 2/28/06	Mon 3/20/06
13	Image Testing	30 days	Tue 9/26/06	Mon 11/6/06
14	⊟ **Device Management Assessment**	**120 days**	**Tue 2/28/06**	**Mon 8/14/06**
15	Evaluate Solutions	60 days	Tue 2/28/06	Mon 5/22/06
16	Select and Design Implementation	15 days	Tue 5/23/06	Mon 6/12/06
17	Purchase and Install	45 days	Tue 6/13/06	Mon 8/14/06
18	⊟ **UH Upgrades**	**91 days?**	**Tue 2/28/06**	**Tue 7/4/06**
19	Deploy Cisco Switchs	90 days	Tue 2/28/06	Mon 4/10/06
20	Complete Cabling	90 days	Tue 2/28/06	Mon 7/3/06
21	Prep for PC Conversion	1 day?	Tue 7/4/06	Tue 7/4/06
22	⊟ **Complete Windows XP Migration**	**60 days?**	**Tue 11/7/06**	**Mon 1/29/07**
23	Build Migration Plan	1 day?	Tue 11/7/06	Tue 11/7/06
24	Begin Migration	60 days	Tue 11/7/06	Mon 1/29/07
25				
26	⊟ **LiveComm Assessment**	**60 days**	**Tue 5/23/06**	**Mon 8/14/06**
27	Roll-Out LiveComm to I.S.	30 days	Tue 5/23/06	Mon 7/3/06
28	Assess and prepare for Business Unit Roll-Out	30 days	Tue 7/4/06	Mon 8/14/06

FIGURE 4.6

Collapsed Project Plan Gantt Chart Showing Only the Critical Path

	Task Name	Duration	Start	Finish
1	⊟ **Infrastructure Upgrades**	**240 days?**	**Tue 2/28/06**	**Mon 1/29/07**
2	⊟ **Novell Client Removal**	**180 days?**	**Tue 2/28/06**	**Mon 11/6/06**
4	⊟ SAN Expansion	15 days?	Tue 2/28/06	Mon 3/20/06
5	⊟ **Build File & Print Architecture**	**135 days**	**Tue 3/21/06**	**Mon 9/25/06**
6	Build File Servers	30 days	Tue 3/21/06	Mon 5/1/06
7	Test/Trial Migration	15 days	Tue 5/2/06	Mon 5/22/06
8	Migrate File Data	90 days	Tue 5/23/06	Mon 9/25/06
13	Image Testing	30 days	Tue 9/26/06	Mon 11/6/06
22	⊟ **Complete Windows XP Migration**	**60 days?**	**Tue 11/7/06**	**Mon 1/29/07**
24	Begin Migration`	60 days	Tue 11/7/06	Mon 1/29/07

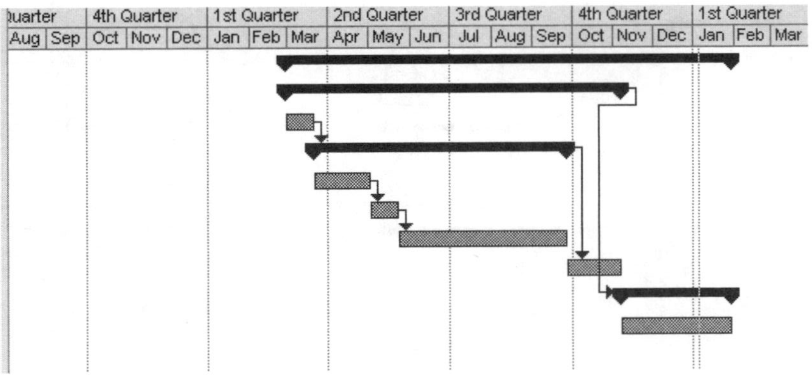

management concerns itself more with doing the right kinds of projects that align with the organization's overall strategic goals and objectives (which is why a PMO must work hand in hand with an organization's IM/IT governance structure, covered in Chapter 3). To illustrate this point, Figure 4.7 shows an IM/IT portfolio of all of the projects that are "in flight" at a for-profit healthcare organization.

Prior to its annual IM/IT capital budget process, this particular organization, using the knowledge gained from professionally managing its portfolio of current IM/IT projects, put together a profile of all of the current IM/IT projects already in flight and rated them based on value and risk. The organization further labeled each quadrant. The lower left quadrant, which represents low-value and high-risk IM/IT projects, is labeled "think twice (or more)." The upper right quadrant represents IM/IT projects that are deemed to both be of high value and have low risk associated with implementing them—this quadrant is labeled "ideal." The size of the bubbles in Figure 4.7 denotes the size in relative dollars of each individual project. Projects are also categorized into nondiscretionary projects (e.g., some projects are mandated by law, such as compliance with the Sarbanes-Oxley legislation), as well as discretionary

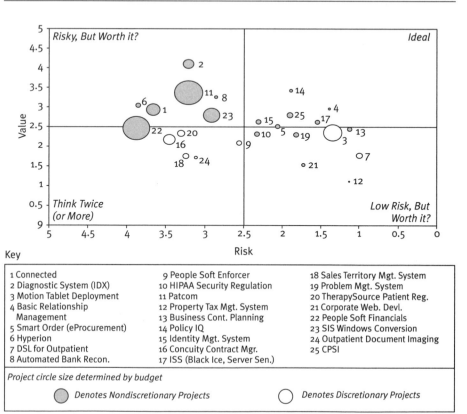

FIGURE 4.7
Illustrative IM/IT Portfolio

Key

1 Connected	9 People Soft Enforcer	18 Sales Territory Mgt. System
2 Diagnostic System (IDX)	10 HIPAA Security Regulation	19 Problem Mgt. System
3 Motion Tablet Deployment	11 Patcom	20 TherapySource Patient Reg.
4 Basic Relationship	12 Property Tax Mgt. System	21 Corporate Web. Devl.
Management	13 Business Cont. Planning	22 People Soft Financials
5 Smart Order (eProcurement)	14 Policy IQ	23 SIS Windows Conversion
6 Hyperion	15 Identity Mgt. System	24 Outpatient Document Imaging
7 DSL for Outpatient	16 Concuity Contract Mgr.	25 CPSI
8 Automated Bank Recon.	17 ISS (Black Ice, Server Sen.)	

Project circle size determined by budget

   ◉ *Denotes Nondiscretionary Projects*   ◯ *Denotes Discretionary Projects*

Source: Carpenter (2005). Used with permission.

projects. Much like an investor reviewing a portfolio of stocks prior to deciding which to divest and which to add to, developing exhibits like the one depicted in Figure 4.7 provides a powerful and succinct means for organizations to evaluate proposed IM/IT projects.

In addition to IM/IT portfolio investment decision support, an IM/IT portfolio management capability also provides regular portfolio status reports to the IM/IT governance entities of an organization. For instance, an IM/IT portfolio dashboard is typically created, sometimes via one of the project/portfolio management applications previously highlighted and sometimes separately via an organization's overall quality or other enterprise dashboard tools, that provides leadership with a view of project progress. Figure 4.8 is a sample of one such view showing all in-flight projects of the organization depicted in Figure 4.7, grouped by strategic categories that are important to the organization along with the dollar amounts budgeted for each project category. The graph on the left of this figure, titled "portfolio by category," depicts the monthly expenditures by project categories. The graph on the right of this figure, titled "resources by category," depicts the amount of full-time equivalent resources being expended on each project category.

While an IM/IT portfolio dashboard can be set up to provide status along any number of dimensions, its greatest impact comes in providing strategic views into the myriad projects the organization is working on to benefit IM/IT governance decision making. In the example provided by Figures 4.7 and 4.8, because this organization is a for-profit healthcare organization that is trying to balance strategically the need for greater regulatory compliance with the Sarbanes-Oxley Act and other legislation with the need for revenue growth, the dashboard quickly provides a view of the last three quarters and the next six quarters with regard to the amount of money being invested in compliance-related projects, operational effectiveness projects, and projects the organization hopes will generate increased revenue. While illustrative and not intended to be a definitive example, the point made by this case example is that organizations must be able to present flexible data representations, like that in Figure 4.7, on the entire portfolio of IM/IT projects to aid its IM/IT governance bodies as they grapple to make informed information technology investment decisions.

The PMO

Generally, these higher functioning portfolio management capabilities are being formalized in many leading healthcare service delivery organizations via the establishment of an IM/IT portfolio management office. Typically, the functions that a PMO will be involved in include but are not limited to:

- Providing regular *communications* to project stakeholders and the rest of the organization regarding progress on projects, programs of projects, and the entire portfolio of projects

FIGURE 4.8
Sample IM/IT
Portfolio
Dashboard

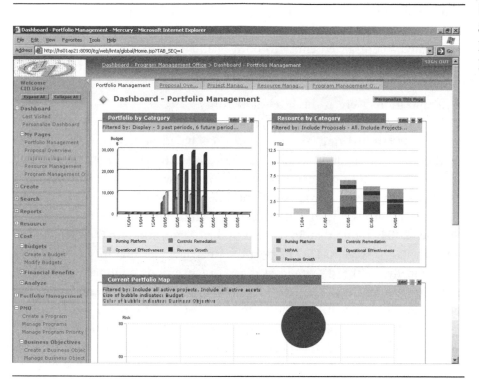

Source: Carpenter (2005). Used with permission.

- Providing authoritative *management and oversight* of all projects within the portfolio
- Providing the *staff function to support the IM/IT governance* of the organization to include accomplishing portfolio analyses as requested by the IM/IT governance entities of an organization and providing recommendations for information technology investments
- Creating *metrics and dashboards* to *facilitate transparency*

While these activities can be accomplished without putting in place a formal PMO function, a number of consultants and researchers suggest that organizations that do so will have a competitive advantage (Light et al. 2005; Kaplan 2005; Jeffery and Leliveld 2004). It is also important to note that putting a PMO in place at an organization is not a quick-fix endeavor but an effort that likely will take most healthcare organizations between two and four years to achieve the full benefits. Jeffery and Leliveld (2004), from data derived in their study of 130 *Fortune* 1000 companies, created the useful IM/IT Portfolio Management Maturity Model, which outlines the four stages of maturity of any organization's IM/IT portfolio management capabilities. Jeffery and Leliveld refer to these four stages as ad hoc, defined, managed, and synchronized.

In the *ad hoc stage,* no formal project management capability is in place at all. Projects are managed informally and inconsistently, and project results are equally inconsistent. Less than 5 percent of organizations find themselves at this level of maturity. In the *defined stage*, the organization has created a centralized entity to both maintain and inventory projects and manage them centrally. In this stage, applications and infrastructure are well defined and documented. Jeffery and Leliveld (2004) found that 25 percent of organizations were at this level of maturity.

Next, in the *managed stage*, the organization has created processes for vetting and rationalizing or ranking projects based on key strategic criteria. Furthermore, investment decisions employ financial metrics to help prioritize projects (e.g., return on investment, return on assets, net present value) and conduct at least annual reviews with business unit leadership on how well the IM/IT portfolio is aligned with overall organizational strategies. Jeffery and Leliveld (2004) found that 54 percent of the organizations in their study were at the managed stage of IM/IT portfolio management maturity.

Finally, in the *synchronized stage*, organizations conduct much more frequent evaluations of the IM/IT portfolio with business unit leaders and include in these evaluations a consistent assessment of returns versus risks in their project portfolios. Typically, organizations at the synchronized level of IM/IT portfolio management maturity have created PMO scorecards or dashboards that provide a means to transparently communicate project status and value. They also consistently conduct postproject benefits realization assessments to see if benefits envisioned prior to the project's adoption are achieved. Jeffery and Leliveld (2004) found that only 17 percent of the organizations in their study were at this level of maturity. The most interesting finding of their study was that organizations that truly want to achieve higher returns from their investments in IM/IT projects must fully move to the synchronized level of IM/IT portfolio management maturity to achieve the higher performance returns. As such, organizations should not come to premature conclusions about the positive impact of their own IM/IT PMO function until all of the capabilities of a synchronized IM/IT portfolio management office, as outlined by Jeffery and Leliveld (2004), have been put into practice.

Summary

This chapter makes the case that many IM/IT projects generally do not achieve the benefits envisioned and that implementing professional project management capabilities is an important first step toward mitigating this project risk. Furthermore, identifying and managing the cross-project interdependencies that a program management approach embodies is an important second step toward mitigating project risk. Finally, implementing an IM/IT portfolio management office that is tightly coupled with an organization's IM/IT governance structures and processes and that also develops the full complement of capabilities outlined in Jeffery and Leliveld's (2004) IM/IT portfolio management maturity model provides the greatest returns to an organization.

Web Resources

Significant, relevant resources are available on the Web to support the information in this chapter:

- Project Management Institute, http://www.pmi.org
- PMI Healthcare Special Interest Group, http://www.pmihealthcare.org/
- PMI Information Systems Special Interest Group, http://www.pmi-issig.org/
- Healthcare Information and Management Systems Society Project Management Special Interest Group, http://www.himss.org/ASP/sigs_project.asp
- American College of Healthcare Executives project management seminar, http://www.ache.org/SEMINARS/ontime.cfm
- *CIO* magazine, http://www.cio.com/topic/1509/Portfolio_Management

Discussion Questions

1. Discuss some of the primary reasons an IM/IT implementation project might fail in a healthcare organization.
2. What are the main differences between IM/IT project management, IM/IT program management, and IM/IT portfolio management?
3. What are the five key processes of project management?
4. What requirements should be considered when selecting project management tools for an organization?
5. Why are project metrics and portfolio dashboards important to IM/IT governance?
6. List and describe the major roles and functions of the PMO.
7. Which two project management knowledge areas described in Table 4.2 do you consider to be the most important? Why?
8. What actions/changes are necessary within an organization to reach the synchronized stage of maturity of IM/IT portfolio management capability discussed by Jeffery and Leliveld (2004)?
9. Even with the development of a PMO, will there be instances in which an IM/IT venture fails? Explain your rationale.

References

Ash J. S., D. F. Sittig, E. G. Poon, K. Guappone, E. Campbell, and R. H. Dykstra. 2007. "The Extent and Importance of Unintended Consequences Related to Computerized Provider Order Entry." *Journal of the American Medical Informatics Association* 14 (4): 415–23.

Bossidy, L., and R. Charan. 2002. *Execution: The Discipline of Getting Things Done.* New York: Crown Business.

Carpenter, R. 2005. "IT Governance." Guest lecture, presented to the University of Alabama at Birmingham, January 8.

Goldman, D., and E. McGlynn. 2005. *U.S. Health Care: Facts About Cost, Access and Quality*. Santa Monica, CA: Rand Corporation.

Han, Y. Y., J. A. Carcillo, S. T. Venkataraman, R. S. Clark, R. S. Watson, T. C. Nguyen, H. Bayir, and R. A. Orr. 2005. "Unexpected Increased Mortality After Implementation of a Commercially Sold Computerized Physician Order Entry System." *Pediatrics* 116 (6): 1506–12.

Hayes, F. 2004. "Chaos Is Back." *Computerworld* 38: 70.

Hunter, D. P., and V. Ciotti. 2006. "IT Disasters: The Worst Debacles and Lessons Learned from Them." *Healthcare Executive* 21 (5): 8–12.

Institute of Medicine (IOM). 1999. *To Err Is Human: Building a Safer Health System*. Washington, DC: National Academies Press.

Jeffery, M., and I. Leliveld. 2004. "Best Practices in IT Portfolio Management." *Sloan Management Review* 45 (3): 41–49.

Kaplan, J. 2005. *Strategic IT Portfolio Management: Governing Enterprise Transformation*. United States: Pittiglio Rabin Todd and McGrath, Inc.

Kendall, G., and S. Rollins. 2003. *Advanced Project Portfolio Management and the PMO: Multiplying ROI at Warp Speed*. Boca Raton, FL: J. Ross Publishing and International Institute of Learning.

Kerzner, H. 2003. *Project Management: A Systems Approach to Planning, Scheduling, and Controlling*, 8th ed. Hoboken, NJ: Wiley and Sons.

Koppel, R., J. P. Metlay, A. Cohen, B. Abaluck, A. R. Localio, S. E. Kimmel, and B. L. Strom. 2005. "Role of Computerized Physician Order Entry Systems in Facilitating Medication Errors." *Journal of the American Medical Association* 293 (10): 1197–1203.

Lee, W. 2006. *The Effect of PMO on IT Project Management: A Summary of Survey Data Results*. Research Report, Hawaii Pacific University.

Light, M., M. Hotle, D. Stang, and J. Heine. 2005. *Project Management Office: The IT Control Tower*. No. G00132836. Stamford, CT: Gartner.

Project Management Institute (PMI). 2004. *A Guide to the Project Management Body of Knowledge (PMBOK Guide)*, 3rd ed. Newtown Square, PA: Project Management Institute.

Smaltz, D., R. Carpenter, and J. Saltz. 2007. "Effective IT Governance in Healthcare Organisations: A Tale of Two Organisations." *International Journal of Healthcare Technology and Management* 8 (1–2): 20–41.

Taylor, A. 2004. "Success and Failure in IT Projects." *CIO Canada*. [Online article; retrieved 5/20/07.] http://www.itworldcanada.com/publication/CIO.htm

EXTERNAL ENVIRONMENT AND GOVERNMENT POLICY

Learning Objectives

1. Describe a justification for government intervention in business processes.
2. List five major types of government intervention into healthcare business, and explain the need for government to invest in healthcare information management/information technology (IM/IT).
3. Describe the eight components of the administrative simplification portion of the Health Insurance Portability and Accountability Act.
4. Assess your organization's readiness for transactions and code set development.
5. Analyze why privacy and security are important and why IM/IT has a key role in protecting privacy and security.
6. Assess four key questions to answer in developing privacy policies.
7. Describe IM/IT leadership's role in responding to legislation.

Much has been written regarding the details of the federal, state, and local governmental policies that have direct and indirect influences on information management/information technology (IM/IT) and its leadership in healthcare organizations (Feldstein 2001; Blumenthal 2006; Kleinke 2005; O'Carroll et al. 2003; Goldsmith, Blumenthal, and Rishel 2003; Taylor et al. 2005; Poon et al. 2006). This chapter does not present an exhaustive list of those impacts. Its goal is to provide healthcare IM/IT leadership with the awareness of the potential effects of healthcare legislation on healthcare IM/IT business practices; the tools to identify and respond to current healthcare legislation; and the strategic vision to plan for future challenges that may arise from governmental interventions. The chapter has three sections, as follows:

- *Government's Role in Healthcare IM/IT.* This section provides the justification of governmental intervention in business processes. Understanding why government gets involved will assist the reader in responding to legislation and anticipating future actions.
- *Health Insurance Portability and Accountability Act (HIPAA).* This major set of government legislative and administrative interventions has fundamentally changed healthcare IM/IT for the last decade and will

likely change it in the future. It is a complex array of interventions that have been implemented in ways not fully anticipated when the legislation was passed in 1996. This section presents some basic policies and procedures designed to respond to select HIPAA requirements.

- *Healthcare IM/IT Leadership Roles.* The external environment and government have direct, indirect, and substantial roles in healthcare operations. Leaders must understand those roles today and anticipate roles in the future. This section presents an action plan for IM/IT leadership.

Government's Role in Healthcare IM/IT

Three questions must be asked in assessing the role of government in healthcare IM/IT:

1. Why does the government (at any level) get involved in regulating healthcare or any business practice? Is there justification for government intervention?
2. If yes, how much and what types of interventions are justified?
3. What triggers those interventions?

The easy answer to these questions is that the government recognizes the challenges that the healthcare field faces regarding cost, quality, and access to care (Gauthier and Serber 2005). Further, it has an obligation to intervene to provide access to high-quality, affordable care to all residents.

Justification for Government Intervention

The generic argument for governmental intervention is that the marketplace does not perform its normal function of optimizing resource production efficiency and resource allocation decision making as classical economics theory suggests (Santerre and Neun 2004). As a result of the market's failure, government can, and some say should, intervene to fix the problem. Key reasons for intervention include problems with public goods, externalities, imperfect consumer information, and monopoly. Public goods are those that producers cannot easily exclude people from consuming, and consumption by one person does not reduce the availability for others to consume. A classic example is national defense, but medical research that leads to cures for disease is another. Externalities are costs or benefits related to a market action that parties not related to the transaction incur. For example, cigarette smoking may impose costs upon those not involved in the decision to smoke. Imperfect information may give rise to government involvement in markets because people are concerned that profit-seeking business may take advantage of their inability to make informed choices. In each of these cases, the market does not reliably provide the optimal quantity. See Santerre and Neun (2004) for an extensive discussion of these issues.

If the market fails to produce a good or service for any of these reasons, government is empowered to intervene in the public interest. Generally, the "fix" is to develop and implement policies that approximate what the market solution would generate, if possible. However, some have argued that government interventions are designed to benefit those special interests that influence politicians rather that society as a whole (Feldstein 2001; Blumenthal 2006; Kleinke 2005; Goldsmith, Blumenthal, and Rishel 2003; Taylor et al. 2005).

Examples of the range of government intervention are included in Figure 5.1. Correcting externalities has been one of the major reasons for government intervention. The Health Insurance Portability and Accountability Act of 1996 (HIPAA), described later, can be considered an intervention to force a market solution that would not occur without direct government support. Funding for medical research is a more traditional example of this type of intervention and will be briefly described as it relates to funding for healthcare information technology. The other categories are not as directly relevant to this book but are still worthy of note in the figure.

A significant amount of research in healthcare IM/IT has been funded by the federal government. A primary source of this funding for research and demonstration projects comes from the National Library of Medicine (NLM) (see http://www.nlm.nih.gov/). The importance of the NLM to current initiatives and emerging features of healthcare IM/IT make it a major change agent. IM/IT leadership should be familiar with NLM funding priorities. Figure 5.2 presents the eight primary functions of the NLM. Assisting healthcare organizations develop the data systems to support both clinical operations and health services research is a major portion of NLM's charge. Using the justification for government intervention argument, the government funds these (and other) crucial activities because it believes that private organizations will not spend sufficiently on them. Further, the benefits from the findings of these

FIGURE 5.1
Types of Government Market Intervention

Purpose	Government Initiative
Provide public goods	Funding of medical research
Correct for externalities	Tax on alcohol and cigarettes
Impose regulations	Federal Drug Administration
Enforce antitrust laws	Limit hospital mergers
Sponsor redistribution programs	Medicare and Medicaid
Operate public enterprises	Veterans Administration hospitals

Source: Reprinted from Feldstein (2001). Used with permission from Health Administration Press, Chicago.

FIGURE 5.2
Primary
Functions of the
National Library
of Medicine

The National Library of Medicine

1. assists the advancement of medical and related sciences through the collection, dissemination, and exchange of information important to the progress of medicine and health;
2. serves as a national information resource for medical education, research, and service activities of Federal and private agencies, organizations, and institutions;
3. serves as a national information resource for the public, patients, and families by providing electronic access to reliable health information issued by the National Institutes of Health and other trusted sources;
4. publishes in print and electronically guides to health sciences information in the form of catalogs, bibliographies, indexes, and online databases;
5. provides support for medical library development and for training of biomedical librarians and other health information specialists;
6. conducts and supports research in methods for recording, storing, retrieving, preserving, and communicating health information;
7. creates information resources and access tools for molecular biology, biotechnology, toxicology, environmental health, and health services research; and
8. provides technical consultation services and research assistance.

Source: Reprinted from the National Library of Medicine. 2004. "National Library of Medicine Functional Statement." [Online information; retrieved 3/1/08.] http://www.nlm .nih.gov/about/functstatement.html

efforts will benefit the entire U.S. healthcare system by enabling the development and testing of new technologies and infrastructure support.

Government Intervention in the Healthcare Field

For most industries, the government largely allows the market to determine costs, efficiency, quality, availability, and firm survival. With the exception of enforcing property rights and legal contracts, the government's role is minor.

Healthcare is different from other industries, however. The government gets involved in healthcare and, by extension, healthcare IM/IT, because the government has a broad obligation to protect the health and welfare of the population. That obligation extends beyond ensuring that markets function and property rights are enforced (Feldstein 2001). Finding that the health of the population is at risk makes intervention to improve patient safety vital. Evidence that this risk is real comes from a series of prestigious Institute of Medicine studies (IOM 1999, 2001). Further, publicized estimates that approximately 45 million people are uninsured and many more underinsured (Gauthier and Serber 2005) bring another call for government intervention. Lack of insurance has an effect on the health of the population because lack of insurance may actually lead to preventable morbidity and mortality (a negative health outcome) that may cost the U.S. health system more than $65 billion per year (IOM 2003; Ayanian et al. 2000). Finally, as we have seen in earlier chapters, healthcare costs have been rising rapidly both in absolute terms and relative to the gross domestic product. These increases in cost are largely paid by governments, thus budget considerations drive government interest as well. In 2005, 45 percent of personal health expenditures were paid through public sources. All levels of government have a major stake in payment rates (CMS 2007). The conclusion is that quality, access, and cost provide a justification of government role in healthcare and thus in healthcare IM/IT.

Government and Business Practice

Given that government intervention can be justified, how much and what types of intervention are justified? With respect to healthcare IM/IT, patient information privacy and security are the major foci of government intervention. The social interest in having patient healthcare information protected cannot, it is argued, be left to individual providers. Good business practice dictates that much of what comes under the guise of government intervention should be followed irrespective of the regulations. As we will see in detail in the next section, HIPAA has, among other features, enhanced privacy regulation. As healthcare delivery organizations are responsible for the health and welfare of their patients, it only makes sense to adopt strict privacy standards even in the absence of government regulation. Therefore, information system managers in healthcare facilities must develop policies and procedures to protect the security of information contained in automated systems throughout the organization.

There are currently a number of potential extensions of the government into healthcare business practices. Goldsmith, Blumenthal, and Rishel (2003) argue for the need for government-sanctioned and supported standardization of at least communication protocols and nomenclature. Without a direct government role, healthcare organizations will adopt technology slowly and in a haphazard fashion. Blumenthal (2006) provides three business arguments justifying government intervention. First, no compelling business case exists for investment in health information technology. Better performance is not routinely rewarded in healthcare, and, in fact, poor performance and providing more services generates greater revenue. The savings from implementing health information technology do not go to providers but rather to benefit insurers and others. Second, for real system benefits to be seen, all components of the fragmented U.S. healthcare delivery system must participate. Without this participation, benefits are incomplete. Interoperability among providers is a necessary step for true sharing to occur, and government needs to impose common communication standards. Third, fraud and abuse regulations do not allow physicians to receive subsidies from hospitals. Blumenthal (2006) makes a strong case for the failure of the market to achieve the desired results, thus government must become more actively involved. Healthcare IM/IT leadership must be aware of specific government interventions to effectively manage their organization.

Health Insurance Portability and Accountability Act

HIPAA

As an example of legislation that has had far reaching effects on healthcare IM/IT, HIPAA has no equal. Begun as a mechanism to ensure that individuals could retain access to health insurance when they changed jobs (portability) (Flores and Dodier 2005; Schmeida 2005), HIPAA also contains a second provision called *administrative simplification* that has far greater impact:

> The Administrative Simplification provisions of the Health Insurance Portability and Accountability Act of 1996 (HIPAA, Title II) required the Department of Health and Human Services (HHS) to establish national standards for electronic healthcare transactions and national identifiers for providers, health plans, and employers. It also addressed the security and privacy of health data. As the industry adopts these standards for the efficiency and effectiveness of the nation's healthcare system will improve the use of electronic data interchange. (CMS 2005a)

As this general provision indicates, HIPAA anticipated the development of electronic record keeping in healthcare. The healthcare field was not able internally to develop the standards and rules governing these new technologies for collecting, storing, and transmitting health information (another example of potential market failure mentioned above). Many realized that strict government controls would have to be put in place to enable healthcare providers to develop systems that met internal needs and facilitated transfer of information across institutions (Blumenthal 2006; Kleinke 2005; Goldsmith, Blumenthal, and Rishel 2003). The electronic medium also raised concerns with security and privacy that the government felt it should address. In simple terms, administrative simplification had five elements (CMS 2005b):

1. Standards
2. Provider and health plan mandate
3. Privacy
4. Preemption of state law
5. Penalties

The complete text of the "Summary of Administrative Simplification Provisions" is provided in Figure 5.3.

Each of these five provisions is important because of what they imply. While the translation of these broad provisions to policy details has evolved incrementally since the passage of HIPAA in 1996, these details are now emerging as a result of a series of negotiations among all of the interested parties. Figure 5.4 details the eight components of the administrative simplification portion of HIPAA that were promulgated to meet the five provisions listed above.

Standards for electronic health information transactions. Within 18 months of enactment, the Secretary of HHS is required to adopt standards from among those already approved by private standards developing organizations for certain electronic health transactions, including claims, enrollment, eligibility, payment, and coordination of benefits. These standards also must address the security of electronic health information systems.

Mandate on providers and health plans, and timetable. Providers and health plans are required to use the standards for the specified electronic transactions 24 months after they are adopted. Plans and providers may comply directly, or may use a health care clearinghouse. Certain health plans, in particular workers compensation, are not covered.

Privacy. The Secretary is required to recommend privacy standards for health information to Congress 12 months after enactment. If Congress does not enact privacy legislation within 3 years of enactment, the Secretary shall promulgate privacy regulations for individually identifiable electronic health information.

Pre-emption of state law. The bill supersedes state laws, except where the Secretary determines that the State law is necessary to prevent fraud and abuse, to ensure appropriate state regulation of insurance or health plans, addresses controlled substances, or for other purposes. If the Secretary promulgates privacy regulations, those regulations do not pre-empt state laws that impose more stringent requirements. These provisions do not limit a State's ability to require health plan reporting or audits.

Penalties. The bill imposes civil money penalties and prison for certain violations.

Source: CMS (2005b).

FIGURE 5.3
Summary of HIPAA Administrative Simplification Provisions

1. Employer identifier standard
2. Enforcement
3. National provider identifier standard
4. Security standard
5. Transaction and code sets standard
6. Place of service codes for HIPAA transactions
7. Health insurance reform for consumers (HIPAA Title I)
8. Medicaid HIPAA administrative simplification

Source: CMS (2005a).

FIGURE 5.4
Eight Major Components of HIPAA Administrative Simplification Provisions

The HIPAA overview reveals specific details of these standards and the timing of their implementation (CMS 2005a). The steps to achieving the goals of improving patient quality and enhancing efficiency through the use of electronic records were developed in stages. Making employers obtain a national identification number for healthcare transactions was the first step. Next, providers were required to have a commonly determined standard identifier, the National Provider Identifier (NPI). These rules set the stage for creating a regional or national data set of electronic information transmission by uniquely identifying the payer source and the provider. This seems insignificant when viewed from within a healthcare organization because healthcare organizations have always used unique numbers to identify patients and to keep patient records distinct. The NPI was novel when applied across organizations, however. The timing of the NPI mandate is current in relation to this discussion in that after May 23, 2007, "healthcare providers may only use their NPIs to identify themselves in standard transactions" (CMS 2005c).

Transactions and code set standards warrant additional commentary because they are so vital to the effective implementation and use of the electronic record. The precise definition of these standards is also still in flux. According to the Centers for Medicare & Medicaid Services (2005d),

> Transactions are activities involving the transfer of healthcare information for specific purposes. Under the Health Insurance Portability & Accountability Act of 1996 (HIPAA), if a healthcare provider engages in one of the identified transactions, they must comply with the standard for that transaction. HIPAA requires every provider who does business electronically to use the same healthcare transactions, code sets, and identifiers. HIPAA has identified ten standard transactions for Electronic Data Interchange (EDI) for the transmission of healthcare data. Claims and encounter information, payment and remittance advice, and claims status and inquiry are several of the standard transactions. Code sets are the codes used to identify specific diagnosis and clinical procedures on claims and encounter forms. The HCPCS, CPT-4 and ICD-9 codes with which providers are familiar, are examples of code sets for procedures and diagnose.

This generic statement gives rise to an array of specific rules designed to enable organizations to collect data in a consistent manner. Unless everyone uses a common nomenclature for defining all clinical and administrative terms, there will be no capacity to communicate. *Interoperability* is the term that describes the goal to its fullest extent. To assist providers and others in this pursuit, CMS has provided information on the Web that can be easily accessed and applied. First, it provides a checklist to be used by healthcare organizations to determine their readiness. That checklist may be downloaded at cms.hhs.gov/EducationMaterials/Downloads/HIPAAChecklist.pdf. Second, CMS makes available a series of ten documents, listed in Figure 5.5, to assist in developing or identifying the checklists appropriate to particular organizations. (Discussing these documents is beyond the scope of this book; however, IM/IT leadership must be aware of their existence and importance.)

The Need for Information Privacy and Security

Healthcare information technology systems contain sensitive information. Clinical systems process medical information about individual patients; human resources information systems contain personal information about employees; and financial and decision-support systems include proprietary data used for planning, marketing, and management of the enterprise. HIPAA has placed

---

The HIPAA Information Series for Providers consists of ten papers that can aid you in transactions and code set development:
- HIPAA 101
- Are you a covered entity?
- Key HIPAA dates and tips
- What electronic transactions and code sets are standardized under HIPAA?
- Is your software vendor or billing service ready for HIPAA?
- What to expect from your health plans
- What you need to know about testing
- Trading partner
- Final steps for compliance with electronic transactions and code sets
- Enforcement

These documents can be downloaded at http://www.cms.hhs.gov/Education Materials/02_HIPAAMaterials.asp.

FIGURE 5.5

Checklist Aids for Transactions and Code Set Development

special emphasis on privacy, and the implications of safeguarding privacy to IM/IT leadership are expansive.

To give some idea of the nature and extent of privacy and security issues even after HIPAA's enactment, the Health Privacy Project (http://www.health privacy.org/) has compiled anecdotes reported in the national press. The shear number of events suggests their importance. A few examples from the Health Privacy Project's (2007) Web publication, *Privacy Stories*, appear below.

The California state Department of Health Services inadvertently revealed the names and addresses of up to 53 people enrolled in an AIDS drug assistance program to other enrollees by putting benefit notification letters in the wrong envelopes. . . . The department learned about the mix-up after 12 people in the drug assistance program phoned to say they had received letters addressed to someone else. . . . The department is looking into ways to make the system more foolproof, such as using envelopes with window addresses, said health services Director Sandra Shewry. HIV/AIDS services and advocacy groups said this was the first known breach of that database. "I would hope this is an anomaly," said Jeff Bailey, director of client services for AIDS Project Los Angeles. (Engel, M., "Mix-Up Breaches Confidentiality of Dozens in State AIDS Program," *Los Angeles Times*, March 3, 2007)

A desktop computer containing personal information for up to 38,000 patients treated at Veterans Affairs Department medical centers in Pittsburgh and Philadelphia over the past four years was reported missing from the Reston, VA offices of VA contractor Unisys Corp. The VA and Unisys [say] the computer contained names, addresses, Social Security numbers and dates of birth. It may also have included insurance carrier and billing information, claims data and medical information. (Robeznieks, A., "Another Computer with VA Data Goes Missing," *HIT Strategist*, August 8, 2006)

Consequently, clinical information systems require comprehensive programs to protect the privacy of patient medical records. The following three categories of clinical systems must be considered:

1. *Patient care systems* (order entry and results reporting; electronic medical records; lab, pharmacy, radiology; etc.) store information about a patient's medical history, diagnoses, and treatment plans. Organizations that provide care are required by law and by ethical considerations to ensure that patient-specific information is available only to authorized users.

2. *Public health information systems* support disease prevention and surveillance programs. Protecting public health requires the acquisition and storage of health-related information about individuals. Public health benefits sometimes conflict with threats to individual privacy. Breaches of privacy of sensitive information can potentially lead to discrimination in employment or insurance eligibility. Individuals concerned about privacy who avoid clinical tests and treatments may endanger the health of others in the community. For example, sexually transmitted infections can be spread by failure to test and/or report the presence of the infections in certain patients (Gostin, Hodge, and Valdiserri 2001).

3. *Medical research information systems* use large repositories of individual patient records to study patterns of health and disease in populations. Data-mining techniques are used to search for potential relationships among patient characteristics and other factors. Research data often are accessible to a number of investigators and their staff, and information security measures are essential to protect patient privacy rights (Lau and Catchpole 2001).

To address privacy concerns, many organizations established HIPAA task forces. Some appointed compliance and/or privacy offices to lead the efforts. Others used existing organizational units, including the offices of the chief information officer (CIO), medical records, and risk management (Marietti 2002). Software vendors played a critical role in HIPAA compliance because most organizations used vendor-supplied software in their information systems. HIPAA patches to existing programs and some in-house work was required to interface applications with one another (Wilson and McPherson 2002). In addition to software updates, changes to business processes and procedures were implemented. Marietti (2002, 55) projected that "80 percent to 85 percent of HIPAA compliance issues will depend on adjusting human behavior." As these regulations have been implemented, some findings are beginning to arise. First, an immediate impact has been on the research community. There is some evidence that HIPAA compliance makes recruitment and retention of subjects into research projects more difficult (Wipke-Tevis and Pickett 2008). In addition, some specific examples now exist regarding how process improvements (automated access verification) can assist organizations to demonstrate compliance (Hill 2006). Finally, the change process is still incomplete because checklists are still being published to help organizations assess their progress (Kiel 2006).

A number of studies have examined the impact of privacy rules on healthcare organizations giving rise to a set of inappropriate responses related to privacy observed by consultants (Upham and Dorsey 2007). Current concerns center on the application of privacy issues to other activities or innovations in healthcare. For example, Paul Tang, chairman of the board of the American Medical Informatics Association, indicated that electronic health record vendors often include contract provisions that may require providers to violate patient privacy standards (Conn 2007). Similarly, in the wake of mass tragedies, access to the perpetrator's health record often is cited as a reason to relax privacy constraints. Peel (2007) discusses this issue in the context of the Virginia Tech massacre in April 2007, in which a student killed 32 people on that campus, and concludes that privacy constraints would not likely prevent these events. Finally, as consumers provide information over the Internet, the collection and availability of that information is a major concern (Nelson 2006).

At the level of sharing information across organizations, a study commissioned by the California HealthCare Foundation looked at privacy from the perspective of developing regional health information organizations (RHIOs). It was trying to determine what needs to be done at the systems level to facilitate RHIO development. The study resulted in a number of findings and substantial recommendations with regard to developing and implementing security policies for RHIOs. The analyses identified the following four key questions that must be addressed to develop privacy policies (Rosenfeld, Koss, and Siler 2007):

1. Who will have access to patient information?
2. Which information will be accessible?
3. What are acceptable purposes of patient information exchange?
4. What circumstances justify patient information exchange?

They also report a number of common elements important for others to consider in the development of privacy policies across organizational entities, including the following:

- Privacy policies are local.
- Organizations participating in the RHIO will influence the privacy policies.
- Privacy policies need to be developed early and revisited often.
- Work on privacy policies is ongoing.
- Privacy policies are unique to the environment; thus, there are not yet best practices to follow.

- Building consensus on privacy policies takes time.
- The consumer role in privacy policy development is limited.

Finally, HIPAA was not the first effort by government to assure the public that the privacy of the medical information would be secure. The Privacy Act of 1974 (CMS 2005e) established key provisions to protect the privacy of patients. Enacted before the conception of electronic records that is prevalent today, this legislation protected all patient records with "personal identifiers" (social security number or other). Every patient can access and, if necessary, correct his or her individual records. The Privacy Act of 1974 generally prohibits disclosure of these records, but it applied only to federal agencies.

The individual's right to genetic privacy was addressed in Oregon's Genetic Privacy Act of 1995, which provides legal protection for medical information, tissue samples, and DNA samples. Harris and Keywood (2001) point out that individuals "have a powerful interest in genetic privacy and its associated claim to ignorance"; however, "any claims to be shielded from information about the self must compete on equal terms with claims based in the rights and interests of others" (415). Cummings and Magnusson (2001) state, "As genetic privacy legislation is developed and enacted at state and federal levels, the needs of individuals must be balanced with the needs of institutions and of research in the larger context of societal needs" (1089).

Healthcare IM/IT Leadership Roles

While governmental involvement through HIPAA may seem difficult to fully understand by information technology specialists, it is particularly baffling for those outside of IM/IT. The consequence of this difficulty is that IM/IT leadership (CIO and others) must be in a position to understand, anticipate, and explain the impact of HIPAA and other legislation. They must be prepared for new and/or changes in government regulations and policies with a number of activities and programs, including comprehensive environmental scanning and organizational education, development of information security policies and procedures, disaster preparedness and recovery planning, and protection of information privacy and confidentiality.

Environmental Scanning and Organizational Education

The first responsibility of IM/IT leadership is to fully understand the operational and resource implications of all legislation of this nature. Internally, the team must understand what it has to do differently as a result and determine what extra staffing, expertise (consultants), technology, software, and time will be needed. The steps for this activity are as follows:

1. Determine breadth and scope of impending or actual legislation
2. Assess current organizational readiness for impact

3. Perform gap analysis within the organization
4. Recommend strategies to meet legal/regulatory changes
   - Develop staffing and critical expertise needed to address changes
   - Specify hardware and software needs
   - Estimate total financial implications of recommendations
5. Identify clinical and other resources within the organization that will be necessary in meeting standards
6. Outline timeline for implementation with key dates and milestones

Naturally, difficulty may be encountered in effectively accomplishing these tasks once the legislation is in place and deadlines are looming. Consequently, IM/IT leadership should be constantly monitoring the horizon for proposed legislation to get a head start on planning for its passage. To do this, IM/IT leadership should be engaged with those responsible for legislative affairs within the organization (if such a role exists). Getting a "heads up" from this source is vital. State and national associations such as the Healthcare Information and Management Systems Society, American College of Healthcare Executives, Healthcare Financial Management Association, and American Hospital Association, among many others, are also good sources of this "pre" data.

There is also a body of literature documenting the many and varied impacts of HIPAA. It is important for IM/IT leadership, either directly or through surrogates, to monitor and stay up to date on this literature. For example, Houser, Houser, and Shewchuk (2007) use the nominal group technique (NGT) for gathering information regarding the impact of HIPAA privacy rules on release of patient information. "The NGT approach is a consumer-oriented formal brainstorming or idea-generating technique that is assumed to foster creativity and to be particularly effective in helping group members articulate meaningful disclosures in response to specific questions" (Houser, Houser, and Shewchuk 2007, 2).

Finally, because the nature of IM/IT legislation, such as HIPAA, can be highly complex, IM/IT leadership should be prepared to educate senior organizational leadership on the implications of these regulatory interventions. Senior leadership includes the chief executive officer, naturally, but also the chief operating officer (if the organization has that position), chief medical officer, chief nursing officer, and chief financial officer. Also, generally, the person responsible for strategic planning, the head of the legal department, the head of human resources, and the head of development should also be educated in IM/IT legislative matters.

Information Security Policies and Procedures

Healthcare organizations must establish enterprisewide standards to maintain data security and protect the privacy and confidentiality of information, particularly patient records. Data security involves two essential elements: (1) protecting against system failures or external catastrophic events, such as fires, storms, deliberate sabotage, and other acts of God, where critical information could be lost, and (2) controlling access to computer files by unauthorized personnel.

Disaster Protection and Recovery Procedures

The information systems steering committee must ensure that effective data backup and recovery procedures are implemented at all processing sites throughout the organization. Critical data files should be copied to removable disk packs or tapes and stored in a secure location away from the processing sites, preferably in a different building. The CIO should develop a data backup plan for approval by the steering committee. The plan should specify which files require duplication and how often backup procedures should be conducted. Recovery procedures to be used if catastrophic events occur should also be included.

The need for disaster planning was underscored by the terrorist attacks in New York City on September 11, 2001. If that event was not convincing, Hurricane Katrina and the resulting challenges surely were. Disaster plans must be implemented, tested periodically, and refined. Testing of the plan provides training for employees and helps identify shortcomings in technology and procedures before they need to be used. A disaster-plan notebook should be developed and stored at the healthcare facility, at an off-site storage location, and at the homes of key employees who will be involved in recovery procedures (Vecchio 2000).

Consultants can be used to assist in disaster planning and recovery. For example, IRM International offers a disaster recovery program that includes four phases: assessment, documentation consolidation, disaster plan development, and testing and refinement. See www.irminternational.com/rptcard .html for a disaster recovery report card that rates disaster-planning readiness.

Data can also be lost through computer viruses, which are increasingly prevalent and destructive. Each computer program should be inspected by virus-protection software every time the program is run. Acquisition of software should be subject to central review and approval, and particular care must be exercised to ensure that software downloaded from the Internet or obtained over networks has been scanned and proven to be virus free. All incoming e-mail messages should be scanned for viruses, and employees should be trained not to open suspicious files attached to electronic mail.

Protecting Information Privacy and Confidentiality

As the discussion above related to the HIPAA privacy provisions suggests, protecting information privacy and confidentiality should be a major concern of the IM/IT leadership. A comprehensive information security policy should include three elements: (1) physical security, (2) technical controls over access, and (3) management policies that are well known and enforced in all organizational units (see Figure 5.6).

Physical Security	Technical Safeguards	Management Policies
Hardware	Passwords	Written security policy
Data files	Encryption	Employee training
	Audit logs	Disciplinary actions for violations

FIGURE 5.6

Components of Information Security

Understanding the processes of information privacy and confidentiality is not a necessary step to successful implementation at the systems level. While there are many examples from the last decade of how individual systems have accomplished these goals, recent evidence indicates that many organizations are not compliant with basic security standards (Davis and Having 2006). Some in the healthcare field have called for systematic incentives from industry or insurers to induce organizations to adopt privacy and security technology (e.g., Lang 2006).

Prior to implementation of HIPAA standards, the Mayo Clinic, based in Rochester, Minnesota, developed a comprehensive set of plans for the security of electronic medical records. A multidisciplinary team formulated the policy and provides management oversight of the security program. Leaders of the Mayo Clinic effort suggest that a confidentiality policy should include the following elements (Olson, Peters, and Stewart 1998, 29):

- Access rights—who has access and for what reasons
- Release of information to the patient, other healthcare providers, and third parties
- Special handling, if any, for specific information (e.g., HIV results, psychiatric notes)
- Special handling, if any, for particular patients (e.g., employees or VIPs)
- Availability of medical information, including retention policies
- Integrity of medical information, including authentication, completeness, and handling of revisions or addenda
- Approved methods for communication of medical information

Summary

The chapter presents three major ideas. First, it presents and explores government's role in healthcare IM/IT. There is a justification for governmental intervention in business processes if markets fail in their role of allocating scarce resources. Understanding why government gets involved will assist the reader in responding to legislation and anticipating future actions. In healthcare, there are compelling reasons for the government intervention, including a weak business case for information technology investment by providers, system fragmentation and lack of interoperability, and regulatory restrictions from fraud and abuse standards.

Second, the chapter explores HIPAA in detail. This major set of government legislative and administrative interventions has fundamentally changed healthcare IM/IT. Passed by the U.S. Congress in 1996, two components of HIPAA have direct impact on healthcare information systems. The administrative simplification provisions of the law are designed to improve efficiency in the healthcare system by establishing uniform, national standards to be used for the electronic transmission of certain financial and administrative transactions. Privacy protection components of HIPAA restrict disclosure of health information to the minimum needed for patient care and administrative support. Patients have gained new rights to access their medical records and to know who has accessed them. HIPAA compliance required that most healthcare organizations and their software vendors make modifications to computer software to meet the data standards and privacy protection provisions of the law. Changes to business processes and procedures were needed as well. Education and training of employees is particularly important.

Healthcare information systems contain sensitive information. Policies and procedures are needed to protect the confidentiality of information about patients, employees, finances, and organizational strategies. This information is contained in patient care systems, public health systems, and medical research systems. While benefits of public health and medical research systems sometimes conflict with threats to individual privacy, the federal and state governments have asserted that providers have a legal and moral obligation to protect patients' rights to privacy. Consequently, laws have been passed at the federal, state, and local levels of government to protect medical information privacy.

Finally, the chapter explores healthcare IM/IT leadership roles. The external environment and government have direct, indirect, and substantial roles in healthcare operations. IM/IT leaders must understand those roles today and anticipate roles in the future. This section presents an action plan for IM/IT leadership.

In response to HIPAA and for ethical reasons as well, healthcare organizations and IM/IT leadership need enterprisewide standards and policies to maintain data security and protect the confidentiality of certain information. A comprehensive information security program requires disaster protection and recovery procedures as well as procedures for limiting access to certain information stored in computer databases.

Web Resources

The information in this chapter is supported by a number of reliable sources.

This chapter's compilation of government and nongovernment information related to legal issues, identifiers, transactions, enforcement, security, privacy, and code sets as well as links to industry collaboration and a vast array of other available resources, all related to HIPAA and its implementation, includes the following:

- General CMS Web pages on HIPAA, http://www.cms.hhs.gov /HIPAAGenInfo/ and http://www.hipaa.org/
- Health Privacy Project website for health privacy guidelines, http:// www.healthprivacy.org/
- U.S. Department of Health and Human Services (HHS) website presenting administrative simplification provisions, http://aspe.hhs .gov/admnsimp/
- National Committee on Vital and Health Statistics, http://ncvhs.hhs .gov/index.htm
- HHS Data Council, http://aspe.os.dhhs.gov/datacncl/index.shtml
- National Uniform Claim Committee, http://www.nucc.org
- Workgroup for Electronic Data Interchange, http://www.wedi.org
- American National Standards Institute, http://www.ansi.org
- Data Interchange Standards Association, http://www.disa.org

A checklist for disaster recovery is available at http://www.irminter national.com/rptcard.html.

Discussion Questions

1. Discuss the effects of government involvement in two other industries. Compare the differences and similarities of these industries to the healthcare field.
2. Discuss the impacts of a breach to healthcare information systems, especially the financial and privacy impacts.
3. What is HIPAA? What are the potential benefits to healthcare organizations to be gained by compliance with HIPAA standards? What are the potential drawbacks?
4. Discuss some of the potential conflicts between a patient's right to privacy and information needed for public health and medical research.
5. Discuss the differences between HIPAA and the Privacy Act of 1974.
6. There are several implications to the use of provider and employer identification. Please discuss the positive and negative implications.
7. Why are the transaction and code set standards important? What is their value to healthcare?
8. What concepts are important to information security policies and procedures? What effect does HIPAA have on healthcare organizations' policies and procedures? Are there any other laws that may affect them?
9. What concepts are important to disaster recovery policies and procedures? What effect does HIPAA have on those policies and procedures? Are there any other laws that may affect them?

10. Is it important to an organization to have a workgroup that focuses on determining the effects of government legislation? Please discuss your rationale.

11. What components should be included in a plan for protecting information privacy and confidentiality?

References

Ayanian, J. Z., J. S. Weissman, E. C. Schneider, J. A. Ginsburg, and A. M. Zaslavsky. 2000. "Unmet Health Needs of Uninsured Adults in the United States." *Journal of the American Medical Association* 284 (16): 2061–69.

Blumenthal, D. 2006. *Health Information Technology: What is the Federal Government's Role?* The Commonwealth Fund Commission on a High Performance Health System #907.

Centers for Medicare & Medicaid Services (CMS). 2007. "NHE Web Tables." [Online information; retrieved 1/2/08.] http://www.cms.hhs.gov/National HealthExpendData/downloads/tables.pdf

———. 2005a. "HIPAA: Overview." [Online information; retrieved 1/2/08.] http://www.cms.hhs.gov/HIPAAGenInfo/01_Overview.asp

———. 2005b. "Health Insurance Portability and Accountability Act of 1996 Summary of Administrative Simplification Provisions." [Online information; retrieved 1/2/08.] www.cms.hhs.gov/HIPAAGenInfo/Downloads/Summary ofAdministrativeSimplificationProvisions.pdf

———. 2005c. "National Provider Identifier Activities Begin in 2005." [Online information; retrieved 1/2/08.] www.cms.hhs.gov/NationalProvIdentStand/ Downloads/NPIdearprovider.pdf

———. 2005d. "Transactions and Code Sets Regulations." [Online information; retrieved 1/2/08.] http://www.cms.hhs.gov/TransactionCodeSetsStands/

———. 2005e. "Privacy Act of 1974: Overview." [Online information; retrieved 1/2/08.] http://www.cms.hhs.gov/PrivacyActof1974/

Conn, J. 2007. "IT Guru Says Some E-vendor Contracts Violate Privacy." *Modern Healthcare*. [Online information last retrieved 2/10/08.] http://www.modern healthcare.com/apps/pbcs.dll/article?AID=/20070719/FREE/70719007/0 /FRONTPAGE

Cummings, L. A., and R. Magnusson. 2001. "Genetic Privacy and Academic Medicine: The Oregon Experience." *Academic Medicine* 76 (11): 1089–93.

Davis, D., and K. Having. 2006. "Compliance with HIPAA Security Standards in U.S. Hospitals." *Journal of Healthcare Information Management* 20 (2): 108–15.

Feldstein, P. J. 2001. *The Politics of Health Legislation: An Economic Perspective*. Chicago: Health Administration Press.

Flores, J. A., and A. Dodier. 2005. "HIPAA: Past, Present, and Future Implications for Nurses." *Online Journal of Issues in Nursing* 10 (2): 5.

Gauthier, A., and M. Serber. 2005. *A Need to Transform the U.S. Health Care System: Improving Access, Quality, and Efficiency*. Washington, DC: Commonwealth Fund.

Goldsmith, J., D. Blumenthal, and W. Rishel. 2003. "Federal Health Information Policy: A Case of Arrested Development." *Health Affairs (Millwood)* 22 (4): 44–55.

Gostin, L. O., J. G. Hodge, and R. O. Valdiserri. 2001. "Informational Privacy and the Public's Health: The Model State Public Health Privacy Act." *American Journal of Public Health* 91 (9): 1388–92.

Harris, J., and K. Keywood. 2001. "Ignorance, Information, and Autonomy." *Theory of Medical Bioethics* 22 (5): 415–36.

Health Privacy Project. 2007. "Health Privacy Stories." [Online information; retrieved 7/1/07.] http://www.healthprivacy.org/usr_doc/Privacystories .pdf

Hill, L. 2006. "How Automated Access Verification Can Health Organizations Demonstrate HIPAA Compliance: A Case Study." *Journal of Healthcare Information Management* 20 (2): 116–22.

Houser, S., H. Houser, and R. Shewchuk. 2007. "Assessing the Effects of the HIPAA Privacy Rule on Release of Patient Information by Healthcare Facilities." *Perspectives in Health Information Management* 4 (1): 1–11.

Institute of Medicine (IOM). 2003. *Hidden Costs, Value Lost: Uninsurance in America*. Washington, DC: National Academies Press.

———. 2001. *Crossing the Quality Chasm: A New Health System for the 21st Century*. Washington, DC: National Academies Press.

———. 1999. *To Err Is Human: Building a Safer Health System*. Washington, DC: National Academies Press.

Kiel, J. M. 2006. "Halfway There? Check to See if You are: Six of 11 Health Insurance Portability and Accountability Act Rules are Set." *Health Care Management* 25 (4): 330–4.

Kleinke, J. D. 2005. "Dot-Gov: Market Failure and the Creation of a National Health Information Technology System." *Health Affairs (Millwood)* 24 (5): 1246–62.

Lang. 2006. "Patient Safety and IT: A Need for Incentives." *Journal of Healthcare Information Management* 20 (4): 2–4.

Lau, R. K., and M. Catchpole. 2001. "Improving Data Collection and Information Retrieval for Monitoring Sexual Health." *International Journal of STD and AIDS* 12 (1): 8–13.

Marietti, C. 2002. "HIPAA: Blueprint for Privacy and Security." *Healthcare Informatics* 19 (1): 55–60.

Nelson, S. 2006. "Privacy and Medical Information on the Internet." *Respiratory Care* 51 (2): 183–87.

O'Carroll, P., W. Yasnoff, M. Ward, L. Ripp, and E. Martin. 2003. *Public Health Informatics and Information Systems*. New York: Springer-Verlag.

Olson, L. A., S. G. Peters, and J. B. Stewart. 1998. "Security and Confidentiality in an Electronic Medical Record." *Healthcare Information Management* 12 (1): 27–37.

Peel, D. 2007. "Will Violating Privacy Preserve Mass Murder?" *Modern Healthcare*. [Online article; retrieved 1/4/08.] http://modernhealthcare.com/apps /pbcs.dll/article?AID=/20070427/FREE/70426007

Poon, E. G., A. K. Jha, M. Christino, M. M. Honour, R. Fernandopulle, B. Middleton, J. Newhouse, L. Leape, D. W. Bates, D. Blumenthal, and R. Kaushal. 2006. "Assessing the Level of Healthcare Information Technology Adoption in the United States: A Snapshot." *BMC Medical Informatics and Decision Making* 6: 1.

Rosenfeld, S., S. Koss, and S. Siler. 2007. *Privacy, Security and the Regional Health Information Organization*. [Online report; retrieved 8/1/07.] http://www.chcf.org/documents/chronicdisease/RHIOPrivacySecurity.pdf

Santerre, R. E., and S. P. Neun. 2004. *Health Economics: Theories, Insights, and Industry Studies*. Mason, OH: Thompson South-Western.

Schmeida, M. 2005. "Health Insurance Portability and Accountability Act of 1996: Just an Incremental Step in Reshaping Government." *Online Journal of Issues in Nursing* 11 (1): 7.

Taylor, R., A. Bower, F. Girosi, J. Bigelow, K. Fonkych, and R. Hillestad. 2005. "Promoting Health Information Technology: Is There a Case for More-Aggressive Government Action?" *Health Affairs (Millwood)* 24 (5): 1234–45.

Upham, R., and A. Dorsey. 2007. "Living Day-to-Day with HIPAA Privacy: The Top 10 Most Inappropriate Responses Overheard in the Healthcare Workplace." HIPAAdvisory. [Online article; retrieved 1/4/08.] http://www.hipaadvisory.com/action/privacy/daytoday.htm

Vecchio, A. 2000. "Plan for the Worst before Disaster Strikes." *Health Management Technology* 21 (6): 28–30.

Wilson, K. J., and C. E. McPherson. 2002. "It's 2002: How HIPAA-Ready Are You? *Health Management Technology* 23 (1): 14–15, 20.

Wipke-Tevis, D. D., and M. A. Pickett. 2008. "Impact of the Health Insurance Portability and Accountability Acto on Participant Recruitment and Retention." *Western Journal of Nursing Research* 30 (1): 39–53.

BLOCKING AND TACKLING

IM/IT ARCHITECTURE AND INFRASTRUCTURE

Learning Objectives

1. Define and use in context technical terms related to information technology architecture.
2. Distinguish between the hardware and software elements of an information system and provide illustrative examples.
3. Identify the elements of a computer network and give examples of various network structures.
4. Distinguish among operating systems, utility programs, and application software.
5. Introduce basic telecommunication concepts.

As many healthcare executives will happily attest, managing information resources and using information effectively do not require an in-depth knowledge of computer technology. However, managers and leaders in information-intensive organizations do need a basic understanding of information systems and their various components. Such an understanding is of particular importance when the manager is part of a multidisciplinary team—along with physicians and other clinicians, financial experts, and technology specialists—charged with the responsibility for defining system needs, negotiating system contracts, or implementing new applications. To be effective, the manager must not be intimidated by technical computer concepts or technology jargon. At a minimum, broad-based knowledge about the various hardware and software elements of an information system and design and configuration principles is needed. Like any other investment decision, consideration must be given to the size and power of the computer to ensure it is appropriate for a given application.

The physical components and devices configured into an information system are known collectively as *hardware*. Computer hardware spans a broad spectrum, from small palm-top computers that can be held in one hand to the personal computer (PC) used by a large segment of the population to extremely large and powerful supercomputers. Computer hardware technology changes at such a rapid pace that keeping up with cutting-edge technology is difficult even for the information systems specialist, let alone the healthcare manager.

In addition, healthcare managers need an understanding of basic software concepts to be knowledgeable participants in the complex processes of selecting, implementing, and testing software. Knowledge needs include a description of application software, an understanding of the distinction between integrated and interfaced systems, recognition of the role of system management software, and some general knowledge about programming languages and language translators.

This chapter discusses the devices, programs, and communication networks that combine to form a computer-based information system. This is not an exhaustive treatment comparable to what is found in computer science texts. Rather, this is an overview that provides the healthcare manager with appropriate background knowledge to understand the various elements of an information system and how they may be configured to achieve desired functionality. The fundamentals discussed in this chapter are designed to make the manager feel comfortable participating in the planning, implementation, and evaluation of new systems.

Computer Hardware

A *computer* is an electronic, digital device characterized by its ability to store a set of instructions, known as a program, and the data on which the instructions will operate. The Electronic Numerical Integrator and Calculator (ENIAC), completed in 1946 at the University of Pennsylvania, Philadelphia, was the first computing device built in the United States (Rosen 1969). ENIAC launched what has since become known as the first generation of computer hardware, consisting of devices that used vacuum tubes. Today, the computer world has evolved to the fourth generation of hardware, which employs microprocessor technology, and is exploring the fifth generation, parallel processing and artificial intelligence. A user can now hold in one hand a device that has more computing power than early computers that required a large, controlled-environment room.

Although this hardware evolution has been impressive in terms of design and functionality, the basic schematic of a computer remains the same. Figure 6.1 depicts the six major components of a computer system. Simplistically, a computing system comprises the central processing unit, primary storage, secondary storage, input devices, output devices, and communications devices. The communications devices "connect" the computer to enable communication with other computers, either within the organization or external to the organization. Such communication gives rise to the concepts of networking and telecommunications.

Central Processing Unit

The central processing unit (CPU), where the actual "computing" takes place, consists of three major subcomponents: the arithmetic/logic unit (ALU), the

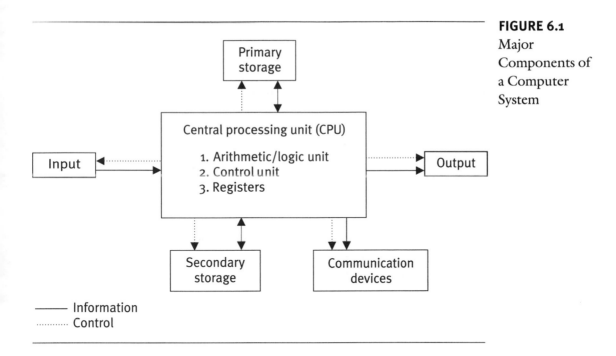

FIGURE 6.1

Major
Components of
a Computer
System

control unit, and registers. The speed and power of the CPU greatly influence the computer's capabilities.

The basic computational and comparison capabilities of the computer lie in the ALU, which has the ability to perform arithmetic functions at high speeds. The ALU also can perform the logical operation of comparison of both numeric and character (nonnumeric) data. The ALU's speed is an important performance characteristic, particularly in applications that involve a large number of arithmetic operations. Examples of such applications include image processing, interpretation of electrocardiogram (EKG) data, and statistical analysis of very large sets of data.

No matter what programming language is used to communicate a problem to the computer, the problem description ultimately is converted to a series of machine instructions stored in primary storage. The control unit orchestrates the sequential processing of these machine instructions by coordinating retrieval of the data to be manipulated, retrieval and application of processing instructions, and storage of the results.

When program instructions or data are transferred from primary storage to the CPU for processing, they are held in a high-speed memory area within the CPU known as registers. Enhancing the computer's performance is possible by increasing the number of operations performed within the CPU's registers and minimizing the number of accesses to data stored in memory.

Primary Storage

Primary storage refers to "internal" memory, where data are stored for access by the CPU. The capacity and speed of the primary storage greatly affect the computer system's performance, and, fortunately, the cost of this component has lessened greatly since early designs. Read-only memory (ROM) is used to store sets of instructions for special tasks such as the computer start-up process. Data cannot be written to this storage area by the user, but the existing readable data are retained even when the machine is turned off. Random access memory (RAM), the largest volume of the types of primary data, stores data and processing instructions in specified locations that can be accessed in any order. The contents of RAM are lost when the computer is powered off. Cache memory stores data to be quickly accessible for high-speed processing. Although most cache storage is cleared when the computer is powered off, some data stored in cache for specific applications may be retained.

Secondary Storage

It is not possible for a computer system to have sufficient primary storage to accommodate all information maintained and used in the many healthcare information system applications required. Secondary storage devices include a variety of devices and media designed to maintain small or large quantities of data. The speed with which data are entered into and retrieved from secondary storage devices is an important specification within the overall system. However, the ability to ensure the security of these devices and media is of paramount importance.

Healthcare enterprises and even individuals need large capacity, nonvolatile storage media from which desired information can be obtained as necessary. Most PC users and large information systems employ a variety of storage media. Table 6.1 provides a summary of commonly used types of secondary storage media and key attributes of each.

Input Devices

The power of an information system can only be realized when data and programs have been entered for processing. A number of peripheral devices are available to facilitate the process of entering data into the computer in a variety of formats, including keyboard entry, scanning, and voice input. The field has progressed tremendously since the era in which keypunched cards served as the exclusive input medium. Users can select one or more input options that meet the organization's needs for speed, accuracy, and cost effectiveness. A selection of currently available devices and techniques used to input data are reviewed in Table 6.2.

Although the keyboard remains a frequently used input device, healthcare organizations have found that other input devices are especially suitable for specific applications. For example, scanning devices provide an efficient and

Medium	Description	Advantage(s)	Disadvantage(s)
Magnetic tape	Data are recorded as magnetized "spots" on tape.	Large amounts of data can be stored at low cost; relatively stable medium.	Older medium; slow speed; sequential access only.
Magnetic disk	Data are recorded as magnetized spots on rigid (hard) or flexible (floppy) disks. Hard disks consist of stacks of "platters" sealed in dust-proof cases and may be internal to the CPU or an external peripheral device. Floppy disks are small (3.50), are removable, and may zip files to increase storage capacity.	Hard disks can store large amount of data in small physical space. Floppy disks are very inexpensive.	Floppy disk storage volume is relatively small; disks are insecure and easily damaged or lost; medium is becoming obsolete.
Optical disk	Data are burned onto a rigid plastic disk with a laser device. Examples include compact-disk (CD) and digital versatile (or video) disk (DVD), both of which may be read-only recordable or rewritable.	Can store large amount of data on small disk; disks are inexpensive, convenient to use.	Disks are easily damaged or lost; portable media pose security issues.
Optical or laser card	Resembles a plastic credit card. Data are permanently written to card with laser; data can be added, but not erased. Could be useful for personal health record.	Large memory capacity; permanent data storage.	Requires special reader; easily lost/portable media pose security issues.
Smart card	Resembles a plastic credit card, but has embedded computer chip to store and process information.	Convenient; good memory capacity.	Requires special reader; easily lost/portable media pose security issues.
USB (universal serial bus) flash drive	Small circuit board encased in metal or plastic that interfaces with the computer via the USB port.	Very small, highly portable storage; inexpensive.	Memory cells eventually fail; easily lost/portable media pose security issues.
Portable hard drive	External (peripheral) hard drive; often used to "back up" data in other storage or to store digital photographs, music, or movies.	Available in many physical sizes and storage capacities; relatively inexpensive.	Portable media pose security issues.

TABLE 6.1

Examples of Secondary Storage Media

TABLE 6.2
Input Devices

Device	Description	Advantage(s)	Disadvantage(s)
Keyboard	Panel of "keys," including alphabetic and numeric characters and special function keys.	Familiar, similar to typewriter; inexpensive.	Poor keying skills result in data-entry errors. Smaller boards on handheld devices may be difficult to use.
Pointing devices (mouse, rollerball, touch screen)	Device that controls the screen cursor; "pointer" may be a finger or special device. Functions are activated at cursor location.	Easy to use; rapid data-entry method.	Precision in pointing required to avoid data-entry errors.
Scanning devices (barcode readers, optical mark readers)	Data are captured by reading differences in light reflection between the mark and white space.	Rapid data entry; good error control; useful in tracking systems.	Limited amount of data captured; fairly limited application.
Handwriting recognition	Stylus or other device used to write data on touch-sensitive screen or optical scanning of writing on paper.	Familiar skill, no training required.	Handwriting must be intelligible.
Voice input	User enters data and instructions via a microphone; software program converts spoken language to machine language by digitizing sound waves.	Technical skills not required.	Expensive, not widely used; machine must "learn" user's voice pattern and pronunciation; vocabulary must be built.

accurate means for tracking many types of inventory items. Medical supplies, pharmaceuticals, and even patient identification bands may be tagged with bar codes or markings that perform several functions when scanned. An item may be removed from current inventory, charged to a patient, and scheduled for inventory replacement with a simple scanning process. Paper documents converted to images for inclusion in an electronic health record typically are indexed for retrieval using a bar code (Dunn 2006).

Physicians may order diagnostic tests or medications simply by touching the monitor screen where a list of options is displayed. Scanning handwritten documents may make the information available to more users much sooner than if the document is transcribed through keyboard entry. Scanned graphical material such as EKG reports can be accessed online from multiple locations, compared with hard copies stored in a single location.

Selection of the best input device for a given application should consider both efficiency and accuracy criteria. While speed of input provides convenience, which is important to time-pressured clinicians, speed should not be gained at the expense of data quality and patient safety.

In the early phases of healthcare computing, data entry typically occurred at centralized locations, such as nursing stations or dictation rooms. More recently, information systems are designed to facilitate data capture at the "point of care," such as the patient's bedside or in other diagnostic or treatment areas. Often data are captured concurrently with patient examination and treatment, through voice recorders or digitally enhanced diagnostic devices. Data also may be entered using computer workstations in or near the patient's room or by using a portable or handheld device.

Output Devices

The actual work performed by the computer system is of little value until it is produced (output) in a usable format accessible to the user, such as in printed form, digitally for future processing, or in audio or spoken form. The goal of the information technology industry is to make data entry and retrieval as simple as possible.

Types of output of particular value to healthcare managers include visual displays, printed documents, and audio (including voice) output. The oldest and still most widely used form of displaying output from an information system is a video display terminal (VDT). Typically called a monitor, the VDT has evolved from small monochrome screens into large, high-resolution liquid crystal displays. These sophisticated monitors can display images at resolutions high enough to support clinical diagnosis and treatment.

Printers, too, have developed extensively from the early impact devices that were similar to typewriters. Today's color laser printers are capable of reproducing artwork and detailed diagnostic images. Key printer characteristics to consider in purchase decisions include memory, resolution, and print speed.

As technology has enabled digitization of sound with good quality, audio output has become a more viable option in clinical technology applications. When digital text is converted to understandable speech by voice synthesis, an ordinary telephone can be used to access healthcare information. For example, a physician needing a patient's test results could use a telephone to call the laboratory system and hear the results read by a voice synthesizer. Clinicians also can listen to body sounds, such as breathing or heartbeat, from distant locations. This capability allows expert consultation without patient travel.

Computer Software

The hardware components of even the most powerful supercomputer cannot by themselves produce output of value to the healthcare manager. The hardware components need a detailed set of instructions that describe, step by step, the tasks that must be performed to achieve a desired objective. This detailed set of instructions is known as a *program*, and programs are collectively referred to as *software*.

Although for many people software is equated with applications, either general purpose or function specific, computer software also includes operating systems, utilities, programming languages, software development tools, and language translators. The healthcare manager must consider many factors in choosing computer software. Among them are the number of existing and potential users, required hardware configurations, security considerations, anticipated future growth in computer applications, and functional requirements for individual applications.

Software issues are important to healthcare managers at a number of levels. First, although most healthcare organizations do little in-house development of software, the manager must be a knowledgeable participant in software acquisition. Managers must acknowledge that the quality of available software is variable, and in some cases software purchased at significant expense fails to meet expectations. Perhaps knowledgeable and informed managers participating in the evaluation, acquisition, and implementation of software will help ensure that installed systems meet their organizations' needs.

Second, all software must be appropriately licensed. It is easy for someone to copy software for personal use or to load a single-license program on multiple machines without any thought of impropriety. Policies should be in place emphasizing the organization's strong stance on exclusive use of legally licensed software.

Third, managers should be aware of the rapid evolution of software versions. Operating systems and application software are constantly being revised. Sometimes, users will campaign to upgrade a software package solely to have the most current version, even when the current version meets their needs. In other cases, the vendor might actually cease to support a given version, thereby forcing the user to upgrade. Again, knowledgeable participation by the manager is valuable in making upgrade decisions.

Finally, and perhaps most important in the current technology environment, the manager must understand the challenges created by the need for interfaces linking disparate software packages.

Application Software

From the user perspective, the most important category of software is application software. After all, this is the software that accomplishes the useful tasks that justify the purchase of the information system. A general overview of application software is provided here, and the topic is covered in greater detail in Chapter 8.

Application software can be further classified as general purpose or application specific. Many computer programs provide an environment in which a user can solve a particular *class* of problems rather than a single, narrowly defined problem. Examples include word processors, desktop publishing software, spreadsheet software, statistical packages, database management software, presentation graphics software, and Web browsers. These types of programs are known as *general purpose* application software. This type of software is generally purchased as a "suite" of integrated, menu-driven module programs.

Application-specific software is a computer program designed to solve a single, specifically defined problem. A good example is a payroll program, which is developed to accumulate labor hours, compute deductions, write payroll checks, post summaries to the general ledger, and complete forms required by federal and state government.

Numerous vendors offer an array of application-specific software aimed at the healthcare industry. *Healthcare Informatics*, a print and online technology journal, publishes a resource guide of information technology companies, products, services, and associations. The online database (available at healthcare-informatics.com) may be searched by product category or by vendor.

Healthcare organizations have the option of developing application-specific software in-house or purchasing (or leasing) a vendor-designed application and installing it on their computer system. However, the process is not as simple as it might sound. Each approach has its advantages and disadvantages. With in-house development, the software can be tailored specifically to the organization's needs, and when changes are needed, they generally are easier to make. Purchased (or leased) software, by comparison, is generally less expensive, requires less time to get running, and requires fewer in-house computer personnel. However, any changes to the program must be negotiated with the vendor. A third approach, modifying an existing package, attempts to integrate the advantages of both alternatives.

In the early years of healthcare computing, in-house development of application software was a favorite choice of many healthcare organizations. Today, most software is purchased or leased. The high cost of specialized software has led some organizations to contract with application service providers (ASPs) that provide needed computing services via a network connection. The ASP may provide a single application, such as billing, or a full range of computing services. This second option might be particularly attractive for a small physician practice. Outsourced computing is not without risks, however, and managers must be savvy when negotiating contracts. Two key issues to include in contract negotiations are data ownership and return of data should the relationship be terminated (Dolan 2006).

Most healthcare managers have concluded that they are in the business of providing healthcare services, not developing software. However, they must still be knowledgeable participants in the process of purchasing or leasing software. In addition, involving key users in software purchasing decisions is very important, especially when major systems are being acquired. Other factors that must be considered when choosing application software are the required staffing and equipment resources, the cost of maintenance, the complexity of the operations being automated, the number of potential users, and data security issues.

Integrated Versus Interfaced Systems Two general approaches are available for acquiring and implementing application software in a healthcare organization. In the first approach, all modules required to satisfy the organization's computing needs are identified and purchased from a single vendor. Typically, these modules will have been designed to work with one another so that data transfer among modules proceeds smoothly. This type of system is known as an *integrated* information system.

By contrast, each of the required modules could be purchased from the vendor thought to be the leader in that particular application area. In some cases, the decision might reflect the personal bias of influential members of a particular department in the organization. In any event, although a given module might work well for its particular application area, connecting the module to other modules could be problematic. For example, the data contained in one module could be incompatible with the data format of other modules. The solution very often is the development of an *interface*, which acts as a bridge between the two modules and which, for example, translates the data format into one that the receiving module can handle.

The use of an interfaced approach is made simpler if the modules comprising the interfaced system have all been developed in accordance with a standard that makes their data formats compatible.

Advantages of an integrated system include compatibility among the modules and the need to have only a single source for system support and maintenance. On the other hand, interfaced systems that allow users to choose the leading system for a given module can sometimes result in lower costs by leveraging one vendor against another, obviating the need to replace all existing modules when updates are considered.

System Management Software

System management software is the group of programs that manage the resources of a computer system and perform a variety of routine processing tasks. Unlike the role of application software, the function of system management software often is not obvious to the user. Thus, many computer users are unaware of the important functions being performed by the operating system and by utility programs.

Operating Systems

Operating systems serve as the interface between the human user and the computer, managing the functioning of the software and hardware. The operating system incorporates a graphical user interface, which uses icons (graphical symbols on the monitor screen) to represent available operating system commands. The user simply clicks on a given icon with the computer's mouse or other pointing device to invoke the desired command.

The complexity of the operating system and the scope of services that it must provide depend on the complexity of the computing environment in which the operating system is installed. An environment that allows only one user to run one program at a time possesses the least complexity and places the fewest demands on the operating system. Examples include the early mainframe computers and the early PCs.

The computing power of a given computer can be more effectively utilized when multiple tasks can be run by either a single user or by multiple users. In such an environment, known as *multitasking*, the operating system plays a more essential role. Operating systems must manage system resources, such as memory, CPU time, and file operations, in a way that results in very efficient multitasking. Multiple users must be able to perform a variety of tasks with no perceptible slowing of processing time.

Utility Programs

Utility programs are software, often incorporated into operating systems, that perform generalized data processing or computational functions. These functions are not specific to any particular computer application. They offer general utility and support to a variety of information-processing tasks, including functions of the operating system as well as application programs. Examples of utility programs include virus scan programs and encryption programs.

Programming Languages

All software—application, system, or utility—consists of a detailed set of instructions describing the specific steps the computer is to perform. This detailed set of instructions must be communicated to the computer in a specific *programming language*. When a spreadsheet user enters a formula in a particular cell on the spreadsheet, that user is actually writing a program statement.

Although the typical healthcare manager will make limited use of programming languages as little in-house program development is done, a few brief comments can illustrate some key points. Despite the number and type of programming languages in existence, the objective of all languages from the user's perspective is simple. The overarching goal is to communicate with the computer in some prescribed format so that useful output can be generated. Whereas skilled programmers may find reward in creating complex code, for the nonprogrammer user, the satisfaction of this communication process lies in the output created, not in the communication process itself.

When computers were first developed, instructions were specified in *machine language*, strings of zeros and ones, which is the only language that a computer is capable of understanding. The progression of programming languages can be tracked through successive "generations," with each generation improving the computer-human interface. The evolutionary goal is to achieve *natural language* input, whereby the user is able to give commands to a computer as easily as communicating with another person. A translator program would convert natural language statements into the binary number commands intelligible to the computer. The technology necessary to recognize the spoken words, interpret their content, transform them into a set of procedures, and translate this sequence into machine commands is complex and has not been perfected.

Networking and Telecommunications

Today's clinicians and managers require information from a variety of sources outside of, as well as within, their organizations. When geographically separated healthcare delivery units are combined to form a healthcare enterprise or an integrated delivery system, sharing information among the system's components becomes increasingly challenging. The implementation of computer networks and the use of telecommunications help these organizations manage their information flow.

The technology associated with data communication systems and computer networks is relatively complex, involving the expertise of communications engineers, computer hardware specialists, and software professionals. While these functional experts assume responsibility for the design and installation of this technology, the healthcare manager must assume responsibility for overseeing these activities and making sure that the organization's information needs are met.

As is true in the areas of hardware and software, the manager will need sufficient understanding of networking and telecommunications concepts to work intelligently with the functional experts in these fields. The following discussion is meant neither to be exhaustive nor to make the healthcare manager a networking or telecommunications expert but to present an introductory overview of these subjects.

A Rationale for Computer Networks

Early applications of computers in hospitals, as in many other industries, consisted of a variety of financial applications such as billing, payroll, and general accounting. These programs typically were run on a large mainframe computer located in the organization's data-processing department. In some cases, the organization might have chosen to have its computing performed by an outside vendor of data processing services. The input data for these programs were contained in handwritten documents such as charge slips, invoices, or time and attendance sheets that were manually or electronically entered. The output consisted of standardized printed reports that were distributed to the appropriate users.

The demise of the mainframe approach can be attributed to two key developments in the computing industry: the introduction of software systems designed to perform specific functions and the introduction of the PC. Special function applications for departments such as pharmacy, radiology, and laboratory systems frequently were run on minicomputers that could be located within close proximity of the department utilizing the system. Using a PC, managers were able to analyze a variety of operational and financial data themselves. They were no longer dependent on the data processing department to run special reports, often with considerable delay.

As department managers purchased minicomputer-based systems and other managers became increasingly dependent on personal computing, they soon realized the various programs were not independent, stand-alone modules. In fact, a high level of interdependence existed among these programs. For example, the laboratory, pharmacy, and radiology systems all needed information captured by the admitting system. Similarly, many of the management reports generated on PCs were derived from data abstracted from a printed report generated by a mainframe financial application.

This situation is particularly problematic in a healthcare system because data on a given patient might be found in a number of locations, and a single laboratory might serve widely separated patient care locations. Data must flow across a large area, and managers often require input from many sources to arrive at a solution to a problem. Clearly, the disparate systems throughout the organization (and even beyond) need to be connected to facilitate the exchange of data and the sharing of resources. The term typically applied to the capability of elements of an information system or network to communicate and exchange information is *interoperability* (Heubusch 2006).

The linkages needed to facilitate data exchange and sharing of resources are accomplished through the construction of a network. When all components of the network are located within relatively close proximity to one another, perhaps within a single facility, the network is generally referred to as a *local area network* (LAN). A network that extends into a broad geographical area is referred to as a *wide area network* (WAN).

Ways of Distributing the Processing Function

One basis for classifying networks is the way in which the processing functions are distributed among the devices comprising the network. Four configurations are in common use, ranging from a *centralized* computing environment, in which the processing functions are concentrated in a single device, to a *decentralized* environment, in which these functions are split, or distributed, among all of the users on the network. Decentralized networks typically create greater managerial challenges, a fact that is particularly relevant for the healthcare manager.

Terminal-Host Systems

In the most centralized computing environment, dating back to the 1960s, users work at devices known as *terminals*. Early terminals had no processing capability and were often known as *dumb terminals*. Today, a PC is used to mimic, or emulate, a terminal. The terminal is connected to a large central *host computer*, typically a mainframe. The important feature of this computing environment is that all computing takes place on the host system. This configuration is depicted in Figure 6.2.

Depending on the level of sophistication of the program running on the host machine, the terminals allow users to perform a variety of functions, including the following:

- Entering a set of data for a program to be run at some later time in batch mode—that is, as part of a sequential stream of programs from several users
- Real-time processing of a program immediately after entering data and/or programming commands
- Responding to a query such as a patient account balance

FIGURE 6.2
Terminal-Host
Configuration

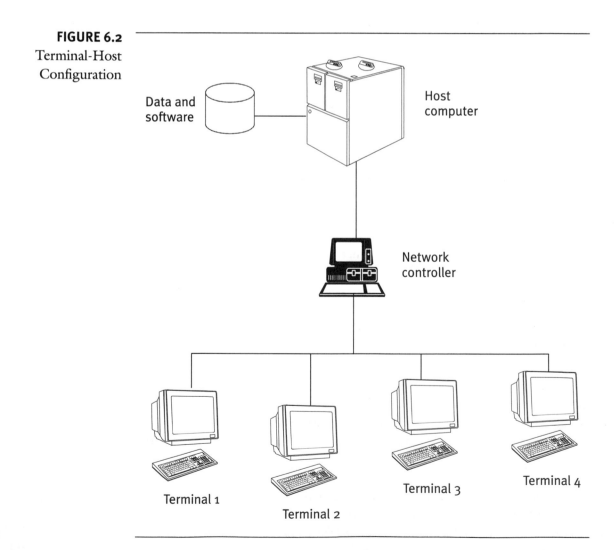

An important subset of a terminal-host configuration is *remote job entry* (RJE), where terminals might be located at considerable distance from the host machine. Several major companies have specialized in providing computing services to healthcare organizations on an RJE basis.

Users of dumb terminals connected to a host computer easily recognized the advantage that would result from their terminals having computing capability. Data could be edited, preliminary computations could be made, and other processing could be done that did not require the power of the host machine. This early conceptualization was predictive of today's client/server computing configuration, which is characterized by less centralization than a terminal-host installation (see Figure 6.3).

Client/Server Computing

Client/server architecture divides applications into two components: (1) client, or *front-end* functions, which include user interface, decision support, and data processing, and (2) server, or *back-end* functions, such as database management, printing, communication, and applications program execution. The server can be a personal, mini-, or mainframe computer, and multiple servers can often be found in a client/server network.

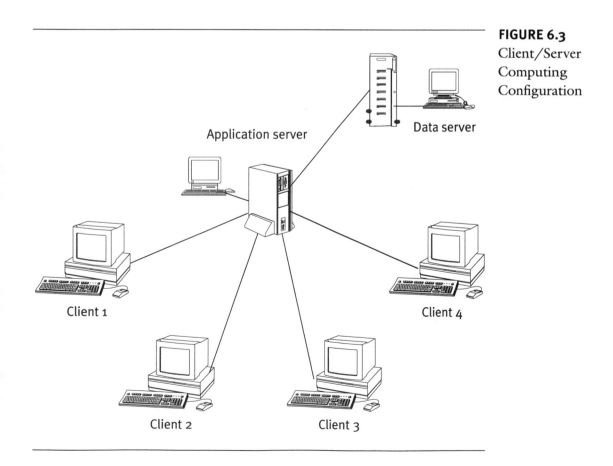

FIGURE 6.3
Client/Server
Computing
Configuration

Data server

Application server

Client 1

Client 4

Client 2

Client 3

When all back-end functions are performed on a single server, the configuration is known as *two-tier* client/server architecture. In a *three-tier* architecture, the user interface resides on the client, the relational databases reside on one server, and the application programs reside on a second server. This configuration is easier to manage and offers faster information processing and distribution.

As managers work with their functional specialists on the implementation of client/server networks, they are likely to encounter two important terms. The first is *thin client*, which means that most processing is performed on the remote server. This offers a cost savings on the client computers, as they need only minimal processing capability. The second is *middleware*, which connects applications in distributed networked systems. Client and server vendors will typically offer middleware packages as options.

File/Server Architecture   Even less centralized than client/server installations is file/server architecture. In a file/server network, a relatively large number of network processors are able to share the data contained in files on the server (see Figure 6.4). The actual processing of data, however, is distributed across the network machines.

Many small LANs are configured with file/server architecture. The file/server typically has a large fixed-disk drive with fast disk-access time. The

FIGURE 6.4
File/Server
Architecture

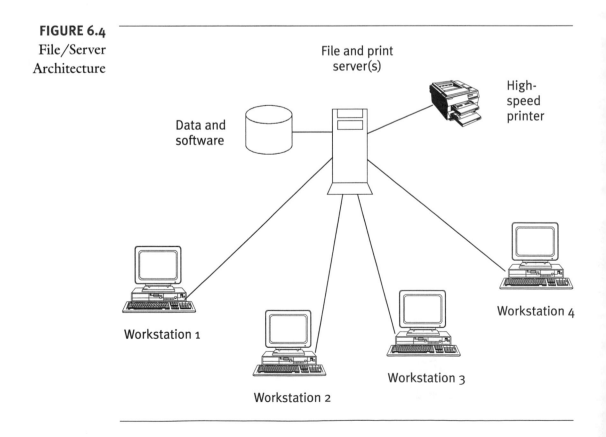

File and print server(s)

High-speed printer

Data and software

Workstation 1

Workstation 2

Workstation 3

Workstation 4

other computers on the network have much more modest fixed-disk drive requirements, but they benefit from fast processors to support their execution of application software.

Peer networks represent a decentralized computing environment, in which each computer on the network has either data or some hardware resource that it can make available to the other users on the network. The key distinguishing feature of peer networks is the fact that there is no server, and all of the computers on the network can be used as workstations (see Figure 6.5). Key advantages of a peer network are the ease of installation and configuration and the relative low expense compared with client/server networks. However, peer networks are generally considered suitable only for small installations, as large peer networks may be nonsecure and unreliable (Hayden 2001, 93).

Peer Networks

Brailer (2001, 29) suggests that the Internet (discussed later in this chapter) provides a viable vehicle for implementing peer-to-peer technology. In addition to offering cost advantages, peer to peer networks implemented

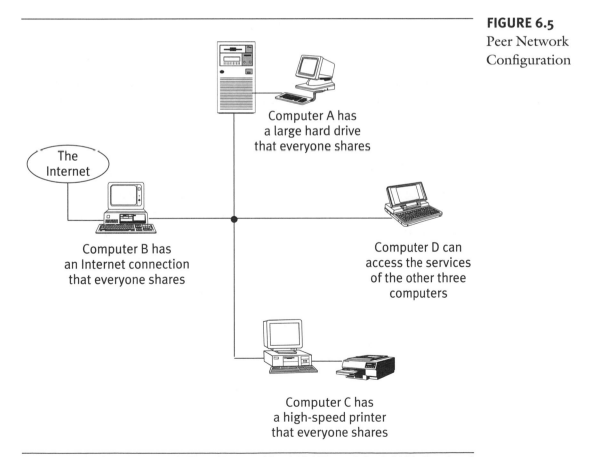

FIGURE 6.5
Peer Network
Configuration

Computer A has
a large hard drive
that everyone shares

The
Internet

Computer B has
an Internet connection
that everyone shares

Computer D can
access the services
of the other three
computers

Computer C has
a high-speed printer
that everyone shares

Source: M. Hayden, *Sams Teach Yourself Networking in 24 Hours,* 2/e, © 2001. Reprinted by permission of Pearson Education, Inc., Upper Saddle River, New Jersey.

via the Internet can address the security concern, as participating organizations maintain control of their own data.

Management Issues

As healthcare managers participate with their functional specialists in selecting the networking configuration for their organization, several issues must be considered. First, the trend is to distribute computing capability down to the user level, as evidenced by the proliferation of microcomputers in most organizations. However, in a highly complex and interrelated field such as healthcare, some degree of centralization of the computing and information storage functions is necessary. Also, the evolution of the field toward integrated healthcare systems and managed care makes information system integration even more vital.

Second, the network configuration can affect the number of copies of application software that must be purchased, licensed, and maintained. A single "network version" of an application package can be installed on a server accessible to the users on the network. Individual licensed copies of the software also can be placed on each user machine. Careful evaluation of these alternatives must consider the purchase price of the software, software licensing fees, and software maintenance costs as well as hardware costs.

Healthcare managers are well advised to monitor closely the architecture being chosen by their functional specialists to ensure that the information systems function is moving in a direction that appropriately supports the organization's strategic direction. Specification of the overall systems architecture and infrastructure is one step in the development of a strategic information systems plan (see Chapter 3).

Network Components

Creating an information network requires the assembly of a variety of hardware and software components. This section presents an overview of these components.

Transmission Media

Early in the process of designing a network, a decision must be made regarding the transmission media to be used. Transmission media, which carry the signal being transmitted from one location to another, include metal wires, which carry electrical signals; fiber-optic cables, which carry optical signals; or air, through which radio waves travel. Each transmission medium is discussed below.

Wired Media

Wired media consist of one or more strands of metal, frequently copper, which is an excellent conductor of electricity. Data are transmitted along these conductors in the form of changing electrical voltages and may be represented as either a *digital* or *analog* waveform. Digital transmission involves the representation of data with binary digits or bits. Analog transmission represents data by varying the amplitude (height), frequency, and/or phase of a waveform. Traditional telephone lines carry signals in an analog format, while integrated services digital network (ISDN) lines, digital subscriber lines (DSL), and the cable in a LAN carry signals digitally.

Data are carried in a fiber-optic medium in the form of light pulses. The electrical data signal is used to turn a light source on and off very rapidly. At the receiving end of the cable, an optical detector converts the light signal back to an electrical signal. Fiber-optic cable is thinner and more durable than copper wiring, provides higher bandwidth, and is not subject to electronic eavesdropping.

Fiber-Optic Media

Unlike copper and fiber media, radio media use radio waves of different frequencies to transmit data through the air. *Broadcast radio* is used to support paging devices and cellular technology. *Microwave radio* is capable of higher data rates than broadcast radio and is used in WANs ands wireless LANs. However, microwave signals travel only in a straight line, so microwave transmission over long distances requires the use of repeaters or satellites. Microwave transmissions are subject to interference from adverse weather conditions as well as any objects that might interfere with their travel from transmitter to receiver. All communication using radio waves is subject to electronic eavesdropping, thus resulting in special security issues that must be addressed.

Radio Media

Transmitters/Receivers

The general process of communication consists of a transmitter sending information (or in some cases raw data) through a transmission medium to a receiver. When two people have a conversation, at a specific point in time the person speaking plays the role of the transmitter, and the person listening has the role of the receiver. During the course of the conversation, these roles alternate many times. Similarly, in an information systems network, at any given time one network component acts as a transmitter while a second component has the role of a receiver. Like personal conversations, the roles of these components can change frequently. The devices used to connect transmitters and receivers to the transmission media depend on the media type and data format.

A network interface card (NIC) serves as an adapter to allow a microcomputer to connect to a high-speed LAN. The specific card that is required depends on the architecture of the microcomputer and the protocol of the LAN. When an NIC is installed, it is also necessary to install appropriate software, known as the *device driver*, which allows the computer to "talk" to the NIC. Finally, one should note that every NIC is assigned a unique 48-bit number (called a media-access control) that identifies the computer to the network (Hayden 2001).

Network Interface Cards

Modems   A modem (modulator/demodulator) is a device capable of changing signals from one format to another and then back again. Two types are available: copper based and fiber optic. The copper-based modem converts a device's digital signals to analog signals appropriate for copper media. It can take the form of a card located inside the computer (internal modem) or a separate component connected to, but located outside of, the computer (external modem). Fiber-optic modems convert a device's digital signals to optical digital signals, which can then be carried over a fiber-optic network.

Multiplexers   Several devices (computer, printer, and scanner) can be connected to a multiplexer. The output of the multiplexer serves as the input to the transmission medium. A multiplexer at the receiving end of the transmission medium separates the signals. Thus, the devices appear to have their own transmission channel when in fact they are sharing the transmission medium. Figure 6.6 graphically represents the function of a multiplexer.

Bridges, Gateways, and Routers   *Bridges* are interfaces that connect two or more networks that use similar protocols (rules or conventions governing the communication process). *Gateways* represent the interface between two networks that use dissimilar protocols to communicate. This allows the users to access data and programs outside of their own region. Gateways are network entrances and play an important role in the interconnection of the many disparate networks that compose the Internet (discussed briefly below).

A *router* is a device located at any gateway to manage the data flow between the networks. The router decides, on the basis of its current understanding of the activity state of the networks, which way to send each packet of information flowing on the network for greatest efficiency.

Network Controller/Servers

A network controller is used in terminal-host networks consisting of a number of terminals connected to one or more mainframe host computers. The function of this controller, which can be a minicomputer or microcomputer, is to "direct" the communications traffic between the host and the terminals and peripheral devices.

LANs do not have a network controller. Rather, communication traffic is directed by a defined protocol that depends on the network topology. The network may have one or more *servers,* which provide network users with a variety of services, including access to files (file servers), help with passing files over the transmission medium (database servers), and a connection to network printers (printer servers).

Network Control Software/Network Operating Systems

Like network controllers, network control software is also associated with mainframe-based telecommunications networks. The software resides on the

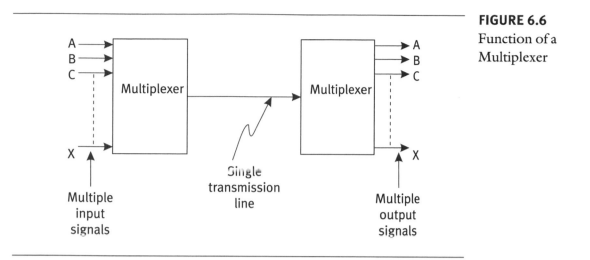

FIGURE 6.6
Function of a
Multiplexer

host (mainframe), on a small computer (front-end processor) connected to the host and dedicated to communications management, and on other processors in the network. Functions of this software include controlling access to resources, regulating data transmission to and from terminals, improving network efficiency, and detecting and correcting errors.

LANs and WANs employ network operating systems to coordinate and support the operation of the network, such as user access, data traffic, and security. Some network operating systems serve as supplements to the computer's existing operating system. Others, like Windows XP, constitute comprehensive computer operating systems where the networking capabilities have been integrated into the operating system.

The information systems manager, when choosing network software, must consider several factors such as the number of existing or potential users, the type of network hardware available, the type of applications software programs needed, available resources (human and equipment), and network configuration costs.

Network Topologies

The configuration used to connect the computers and peripheral devices in a LAN is known as the network's *physical topology*. Three alternative configurations are available to network designers: bus, ring, and star topologies. These topologies can be used singly or in combination with one another to form a *hybrid network*.

Closely related to these physical topologies are *logical topologies*, which "lay out the rules of the road for data transmission" (Hayden 2001, 36). These topologies are largely abstract and not as easily visualized as the physical topologies. This section presents an overview of four physical topologies (bus, ring, star, and hybrid) and four common logical topologies (Ethernet, including fast and switched Ethernet; token ring; fiber distributed data interface; and asynchronous transfer mode).

Bus Networks

In a bus network, a single circuit, or bus, is used to link the computers and other devices composing the network (see Figure 6.7). The medium employed for this single circuit can be twisted wire, coaxial cable, or fiber-optic cable. A hardware device known as a terminator is used at either end of the bus. Advantages of a bus network are the relative ease of wiring the network and the relatively fast communication rate. Disadvantages are limitations of length of the bus because of signal attenuation and the fact that if a break in the bus were to occur, then all of the devices beyond the break would be disconnected from the network.

A device instructed to send a message listens first to see if the bus is busy. The message is then sent out and received by every other device. Only the intended recipient, however, pays attention to the message. If by chance two devices send out messages at the same time, a collision will occur, which will be detected. This problem is resolved by having the two devices involved wait for a random time interval and then resend the message. This protocol is known as *carrier sense multiple access with collision detection* (CSMA/CD). The trade name for this protocol is *Ethernet.* When a large number of users are attempting to use an Ethernet network, a bottleneck can occur. Fast Ethernet and switched Ethernet represent two possible solutions for this bottleneck. *Fast Ethernet* simply uses a higher-quality line and operates at ten times the

FIGURE 6.7
Bus Network
Topology

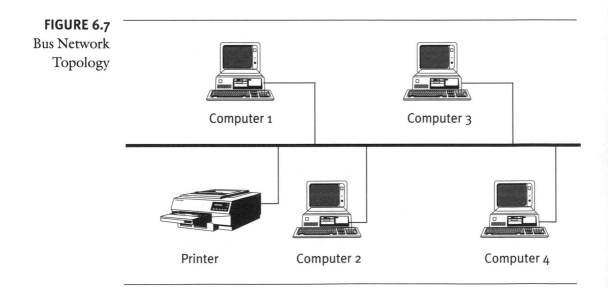

Computer 1   Computer 3

Printer   Computer 2   Computer 4

speed of traditional Ethernet. *Switched Ethernet* dedicates bandwidth space to segments of users.

Ring Networks

A ring network can be conceptualized as a group of devices (nodes) arranged in a circle with a connection between adjacent devices to form a closed loop (see Figure 6.8). Data travel in a single direction around the ring, and each device on the network retransmits the signal it receives from the previous device to the next device in the ring. Ring networks offer the advantage of facilitating the construction of high-speed networks that operate over large distances. This is accomplished through the use of a fiber-optic transmission medium for the connection between adjacent nodes along with the use of an amplification device (repeater) at each node. In addition, the operation of the network is not affected by removal of a node from the ring. Disadvantages include difficulty in troubleshooting the network and adding new nodes to the ring.

A protocol often used with ring networks, the *token-ring* protocol, passes an electronic token along the loop. Only the node computer that holds the token at a given time can place a message on the network. The token is then passed on to the next node. The message passes from node to node until it reaches its destination. Because only one node can access the network at a time, the collisions that are possible with the CSMA/CD protocol (Ethernet) cannot occur here. A fiber distributed data interface (FDDI) utilizes a backup token ring that becomes operational in the event that the primary ring fails.

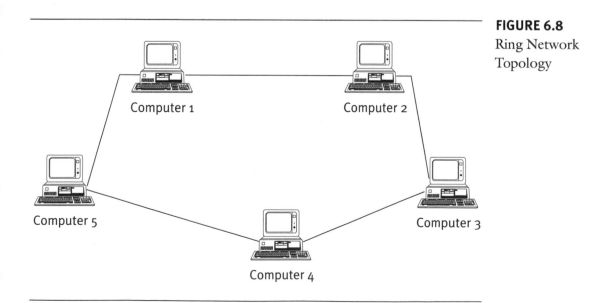

FIGURE 6.8
Ring Network Topology

Computer 1   Computer 2

Computer 5   Computer 3

Computer 4

If the second ring is not needed for backup and can be used to carry data, the network can operate at rates up to 200 million bits per second.

Star Networks

In a star network, each node has a single point-to-point connection to a center node, called a *hub*, or *concentrator* (see Figure 6.9). When a given node wants to send a message to a second node, the message must first travel through the central hub. A *passive hub* simply serves as a connector for the wires coming from the various nodes. A message sent from a given node goes to every other node, and the intended recipient node is responsible for claiming its own messages. An *active hub* not only serves as a connector but also regenerates message signals before sending them on to the other nodes. The message signal still goes to all of the nodes, and the appropriate node claims its own messages. Finally, *intelligent hubs* are able to determine the destination address for a particular message and to route the message to that address only.

Advantages of a star network include the ease with which it can be initially wired and repaired and the relative ease with which nodes can be added to an existing network. One disadvantage of a star network is the fact

FIGURE 6.9
Star Network
Topology

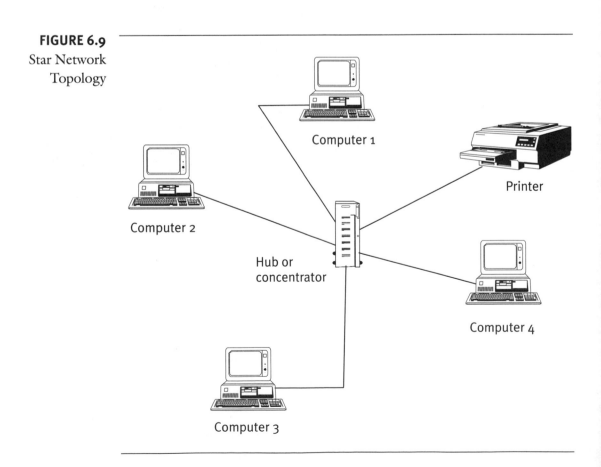

Computer 1

Printer

Computer 2

Hub or
concentrator

Computer 4

Computer 3

that a malfunctioning hub can bring the entire network down. The use of backup hubs can help to address this difficulty. Additionally, star networks can require more cabling than networks using other topologies. Nevertheless, this topology is in wide use in many network installations.

Hybrid Networks

Two or more of these network topologies are often combined into a single network known as a *hybrid network*. One example is a WAN formed by linking several LANs having different topologies. Another example is the Internet (discussed briefly later in this chapter), which consists of an interconnection of a variety of network types.

Asynchronous Transfer Mode

Asynchronous transfer mode (ATM) refers to a logical network topology that segments data to be transmitted into small packets, called *cells*; directs the cells through switches to the appropriate destination node; and then reassembles the data. It allows voice, data, and video to be mixed over the network, and it can run at speeds up to 1.5 billion bits per second (Hayden 2001, 40).

Electronic Data Interchange

The networks described in this chapter can serve as the medium for transferring structured information from one computer to another without human intervention, a process known as *electronic data interchange* (EDI). This process needs to incorporate standards and procedures so that the receiving computer will be able to interpret the output of the sending computer. The fact that the information is structured serves to differentiate EDI from electronic communication such as e-mail in which unstructured text is transferred in the form of messages.

Early applications of EDI in the healthcare field involved the electronic processing of health insurance claims, and claims processing remains an important role for EDI today. Geometrically increased numbers of claims can be processed daily, and turnaround time is improved dramatically over paper-based claims. EDI can also play a part in a healthcare organization's supply chain management by monitoring utilization, forecasting demands, and generating orders.

Wireless Communication

In each of the computing configurations described earlier, users interact with the information system at a fixed location, often called a *workstation*. However, healthcare practitioners deliver their expertise at the site of the patient, and at that site is where they must be able to retrieve needed information and record newly acquired patient data. Mobile computing and wireless communication make this flow of data at the point of care possible.

Mobile Computing Versus Wireless Communication

Mobile computing and wireless communication are in fact two separate concepts. *Mobile computing* refers to the use of a portable computing device such as a laptop, notebook, or palm-top computer. For example, nurses and other caregivers providing healthcare services in patients' homes can *download* the records of their patients for a given day from a central database into their laptop computer's hard disk, enter new data and notes into their laptop computer over the course of the day, and then *upload* the newly acquired information back to the central system at the end of the day.

Although this procedure is workable, it recreates the very difficulty that led hospitals to adopt networking technology. Because the laptops function as stand-alone computers, the information in the central database is not current until data collected by the portable devices are uploaded back to the central system. If a second provider, say, a physical therapist, calls on the patient later in the day, the nurse's notes, collected earlier but not yet uploaded, will not be available to the therapist.

Even within an inpatient setting, similar problems result when independent mobile computers are used. Until newly acquired information within the hard disk of the mobile computer is transmitted back to the central database or information from the central computer is sent to the mobile computer, a discrepancy remains between two or more databases relative to a given patient. This "mismatch" is not always considered to be a serious problem. For some applications, merely updating the wireless device on a periodic basis is sufficient. For example, physicians may use personal digital assistants (PDAs) at the bedside that contain clinical data, including basic patient data, lab results, and medications prescribed and administered. Updated data are available for download from syncing stations (Briggs 2002, 46). A *syncing station* is a cradle that is wired to a PC. When the PDA is placed in the cradle, data and systems are updated on the PDA and the PC.

On the other hand, the combination of mobile computing and wireless communication enables portable computers to be connected to an established information systems network. In this way, the computing activities performed on the portable devices occur in real time, and the central database, as well as the mobile device, always stays current. Installing a wireless network is considerably less costly than installing additional cabling to create a hardwired system (Sislo 2002), and clinicians typically are supportive of wireless technology (Gillespie 2001, 27).

Despite the obvious benefits of data accessibility, mobile devices are not without drawbacks. Portability, the feature that is a prime benefit, makes the devices physically insecure. Devices may be lost or stolen, creating problems of data security. Due to their size, devices may be easily damaged or need frequent replacement. Special attention must be paid to removing or destroying data on devices that are taken out of service or reissued to new users (Southerton 2007).

Wireless Topologies

Expansion of radio frequency and microwave technologies has enabled broadband wireless options with various ranges, many of which are well suited to use in health facilities. Ultimately, it is expected that availability of low-cost, open-standard wireless technology will lead to cable replacement (Ng et al. 2006). With wireless communication networks, even patients and visitors can use their personal communication devices while inside the facility.

The advent of wireless networks has expanded the traditional classification of networks as LANs or WANs into five classes: (1) wireless global area networks, (2) wireless regional area networks, (3) wireless metropolitan area networks, (4) wireless local area networks, and (5) wireless personal area networks (Siep 2007). As indicated by the labels, the network range may be as extensive as nationwide or limited to a single room.

Three wireless communication topologies are commonly used in networks. Two are typically associated with LANs, while the third is used in a WAN. Each is briefly described below.

Spread Spectrum

Spread spectrum is a type of radio frequency technology widely used in healthcare today for wireless communication between devices on a LAN. Benefits of this transmission approach include improved privacy and decreased signal interference. Of the four basic techniques—frequency-hopping spread spectrum (FHSS), direct-sequence spread spectrum (DSSS), time-hopping spread spectrum (THSS), and chirp spread spectrum (CSS)—only FHSS and DSSS are widely used.

Decisions to use this technology in wireless LAN installations should be informed by *range* of the transmitted signal (to determine network access points), signal *frequency* (to avoid interference with other systems), and aggregate *throughput* (data transfer rate).

Infrared Technology

Infrared radiation is a wavelength between visible light and radio waves. Because infrared technology is "line of sight" and cannot pass through walls, it can only be used in a single room. It has found common use in wireless keyboards and mouse devices, remote control units, and cordless modems.

Cellular Digital Packet Data

Cellular digital packet data (CDPD) is a WAN architecture used in cellular networks, like those of cellular telephones, except the CDPD transmits and receives packets of data rather than continuous voice signals (Wu et al. 1996, 179). CDPD allows remote users to connect to a network without a telephone jack.

Communicating via the Internet

The LANs described in this chapter can be connected to form larger networks, known as *internets* (note the use of a lowercase *i*). For example, the LANs within each institution comprising an integrated delivery system can be linked to form an internet known as an enterprise computer network.

The largest interconnection of networks in the world today is known as the *Internet* (note the uppercase *I*). The Internet began in 1969 as a U.S. Department of Defense project designed to connect various government laboratories and contractors. However, as the "Net" began to be used, it was soon recognized as an indispensable data link between researchers. By the 1990s, the Internet had entered the domain of the general public.

The Internet has become a ubiquitous business and personal tool, bringing instant access to information on almost any topic imaginable, not the least of which is healthcare. According to Internet World Stats (2007), North America boasts 233 million Internet users, about 69 percent of the population. This figure represents more than 100 percent growth in number of users since 2000. The United States contributes 19 percent of all Internet users in the world.

The World Wide Web (www), developed in 1991, is a collection of electronic resources distributed over the Internet that combine text, graphics, sound, and video. Not only have individuals found the Internet and the Web to be valuable tools, but a wide spectrum of businesses has also developed numerous applications using these resources. The healthcare field is no exception. This section provides an overview of the technology issues associated with communication on the Internet, including connecting to the Internet, the concept of a website, the role of an intranet, and the use of a thin client network computer.

Connecting to the Internet

Except for the very few institutions with a staff of in-house engineers, computer specialists, and networking experts who are capable of connecting directly to the Internet, the majority of healthcare organizations will obtain their Internet services through an intermediate provider. This provider can be an *online service connection* such as America Online, which provides an array of information services, or an *Internet service provider* (ISP), whose function is to provide users with a link to the Internet. A list of ISPs can be obtained on the Internet at www.thelist.com. The Internet provider can be reached using a dial-up connection or a direct network connection.

Dial-Up Services Users of dial-up services typically have a high-speed modem (56 kilobits per second) connected to a standard telephone line, or they make use of an ISDN line with an appropriate card to connect their computer to the line. The data transfer rate is typically 64 or 128 kilobits per second.

Direct Network Connections A direct network connection uses dedicated digital telephone lines that go directly from the computer to the ISP. They can be fractional T1 lines (about 1 megabit per second) or T3 lines (45 megabits per second). Telephone companies now offer DSL service, which runs over standard telephone wire. It is priced affordably and is found in many home-computing environments.

Many cable companies offer direct connections between a computer and the cable television network. The cable company then provides a connection between its cable network and an ISP, or the company might serve as the ISP. A cable modem must be added to the computer to facilitate making a connection into the cable network.

Once a connection has been made between a computer and the Internet, a program is needed to manage the assembly and routing of the messages being transmitted. The *transmission control protocol/Internet protocol (TCP/IP)* is such a program. Although the IP takes care of handling the actual delivery of the data, the TCP takes care of keeping track of the individual units of data (called packets) into which a message is divided for efficient routing through the Internet.

The Role of an Intranet

Once the Internet infrastructure is in place, the same technology can also support communication *within* the organization; this structure is referred to as an *intranet*, or private network. When an organization shares part of its intranet with customers, strategic partners, and other stakeholders, the intranet becomes an *extranet*. An intranet or extranet uses the same protocols as the Internet and in general looks no different.

A *firewall* is a security protocol to protect the intranet from outside access while permitting organizational access to the Internet. The firewall can also contain software that establishes a *virtual private network* that allows organizations to maintain privacy while sharing public networks for transmission of their data. Data are encrypted before they are sent through the public network and then decrypted at the receiving end. This methodology makes customers feel more comfortable about providing personal information, such as a credit card number, "online." Transmission of sensitive patient information can use this same protocol.

As developments in intranet applications continue, healthcare managers should monitor how their organizations are using this technology. Special attention should be directed toward the security and confidentiality issues created by intranets. Chapter 5 addresses security and confidentiality.

Thin Clients and the Internet

Thin client computers are minimally configured PCs that were described earlier in the chapter as suitable client machines in a client/server network. These machines can also serve as user workstations on the Internet. The healthcare manager will encounter a variety of terminology associated with this type of installation, including *network computer*, *net PC*, and proprietary names like Windows Terminal or Winterm.

Two major advantages result from the use of thin clients rather than fully configured PCs. The first, and most obvious, advantage is cost. Thin clients carry a lower purchase price that can become significant as the number of computers connected to the Internet in typical healthcare settings continues to increase. A second, and somewhat related, advantage relates to the maintenance of these machines. The typical PC has a number of applications packages residing on its hard drive. As software changes, the information technology department has a formidable task of updating all of the machines. In an environment where thin clients are used, the software resides on the Web server and can be updated relatively easily.

A disadvantage that the manager will face in moving toward the use of thin clients is a cultural one. Users have become accustomed to the power of a fully configured PC on their desk. Making a change to thin clients could face opposition from these users. Another disadvantage, as in all networking situations, occurs when the server is "down;" the user of a thin client is also "down."

In this area, as in all decisions concerning information systems acquisition and installation, the healthcare manager is well advised to be aware of all alternatives and select the one best suited for his or her organization.

Summary

The trend toward the creation of integrated health systems and other industry environmental changes has made the information needs of healthcare organizations increasingly complex. Among the strategies necessary to respond to these changes are the development of interoperable computer networks and the use of telecommunications. These technologies are necessary for EDI between and among organizations.

Networks also can be classified according to the manner in which the processing function is distributed among the devices comprising the network: (1) terminal-host systems, (2) a client/server network, (3) a file/server configuration, and (4) a peer network. Each alternative has its own strengths and weaknesses, and the appropriate configuration is dependent on the organization's strategic direction.

A variety of components compose an information network. Transmission media include wired media, fiber-optic media, and radio media. Transmission and receiving components include NICs, modems, multiplexers, bridges, gateways, and routers. Network controllers and protocols associated with the network servers help to direct the communication traffic on the network. Finally, network control software and network operating systems control the accessing and use of network resources and help improve network efficiency.

The configuration with which devices are connected to form a network is known as the network physical topology. Three alternative configurations, each with pros and cons, are a bus, ring, and star topology. Two or more topologies can be combined to form a hybrid network. Networks also have logical topologies that guide data transmission. Four logical topologies are Ethernet (including fast and switched Ethernet), token ring, FDDI, and ATM.

Mobile computing makes information available at the point of care. The addition of wireless communication to the mobile computing device allows the transfer of information between the device and central database to occur in real time. Spread spectrum technology serves as the basis for wireless LANs. CDPD is a WAN architecture that makes data transmission across cellular networks possible.

The Internet is an important resource for healthcare organizations. It provides access to a wide range of information, allows the organization to achieve a presence on a worldwide information network, and provides an infrastructure for communication within the organization.

Networking and telecommunications are highly technical and rapidly changing areas. Gaining a basic understanding of these areas, staying abreast of the changes, and knowledgeably interacting with the technical specialists in the field are ongoing challenges for the healthcare manager.

Web Resources

Additional information about the infrastructure elements of an information system is readily available through various websites, particularly those hosted by leading technology vendors and industry advocacy groups.

McKesson (mckesson.com) has extensive information about its technology products.

The archive library and current content on Microsoft's websites (www.microsoft.com) contain user tips and guides as well as product information.

As noted earlier in the chapter, *Healthcare Informatics* magazine (healthcare-informatics.com) publishes a resource guide of information technology companies, products, services, and associations.

Discussion Questions

1. Name each of the six components of a computer system and indicate the function of each.
2. Give a brief description of three secondary storage media, including advantages and disadvantages.
3. Discuss the relative advantage of using a pointing device to enter a patient's vital signs compared with simply typing in the values using a keyboard.
4. Suggest how the use of a patient ID bracelet containing a bar-code representation of the patient's ID and a bar-code scanner can lead to improved quality of care in a hospital.

5. Explain the difference between devices capable of voice input and voice recognition.
6. Explain what is meant by the resolution of a VDT, and indicate applications where high resolution is important.
7. List the four generations of programming languages and briefly describe the characteristics of each.
8. Why are users doing so little in-house development of software today?
9. Explain the difference between interfaced and integrated systems, and state one advantage of each.
10. List three specific functions of an operating system.
11. Describe how the development of integrated healthcare systems has created an impetus for installing computer networks.
12. What is the difference between digital and analog waveforms?
13. What are the advantages of fiber-optic media compared with copper media?
14. Name and describe the three physical network topologies.
15. Describe some important applications of electronic data interchange in the healthcare field.
16. What is the difference between mobile computing and wireless communication?
17. Explain the difference between internet and Internet.
18. What is the purpose of a firewall?
19. What are the benefits of using a thin client for Internet connection?

References

Brailer, D. J. 2001. "Connection Tops Collection. Peer-to-Peer Technology Lets Caregivers Access Necessary Data, Upon Request, Without Using a Repository." *Health Management Technology* 22 (8): 28–29.

Briggs, B. 2002. "Is the Future in the Palm of Your Hand?" *Health Data Management* 10 (1): 44–62.

Dolan, T. G. 2006. "Contracting for ASP Services: When Signing On for the Benefits, Remember to Manage the Risks." *Journal of AHIMA* 77 (5): 48–50.

Dunn, R. 2006. "A Quick Scan of Bar Coding." *Journal of AHIMA* 77 (1): 50–54.

Gillespie, G. 2001. "Wireless Catching Up, Catching On in Health Care." *Health Data Management* 9 (8): 26–34.

Hayden, M. 2001. *Sams Teach Yourself Networking in 24 Hours*. Indianapolis, IN: Sams Publishing.

Heubusch, K. 2006. "Interoperability: What It Means, Why It Matters." *Journal of AHIMA* 77 (1): 26–30.

Internet World Stats. 2007. "Internet Usage Statistics for the Americas." [Online information; retrieved 6/28/07.] www.internetworldstats.com/stats2.htm

Ng, H. S., M. L. Sim, C. M. Tan, and C. C. Wong. 2006. "Wireless Technologies for Telemedicine." *BT Technology Journal* 24 (2): 130–37.

Rosen, S. 1969. "Electronic Computers: A Historical Survey." *Computing Surveys* 1 (1): 7–36.

Siep, T. 2007. "Bluetooth Bolsters UWB Performance." *Microwaves and RF* 46 (2): 86–89.

Sislo, W. 2002. "What Works: Reaping the Benefits of Wireless." *Health Management Technology* 23 (2): 50.

Southerton, L. 2007. "Mobile Device, Use, Reuse, and Disposal." *Journal of AHIMA* 78 (6): 68–70.

Wu, J. B., J. Colon, J. Lauer, and J. Kromclow. 1996. "Wireless Data Transmission: How to Implement Remote Data-Access." In *Proceedings of the 1996 Annual HIMSS Conference*, vol. II, 175–87. Chicago: Health Care Information and Management Systems Society.

IM/IT SERVICE MANAGEMENT

Learning Objectives

1. Articulate the impact that unplanned work has on an information management/information technology (IM/IT) department.
2. Identify a number of different process improvement frameworks that could be applied to the management of the IM/IT department and the advantages and disadvantages of each approach.
3. Describe the Information Technology Infrastructure Library (ITIL) service support components and how they are interrelated.
4. Articulate why the configuration management database is critical to the service support processes.
5. Describe the ITIL service delivery components and how they are interrelated.
6. Describe what service level agreements are and why they are important to an IM/IT department.
7. Describe some of the reasons given for IM/IT service continuity plan failures.

A consistent area of focus throughout a healthcare manager's career, regardless of his or her area of responsibility, is the constant effort to achieve efficient, cost-effective operations. While it is certainly true that all healthcare managers will continually be asked to think more strategically, a focus on the strategic aspects of the job at the expense of the operational aspects is a sure recipe for failure as a manager. Debra Walker, former chief information officer (CIO) of Goodyear Tire & Rubber Company, provides a framework for how to think about the effective management of an information management/information technology (IM/IT) department for both operational effectiveness and strategic impact. She suggests that the IM/IT department must master three levels of services. The base level provides a robust and reliable infrastructure for the organization, which was covered in Chapter 6. The second level, which builds on the base level, provides excellent IM/IT services, which is the focus of this chapter. Walker characterizes the third level by noting that "if [the IM/IT department] achieves those two things, then [it] gets the credibility that allows [it and the CIO] to play in the third level: partnering with the business to do the very high value-added activities and create competitive advantage" (Field 1998).

Why IM/IT Service Management Matters

The assertion that the more tactical or operational elements of IM/IT services are critical to strategic IM/IT value delivery is consistently reinforced in a number of academic studies (Singleton, McLean, and Altman 1988; Watson, Pitt, and Kavan 1998; Agarwal and Sambamurthy 2002; Smaltz, Sambamurthy, and Agarwal 2006). Much in the same way that Maslow's (1970) hierarchy of needs works in the field of psychology, if lower-level organizational IM/IT needs (reliable infrastructure, consistent and effective IM/IT support services) are not being met, chief executive officers (CEOs) wonder if the CIO and his or her organization can be effective in delivering the higher-level strategic IM/IT needs of the organization.

Ironically, only the most progressive organizations are adopting best practices in IM/IT service management, while many IM/IT departments continue to rely on informal, "seat of the pants," error-prone processes (Schick 2001). This leads to reactive "fire fighting" operating norms within IM/IT departments, when formal, proactive approaches would be more effective. Recent studies suggest that one of the most accurate indicators of IM/IT departmental effectiveness in delivering quality services is the percentage of unplanned work in which the department is engaged. *Unplanned work* is any activity in the IM/IT organization that cannot be mapped to an authorized project, procedure, or change request. While unplanned work can never be entirely eliminated from an IM/IT department, Kim (2006) suggests that the nature of the unplanned work is very different for high- and low-performing IM/IT departments. In Kim's study, low-performing IM/IT departments' unplanned work includes the following:

- *Failed changes*: The production environment is used as a test environment, and the customer is the quality assurance team.
- *Unauthorized changes*: Engineers do not follow the change management process, making mistakes harder to track and fix.
- *No preventive work*: Failing to conduct preventive work makes repeated failures inevitable. Mean time to repair may be improving, but without root-cause analysis, the organization is doomed to fix the same problems over and over.
- *Configuration inconsistency*: Inconsistencies in user applications, platforms, and configurations make appropriate training and configuration mastery difficult.
- *Security-related patching and updating*: Inadequate understanding and inconsistency of configurations make applying security patches extremely dangerous.
- *Too much access*: Too many people have too much access to too many IM/IT assets, causing preventable issues and incidents.

In contrast, Kim (2006) found that high-performing IM/IT departments had very different types of unplanned work, which included the following:

* Product failures
* Release failures
* Human/user errors

The key difference between low- and high-performing IM/IT departments is that high-performing IM/IT departments put in place holistic controls and processes that cut horizontally across the IM/IT department, whereas low-performing IM/IT departments often operate in vertical function-based silos with little to no formal cross-functional controls or processes. Interestingly, the Sarbanes-Oxley Act, passed by Congress in 2002, now mandates that holistic and formal controls be put in place for all for-profit organizations (Library of Congress 2002). However, these controls are not mandated for not-for-profit organizations, which make up the majority of the healthcare service delivery field. As such, many IM/IT departments will continue to have high levels of costly, unplanned work as a result of poor adoption rates of leading-practice process frameworks that include but are not limited to the frameworks outlined in Table 7.1.

Sundaresan (2005) notes that "while transforming a typical IT organization into an efficient service delivery organization is difficult, companies that don't make the transition face loss of competitiveness, while the IT organization faces loss of credibility, influence and most importantly impact." Kim (2006) illustrates this sentiment via the following scenario:

> Suppose someone changes an IT asset [such as releasing a small software patch to a major enterprise application] but the change fails catastrophically due to lack of preproduction testing and change management authorization. The failed change results in an "all hands on deck" situation for the IT operational staff; IT drops planned work to remedy the results of the changes. The service disruption causes an incident that takes four hours to repair and involves 25 IT staffers from all functional roles: application developers, QA [quality assurance] workers, database administrators, network and systems administrators, and security. Lost IT staff productivity is the first cost of this episode of unplanned work.
>
> Unplanned work also comes at the cost of planned project work. In this case, the application developers and QA staffers are taken from the critical path of an important sales support project, and the project ship date slips one week. In addition, to address this project delay, IT has to employ a team of contractors longer.
>
> The costs continue to mount. While the IT staff works to restore service, external customers call the service desk to find out why they can't access their billing information. Because of the large customer base, thousands of customers

TABLE 7.1
IM/IT Process Improvement Frameworks

IM/IT Process Improvement Framework	Description
Capability Maturity Model (CMM)	An IM/IT process improvement framework best suited to process improvements surrounding the application development and maintenance domain. The model is based on five levels of maturity (Gartner 2001): • Level 1: Initial—No repeatable processes • Level 2: Repeatable—Requirements identification process in place, policy compliance in place, and basic project management • Level 3: Defined—Application development processes are well defined, as are applications training and coordination processes • Level 4: Quantitatively managed—Adds precise measurement, forecasting, and predictability and seeks to reduce special cause process variation • Level 5: Optimizing—Adds continual process improvement efforts at reducing common cause process variation CMM describes what characterizes an organization at each level but does not describe "how to" get there.
Control Objects for Information Technology (CobiT)	An IM/IT governance, oversight, and process audit framework recently linked to Sarbanes-Oxley Act of 2002 corporate financial reporting compliance law. CobiT is made up of four main areas of control objects (IT Governance Institute 2005): • Planning and organization—Assess strategic plan creation, how projects are managed, communications and messaging, and human resources • Acquisition and implementation—Assess how the organization acquires IM/IT assets, how it implements information technology, and how changes are inserted into existing assets • Delivery and support—How end users are supported and serviced • Monitoring—Ensuring that regular audits of IM/IT controls are accomplished and that reporting is available on internal financial controls In addition, there are two supporting areas of focus: • Information—The degree to which information about the IM/IT operations and internal controls is available for proactive management action • IM/IT resources—The degree to which adequate IM/IT resources are in place to ensure effective internal controls are in place Like the CMM, it tends to describe what characterizes an organization that has solid internal control mechanisms in place but falls short of "how to" descriptions.

TABLE 7.1 Continued

ISO 9000	Also from manufacturing, requires that organizations become accredited or registered, thereby assuring customers that the organization adheres to the ISO quality assurance standards. Some criticisms of ISO 9000 include: • Requires a great deal of administrative overhead to employ ISO 9000 standards and become registered • May not be well suited to hospital IM/IT departments that tend to implement vendor applications, rather than develop their own applications
Information Technology Infrastructure Library (ITIL)	An IM/IT process improvement framework centered on seven main IM/IT management domains (itSMF 2004): • The business perspective—Processes focused on aligning IM/IT investments and activities with the business's strategic and operational needs • IM/IT service management (service delivery)—Processes focused on ensuring the long-term availability and capacity of IM/IT assets • IM/IT service management (service support)—Processes focused on holistic approaches to change, release, incident, problem, and configuration management • Information communication technology infrastructure management—Processes associated with the full lifecycle of IM/IT assets from requests for proposals to acquisition, testing, implementation, and retirement of the IM/IT infrastructure asset • Planning to implement service management—A planning framework for implementing an IM/IT service management improvement program to include the cultural and organizational change issues associated with it • Application management—Processes focused on all stages of an application's lifecycle • Security management—Processes focused on information security to include assessment of information security risks and mitigation strategies ITIL is well suited to organizations whose CIO or IM/IT leader are championing IM/IT process improvements. As opposed to some of the other process improvement models, ITIL provides high-level "how to" guidance via its many generic ITIL process flow diagrams and descriptions.

call the service center. The excess calls require the service center to activate the overflow call center, which costs tens of thousands of dollars. Revenue is also disrupted because the service center staff can't take orders while processing the customer incidents.

Downtime and IT project-resource costs run in the thousands of dollars; service center costs, lost revenue and the delayed IT project costs are in the tens of thousands. Let's take it one step further. Maybe customers become so unhappy that 2% of them leave. The business now has to spend hundreds or thousands of dollars to recapture each of those customers.

Now that your single rogue change affects customers, costs increase almost exponentially. With unhappy customers, you now have marketing and public relations problems. Your marketing department has to both gain new customers and win customers back—a feat more difficult and more expensive than gaining brand-new customers.

(And, there is one more extremely high cost of unplanned work. Each one of those late projects, which are getting even further delayed, had some ROI that the business attached to it. So, every moment of unplanned work delaying that project has a quantifiable opportunity cost. . . .) (Kim 2006)

The scenario is all too common in most hospital and healthcare service delivery organizations. As such, doing nothing to improve these broken IM/IT processes will make it increasingly difficult for the CIO and the IM/IT department to take on the even more challenging strategic IM/IT issues facing the healthcare field. It is beyond the scope of this text to expand on each of the various IM/IT process improvement frameworks listed in Table 7.1. While each has its own advantages and disadvantages, the Information Technology Infrastructure Library (ITIL*) is an IM/IT process improvement framework that is well suited to improvement efforts led by the CIO or IM/IT department (Young and Mingay 2003).

The Information Technology Infrastructure Library

While Control Objects for Information Technology (CobiT) (see Table 7.1) can be thought of as a framework for *what* sorts of things an IM/IT department should consider having in place, ITIL can be thought of as a framework of *how* IM/IT department processes should be interlinked to gain optimum proactive IM/IT service management. The ITIL was originally created by the Office of Government Commerce (OGC) in the United Kingdom. It is intended to be a holistic framework for providing both the lower-level and higher-level IM/IT needs of an organization (Figure 7.1). Arguably, current healthcare IM/IT operating budget levels, which typically average 2 percent

*ITIL® is a registered trademark and a registered community trademark of the United Kingdom Office of Government Commerce (OGC) and is registered in the U.S. Patent and Trademark Office.

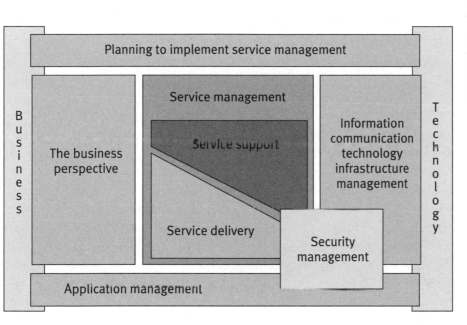

FIGURE 7.1

The
Information
Technology
Infrastructure
Library

Source: © Crown Copyright material reproduced with the kind permission of the United Kingdom Office of Government Commerce and the Controller of Her Majesty's Stationary Office (HMSO); © Copyright itSMF®, 2001.

of operating expenses in community hospitals and nearly 3 percent in large integrated delivery systems (Ciotti and Birch 2005), may make full adoption of the entire ITIL framework challenging. By this we mean that ITIL requires organizations to dedicate some of their resources toward putting in place the more proactive ITIL processes. However, the low-operating IM/IT budget levels that exist within the healthcare industry mean that most IM/IT departments do not perceive that they have excess resources needed to break out of their reactive, fire-fighting mode. By comparison, the financial services industry expends 5 percent to 7 percent on IM/IT operating budgets (Baschab and Piot 2003) and, not coincidentally, is a robust adopter of both the CobiT and ITIL frameworks. It also enjoys far fewer interruptions to IM/IT services (Sallé 2004; Potgieter, Botha, and Lew 2004).

IM/IT services in most healthcare organizations will, out of necessity, most likely require more proactive approaches with the increasing use of mission critical automation like electronic health records (EHR) with clinical decision support (CDS) and computerized physician order entry (CPOE). The service management (service support and service delivery) components of the ITIL framework (the middle box in Figure 7.1) are particularly well suited to healthcare IM/IT departments that seek to improve their service delivery and support via more proactive, holistic, and integrated IM/IT service workflows (Grajek and Cunningham 2007).

The IT Service Management Forum (2004) notes that "ITIL . . . provides a framework of 'best practice' guidance for IT service management and is the most widely used and accepted approach to IT service management in the world." IM/IT service management is composed of two main domains: service support and service delivery (see Table 7.2).

The ITIL processes outlined in Table 7.2, along with project management concepts and practices discussed in Chapter 4, can be thought of as the fundamental IM/IT services in which every IM/IT department must excel to be successful, particularly as hospitals and healthcare service delivery organizations become even more automated. While informal, seat-of-the-pants IM/IT service management processes may have been adequate for organizations with largely paper-based records and manual processes, these informal service management processes will no longer be adequate for organizations that increasingly rely on digitally enabled workflows such as EHRs with CDS and CPOE. IM/IT service support processes are now discussed in more detail.

IM/IT Service Support

All of the IM/IT service support processes identified in Table 7.2 are heavily interrelated and should be put in place with forethought. Figure 7.2, for example, provides some insight into how these processes are related.

Service Desk

Almost all hospitals or healthcare service delivery organizations provide "help desk" or "service desk" services, which users call or access online to obtain assistance with computer-related problems. This service is likely the most misunderstood and underappreciated service provided by the IM/IT department. Best practices in providing services for incidents (when malfunctions occur that require IM/IT support services to repair) are discussed later in the chapter. Here, it is important for the healthcare manager to recognize that because the service desk provides such wide exposure into the customer interfacing operations of the IM/IT department, for better or worse, it becomes one of the main ways that healthcare executives and managers throughout the organization gauge effectiveness of the IM/IT services delivered. Therefore, it behooves CIOs and IM/IT department managers to ensure that the leading customer service practices discussed later in this chapter are in place. The IT Service Management Forum (2001, 11) notes that the service desk is "often a stressful place for staff to work, [and] underestimating its importance, high profile, and the skills required to perform the duties well, can severely hinder an organization's ability to deliver quality IT services."

For most of the users of computer resources, the help desk represents the face of the IM/IT department. While some of the employees of the

TABLE 7.2

Elements of IM/IT Service Management

IM/IT Service Support

Service Desk	The single point of contact for users to report incidents and seek troubleshooting resolution
Incident Management	The process by which "trouble calls" or incidents are managed to resolution
Problem Management	The process by which recurring incidents are analyzed to determine and provide permanent solutions for root causes
Change Management	The process by which changes are introduced into the computing environment of an organization
Release Management	The process by which major new releases of application or operating system software are implemented
Configuration Management	Closely tied to all of the above IM/IT service support processes, configuration management is the process by which the computing environment is documented, typically in a configuration management database

IM/IT Service Delivery

Service Level Management	The process by which service levels are negotiated with end users and tracked for performance adherence
Availability Management	The process focused on ensuring that the IM/IT infrastructure and support services are available to the business functions
Capacity Management	The process focused on ensuring that the IM/IT infrastructure has the processing capacity needed by the business functions
Financial Management for IM/IT Services	The process of accounting for the complex nature of IM/IT services, understanding cost by unit of service, and assisting in management decisions relating to IM/IT services
Service Continuity Management	Formerly known as the "disaster recovery" or "business continuity planning" function, this is the process by which organizations identify their most critical applications and design, test, and maintain alternatives for providing IM/IT services in the event of a major service interruption

Source: Adapted from itSMF (2004).

FIGURE 7.2
ITIL Service
Support
Processes

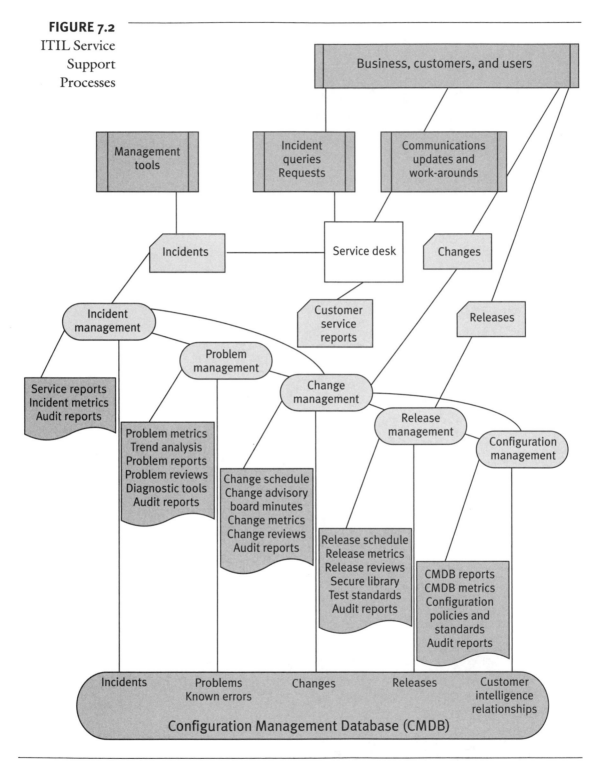

hospital or healthcare service delivery organization have the opportunity to interact with the other service delivery teams within an IM/IT department, statistically *all* employees, at some point in their tenure, will have a need to contact and use the services of the information technology help desk. Gartner Research suggests that, on average, users will place 1.1 to 1.6 calls per month to the help desk (Holub 2007). This does not necessarily mean that each and every user will call the help desk at least once a month (e.g., a single user may place six calls in one month and six more the next month to the help desk, while another may not place a call for a year or more). Because many help desks address not only malfunctions or incidents but also "how to" type questions, it is easy to see how a user over time can average 1.1 to 1.6 calls per month. Additionally, as Figure 7.2 indicates, a second source of incidents comes from IM/IT operational management tools that can monitor the IM/IT infrastructure. When certain thresholds are met (e.g., central processing unit [CPU] capacity on a critical server reaches 75 percent; disk space in the storage area network reaches 85 percent capacity) these management tools will automatically trigger an incident that initially gets sent to the service desk for action.

Hospital or healthcare service organizations typically have one of three different types of IM/IT service desks:

- *Decentralized.* This is typical of many academic medical centers where often a central service desk exists, but many departments historically retain their own IM/IT staff to deal with incidents within the department.
- *Virtual.* This is a new form of service desk whereby a single contact phone number or website is provided for initiating incidents; however, the actual services may be delivered by a number of different service providers, including internal staff and a third-party provider.
- *Centralized.* A central pool of resources typically within the IM/IT department provides centralized service desk support.

While there are pros and cons for each type of IM/IT service desk, the key feature that all three must put in place to optimize service support is an integrated view of all incoming incidents not only to facilitate a coordinated resolution of the incident but also to ensure that trends across the enterprise can be spotted and more proactive approaches can be applied to prevent incidents in the first place (as opposed to simply reacting to them each time they recur).

Incident Management

The goal of incident management is "to restore normal service operation as quickly as possible with minimum disruption to the business [or clinical workflows], thus ensuring that the best achievable levels of availability and service are maintained" (itSMF 2001). In most organizations with a central service desk function, all incidents are channeled through the service desk. Typically, central IM/IT service desks are organized to provide three levels of support.

First-level support services. All incidents initially come to the individuals that staff the first-level support services. These individuals typically log the call or request into a "trouble ticket" or "incident management" database so that incidents can be tracked from start to finish. Additionally, the first-level support staff are typically trained to handle most routine, recurring incidents such as resetting a user's password, assisting with routine office automation software, and answering how-to questions. When IM/IT service desk technicians are armed with service desk tools that allow remote control of a user's desktop device, organizations can expect 65 percent resolution on the first call into the first-level support technicians. With increased training and access to a knowledge base of symptoms/resolutions, first-call resolution rates above 80 percent can be obtained (Anton 2001).

Second-level support services. Incidents that cannot be addressed by the first-level support technicians because they require greater expertise and training or require that a technician physically go to the user's location are handed off to dedicated desktop or field support technicians for resolution.

Third-level support services. Incidents that are routed to third-level support are typically the most difficult and unique problems and often require deep root-cause analysis and reengineering of the application or system affected.

Figure 7.3 depicts a sample workflow diagram showing how incidents may flow through the various levels within a service desk.

In this example of a typical organizational central IM/IT service desk, the end user can either call in his or her incidents, requests, problems, or questions (IRPQ) or, for nonurgent IRPQs, simply open an incident report via the service desk's Web-based incident portal application. In either case, first-level service desk technicians will initially address the IRPQ and attempt to resolve it on the spot. In this example, the service desk technicians also have access to an ITIL best practice, a configuration management database (CMDB), which will be covered later in this chapter. In short, this is essentially a knowledge store of solutions, answers, and temporary fixes (SAT) as well as a knowledge store for system configuration settings that first-level technicians can use to potentially expedite the resolution of an end user's incident. However, if the first-level service desk technician cannot immediately resolve it, the IRPQ gets escalated to a second-level service desk technician. Finally, for organizations that have implemented a portfolio or program management office (PMO) as outlined in Chapter 4, often the service desk becomes the "front door" for requesting new IM/IT projects, which, as the figure suggests, get escalated immediately to the PMO.

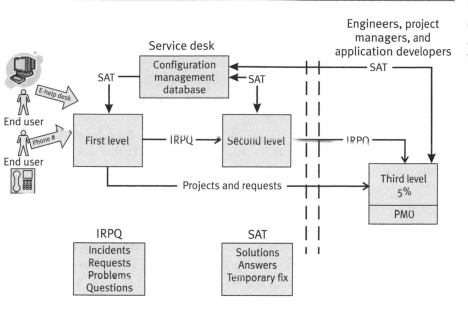

FIGURE 7.3

Sample IT
Service Desk
Workflow

Second-level IM/IT service desk technicians also make use of the configuration management database and may create new knowledge within it when they discover a permanent solution or find a reliable temporary workaround or fix to a recurring problem. As the figure indicates, when second-level service desk technicians cannot resolve the issue, IRPQs are then escalated to the third-level service desk technicians, who typically are located within an organization's IM/IT network engineering, server administration, or applications development group where root-cause analysis occurs as well as efforts to engineer a permanent solution to the IRPQ. Typically, first- and second-level service desk technicians should be able to find permanent solutions, answers to questions, and devise temporary fixes 95 percent of the time, while third-level service desk technicians should only be needed for 5 percent of the IRPQs.

Without a disciplined, effective front-door approach to all trouble calls and request for services, an IM/IT department can quickly become swamped with requests that circumvent the service desk process. Additionally, without the integration with some of the other ITIL processes (like change management, release management, and configuration management, discussed later in this chapter) the service desk can be seen as largely ineffective. Ciccolini and McDermott (2005) suggest that

in many cases, the front-line service desk acts as little more than an answering service, logging incidents and forwarding them to a more senior IT person [second- or third-level support technicians] for resolution. Further, service desks often lack the information needed to address end-user incidents—particularly those that involve proprietary applications. The under-utilization of front-line service desks poses both cost and credibility problems for IT organizations. Incident resolution costs (and indirect opportunity costs) increase as cases are passed on to more senior IT specialists. Business users suffer from productivity declines and perceptions of IT often sour as customers fail to see their issues being addressed in a timely fashion.

Best practices in incident management to overcome these costs and productivity declines include the following:

- Insisting that all users employ the service desk as the front door for submitting all incidents, requests for service, and problems
- Using effective automated service desk tools such as telephony to track phone metrics (e.g., average time a customer is on hold) and service desk management software to log and track all incidents through to resolution
- Service desk technicians with access to an effective CMDB that serves as an effective knowledge base of system configuration settings, upcoming changes to the infrastructure, upcoming new releases, known problems and errors, resolutions, and work-arounds
- Service desk technicians with access to service level management data (covered later in this chapter)

One of the most important functions of the service desk, in addition to quickly finding a resolution to an incident and returning users to productive use, is in providing data to spot trends that require root-cause analysis and a more permanent resolution. For instance, in tracking monthly incident metrics, the IM/IT manager spots the same incidents recurring each month. As Figure 7.2 indicates, these recurring incidents become the input to the next IM/IT service support process, problem management.

Problem Management

The goal of problem management is "to minimize the adverse effect on the business of incidents and problems caused by errors in (any of the components of) the infrastructure and to proactively prevent the occurrence of incidents, problems, and errors. . . . A problem is the unknown underlying cause of one or more incidents. It will become a known error when the root cause is known and a temporary workaround or a permanent [solution] has been identified" (itSMF 2001, 19).

With incident management, the primary goal is to restore service to end users as quickly as possible. This often results in temporary work-arounds or "Band-Aid" solutions being implemented to allow the end user to use whatever IM/IT asset is needed to perform his or her job. Problem management, on the other hand, is focused on determining the underlying root cause(s) of incidents. Root-cause analysis should not be a foreign concept, as The Joint Commission (2003) now requires root-cause analysis to be conducted to get to the underlying causes of sentinel events that occur in healthcare settings. Furthermore, the National Aeronautics and Space Administration uses root-cause analysis routinely to determine underlying causes of spacecraft system malfunctions. These same root-cause analysis processes are applied by leading-practice healthcare IM/IT departments as a means of providing world-class IM/IT support services. Root-cause analysis is composed of the following four elements (Rooney and Vanden Heuvel 2004):

1. *Data collection.* IM/IT department analysts collect all known information about a particular problem from myriad sources, which include but are not limited to the incident management database, the configuration management database, and change control logs.
2. *Causal factor charting.* Analysts create a flowchart of events, configuration settings, and other known facts that created the problem. This charting process often identifies gaps in knowledge that require more data collection to investigate the problem. Therefore, the data collection and causal factor charting should be viewed as iterative processes that work in tandem. Additionally, it is not uncommon for multiple contributing causes to problems to exist.
3. *Root-cause identification.* After all of the potential contributing causes have been identified in a flowchart, analysts identify the underlying root causes for the problem.
4. *Recommendation generation and implementation.* Based on the particular root causes, people from the IM/IT department with the relevant key skill sets are gathered to generate ideas about resolving the identified root causes, select the "best" recommended solution(s), develop and implement the plan (this typically involves the change management process discussed later in this chapter), and then execute that recommended solution.

Healthcare organizations with formal problem management processes in place can expect to see a reduction in the number of overall incidents that are generated, a reduction in average time to resolve incidents, and an increase in customer satisfaction over time.

Change Management

To effectively administer needed changes to the IM/IT infrastructure (broadly defined as any IM/IT application or architecture component), or-ganizations generally have in place a change review committee or change advisory committee. This committee is made up primarily of IM/IT personnel from all of the various teams within the IM/IT department along with key users from the business and clinical areas. Typical representation of such a group includes but is not limited to the following:

- Network engineer or architect
- Server/hardware engineer or architect
- Key application analysts
- Support center managers
- Nurse manager
- Business office manager
- Physician (as needed for changes that involve physician workflow)
- Vendor representatives (as needed when changes affect a vendor-supplied application or hardware device)
- Third-party consultants and other technical experts (as needed)

This group meets as often as needed to proactively manage upcoming changes. Typically, organizations should have in place a means of dealing with both urgent changes, which follow a "fast track" approach (such as quickly rolling out the latest virus protection signature files to all end-user devices after an organization is hit with a new virus), and routine changes, for which lead times are known and can be planned in a less hurried manner (such as adding disk encryption software to all end-user devices, which can be planned far in advance and rolled out in a measured way).

As Figure 7.2 indicates, requests for changes can come from the business or clinical units (e.g., request to interface two preexisting applications that have not previously been interfaced), can come from incidents, or can be necessitated by a problem management process that has recommended changes to alleviate root causes to identified problems. Additionally, change management process must also ensure that ongoing changes are documented in the organization's configuration management database (covered later in this chapter), which serves as the IM/IT department's central knowledge base to inform all of the processes within the ITIL framework.

Release Management

The purpose of release management processes is to ensure that either new software or new hardware being added to a live environment has been built and tested in such a way that it is put into service without causing negative impacts described earlier in this chapter. For instance, as a part of the healthcare organization's testing of a new version of a mission critical software application, an IM/IT manager discovers that it will only run on hardware with upgraded operating systems and upgraded hardware memory. In this case, the decision is made to release this new version of software as part of a package that includes an upgrade of its associated hardware. Organizations without rigorous release management practices suffer from disruptions in service due to unplanned work as described by Kim (2006) earlier in this chapter.

The full release management process as outlined by the IT Service Management Forum (2001) includes the following processes, all of which are tied to the configuration management database at a minimum (as the definitive knowledge source to document changes to all IM/IT resources):

- Release policy (to clarify roles and responsibilities within the IM/IT department and establish business rules or operating norms associated with how releases will be managed)
- Release planning (development of a succinct but comprehensive plan for each specific release to include a contingency plan to remove the release and return to a preexisting version should the release fail)
- Develop or buy software/hardware (determine if the release requires the purchase of hardware or software components)
- Build and configure the release to include development of detailed instructions for implementing the release
- Test the release (conduct a performance test of the release, ideally with end users of the product, to ensure it operates as expected)
- Release acceptance (formal process of acceptance by the end users and the IM/IT manager[s] responsible for the release)
- Roll-out planning (essentially extends the release plan that was initially developed at the beginning of the project to add specific details of the exact installation process)
- Communication preparation and training (plan and develop the communications targeted at end users as well as the training that end users and system administrators may need prior to the release implementation)
- Distribution and installation (the process of distributing the release and installing it as appropriate)

In essence, the release management process requires explicit and deliberate coordination and communication mechanisms to be evident within and beyond the IM/IT department.

Release management processes are closely tied to both change management and configuration management. In fact, leading-practice organizations are advised, when putting in place these ITIL processes, to centralize oversight of the change, configuration, and release management processes (OGC 2005; Farah 2004) and closely tie this centralized oversight into the project management process identified in Chapter 4 (Moreira 2004).

Configuration Management

A common feature of almost all hardware and software is the ability to manipulate its configurations. Examples of configuration settings can be simple, such as the screen saver that can be selected on a personal computer, or complex, like the fail-over settings for adding CPU capacity to a virtual server environment. Most hospitals and integrated hospital delivery networks use a hundred or more different applications and dozens of different hardware platforms. Thus, maintaining comprehensive knowledge of the configuration settings on each becomes an important task for IM/IT departments that want to avoid all of the reactive, unplanned work that results when new changes or releases are introduced without knowledge of their impact on preexisting configurations (Kim 2006). Configuration management processes focus on the identification, recording, and reporting of IM/IT components to include versions and the interrelationships between the components (itSMF 2000, 2001).

Configuration management includes the following five subprocesses:

1. *Planning*—High-level outline planning and more detailed three- to six-month planning that address envisioned additions to the hardware or software environment that likely will have an impact on configuration settings of one or more of the IM/IT assets within the healthcare organization.
2. *Identification*—Explicitly identifying configurable components of the IM/IT infrastructure and documenting their ownership and the interrelationships between them. Examples include but are not limited to servers, network components, software licenses, desktops, and computer facilities.
3. *Control*—Ensuring that no change is enacted within the IM/IT infrastructure without appropriate documentation validating that the envisioned effected configuration items have been adequately tested prior to implementation.
4. *Status accounting*—Ensuring accurate reporting of the configuration setting of all of the items that make up an organization's IM/IT infrastructure throughout their lifecycle.
5. *Verification and audit*—Routinely auditing the documentation that exists on configuration items to ensure accuracy.

One tool that can facilitate the configuration management process is the configuration management database. As noted in Figure 7.2, all of the IM/IT service support processes (incident management, problem management, change management, and release management) can have an effect on IM/IT asset configuration settings. As such, a single CMDB that is used by the entire IM/IT department can provide a powerful means of dynamically documenting change states in asset configurations as well as serving as an up-to-date tool to plan changes and releases.

IM/IT Service Delivery

The previous section of key IM/IT departmental processes was largely focused on putting in place a rigorous, interconnected set of operational methodologies. This section, on IM/IT service delivery, focuses on tactical methodologies that focus on ensuring that expected services are delivered as expected by the IM/IT department's customers. Figure 7.4 depicts how the IM/IT service delivery processes work together. (For definitions of IM/IT service delivery processes, please refer back to Table 7.2.)

Service Level Management

The purpose of service level management is to proactively review, with the IM/IT department's customers, the value of the services being delivered. Service level management is typically operationalized via the establishment of service level agreements (SLAs) between the IM/IT department and specific sets of customers. The contents of a typical SLA include the following (itSMF 2004):

* A description of the services to be provided or a particular deliverable (e.g., provide dual power and redundant server hosting services in the hospital's central computer room)
* Agreed-upon service hours (e.g., to provide help desk services from 7:00 a.m. to 7:00 p.m.)
* A description of the response times and resolution times for various scenarios (e.g., resolve within two hours all personal computer support incidents categorized as "urgent")
* A description of service availability, security, and business continuity expectations (e.g., in the event of catastrophic loss of the hospital's central computer room, inpatient electronic medical record application will be available via our disaster recovery remote site within 72 hours)
* Explicit articulation of customer responsibilities and IM/IT department responsibilities (e.g., customer is required to initiate all requests for service via the IM/IT central service desk)
* Explicit articulation of critical business periods (e.g., end-of-year financial closeout may require heightened service levels and responsiveness) and exceptions (e.g., holidays)

Some IM/IT departments do not enter into SLAs at all—hospital users simply get whatever service the IM/IT department is able to provide. Others enter into SLAs whereby the IM/IT department specifies the terms or conditions of the services they are able to provide within specified time periods without any input from its customers. Both of these examples (no SLAs and SLAs dictated by the IM/IT department) are suboptimal practices that do not align IM/IT service delivery expectations with the drivers of the hospital's business. High-functioning IM/IT departments, on the other hand, take the time with all of their major customers to negotiate and agree upon specific service level expectations at a given cost. Typically, IM/IT departments can be more responsive with more resources. But often, hospital budgets limit the

FIGURE 7.4
ITIL Service
Delivery
Processes

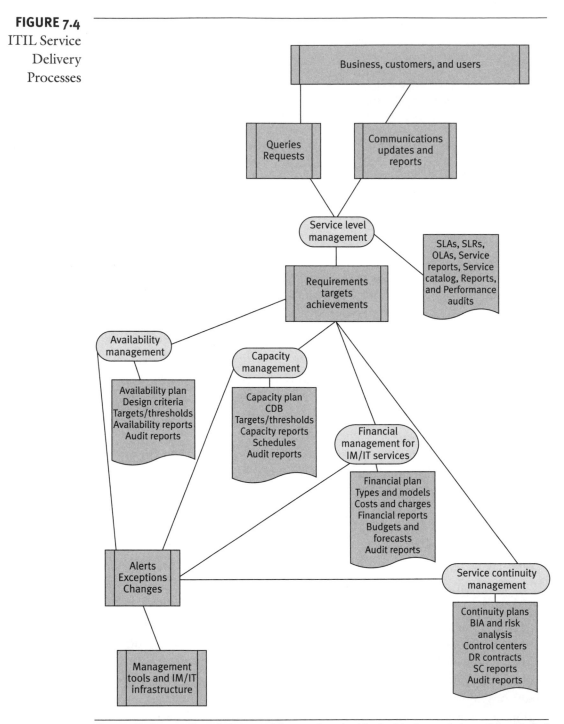

amount of dollars available for the delivery of IM/IT services. For this very reason, it becomes paramount that IM/IT managers put in place service level agreements with their customers not only to set realistic expectations (in the case of the budget-constrained hospital) but also as a means of continually working together to assess performance against the service level agreement and continually making adjustments (perhaps by increasing the IM/IT budget to attain higher service levels).

Another important component of service level management is the development of a service catalog, which describes all of the IM/IT services that the healthcare organization's customers can expect to receive from the IM/IT department. These service catalogs can range from simple brochures detailing the services and means of accessing the services to fully Web-enabled dynamic service catalogs that link to various applications that serve as entry points to numerous IM/IT services.

Capacity Management

The Information Systems Audit and Control Association, considered the definitive professional society for certifying and educating information systems audit professionals, defines *capacity management* as "the process of monitoring, analyzing and planning the effective use of computer resources" (Anderson and Peris 2007). Specifically, capacity management is an explicit process that attempts first to create better understanding of the business and clinical needs for computer resources (such as the impact that adding a patient portal to a preexisting EHR system will have on existing computer resources). This is largely an outward-looking analysis of the organization's changes in business goals and approaches and how they might necessitate changes in the hardware or software environment that supports the business and clinical processes. The second focus of capacity management is more inwardly focused, whereby CPU performance, disk space utilization, growth of applications running on computer resources, growth of users accessing computer resources, and network traffic patterns are constantly monitored so that IM/IT managers can proactively address potential problems that can be forecasted as a result of this rigorous monitoring. As such, the definitive goal of capacity management is to consistently and accurately predict and implement needed changes in the computer resources of an organization to ensure that sufficient capacity exists within the computing resources for unimpeded business and clinical operations. Organizations that do not have capacity management processes in place experience higher amounts of unscheduled downtime and greater costs associated with mitigating the impact of unforeseen computer resource upgrades needed to restore capacity (Schess 2002).

Availability Management

Availability management is closely related to capacity management in its focus on ensuring that computer resources are available when users need them.

Availability management consists of the following five components (itSMF 2001):

1. *Availability*—The percentage of agreed-upon service hours that a particular computer resource or service is available for use (e.g., the service center will be available for taking trouble calls from 7:00 a.m. to 7:00 p.m.)
2. *Reliability*—The prevention of malfunctions and the ability to keep services and computer resources operational (e.g., via use of backup power distribution units, power-related failures are mitigated)
3. *Maintainability*—The ability to quickly restore services or computer resources back to normal operations (e.g., an effective service center that can quickly resolve incidents and restore computer resources to an operational state)
4. *Serviceability*—The ability for external contractors to augment internal IM/IT department resources to service parts of the IM/IT infrastructure (e.g., an effective escalation process whereby vendor specialists can be called in to help resolve vendor-specific hardware or software issues)
5. *Security*—The implementation of appropriate access controls to ensure continued services (e.g., the ability to accurately restore user passwords for bona fide employees when such a need arises)

The availability management process focuses on measuring system downtime, network downtime, average time it takes to resolve an incident, and other metrics that describe when systems and services are not available to users. These metrics then become the internal benchmarks with which IM/IT managers assess improvements in availability of computer resources.

Financial Management for IM/IT Services

Many smaller healthcare IM/IT departments do not set up a distinct function to holistically manage the finances associated with providing IM/IT services. As healthcare institutions continue to automate an increasing number of their operational processes and as the complexity of managing computer resources increases as a result of this significant growth in automation, the need to effectively manage IM/IT as a business in and of itself will also continue to grow (Lutchen 2004). In fact, Ferranti (2007) suggests that organizations with more than 100 IM/IT employees will typically have a senior manager who oversees the IM/IT department finances and reports directly to the CIO. Typical functions associated with the financial management of IM/IT services include but are not limited to:

- Creating the annual IM/IT budget; managing the IM/IT budget to ensure annual expenditures do not exceed the annual IM/IT budget
- IM/IT asset procurement management to ensure purchased items are within the budget and to seek maximum volume discounting on purchases

- Creating the schedule of costs and overseeing charge-back processes and receipt of funds from customers
- Vendor management to continually seek vendor discounts and manage relations with vendors
- Overseeing anti-fraud policies and procedures such as Sarbanes-Oxley Act compliance (particularly true of for-profit healthcare organizations)

As noted in Figure 7.4, the finances needed to provide a given level of IM/IT services are driven by the clinical and business needs of the healthcare organization. As the need for responsiveness goes up, so, too, does the need for additional finances to support these higher service level targets. Likewise, if organizations attempt to increase the number of IM/IT development initiatives they wish to undertake within a budget cycle, this typically will also drive up the funding levels needed to support increased simultaneous development efforts. Thus, it is critical to negotiate definitive service level agreements with all of the customers of the IM/IT department to ensure that adequate funding needs can be identified that align with the desired service level needs. Often, cutting back on IM/IT budgets forces organizations to remove resources that had previously been assigned to providing IM/IT services. In these situations, it is paramount that IM/IT leaders renegotiate service level agreements to ensure that misunderstandings about service level expectations can be avoided. The old adage "you get what you pay for" holds particularly true in providing IM/IT services to healthcare organizations. To avoid a mismatch in customer expectations, fully understanding the service level constraints of given levels of funding are important to effective financial management for IM/IT services.

Service Continuity Management

While service interruptions due to unforeseen downtime of healthcare IM/IT assets are fairly well understood, expected, and largely routinized, major service interruptions due to natural disasters such as earthquakes, hurricanes, or fires typically require a much different response. IM/IT *service continuity management* is the process for restoring the healthcare organization's IM/IT services as quickly as possible after a service interruption (itSMF 2001). Examples of devastating impacts on healthcare operations were plentiful in the New Orleans area following Hurricane Katrina in 2005. Some healthcare operations, such as Charity Hospital, simply ceased to exist as a result (Rowland 2007). As noted previously, healthcare service delivery organizations' lack of financial health often makes it difficult to invest adequately in IM/IT services such as continuity plans. While it is not uncommon for organizations to have continuity plans, in the event of a real disaster or major disruption in service, these plans often fail when executed. Clarke (2004, 21, 22) refers to these types of plans as "symbolic plans" or "fantasy plans." He notes, "symbolic [continuity] plans are the ones that are charade. They're touted as workable but, in fact, they're not based on actual expertise or experience and, by definition, they over promise. . . . [Furthermore,] symbolic plans can create a dangerous false sense of security."

To ensure that your IM/IT department has workable IM/IT service continuity plans in place, the United Kingdom's OGC (2005) suggests that first a business impact analysis be conducted whereby the senior leadership team of the healthcare organization identifies the business and clinical processes that are absolutely critical to the functioning of the enterprise. For instance, a balanced scorecard performance reporting application may not be essential but the admissions, discharges, and transfers application, as well as the billing application, will likely be considered critical. The business impact analysis also assesses the following for each critical process:

- Lost revenue or costs associated with the disruption that may accrue
- How the degree of damage or loss is likely to escalate after a disruption
- The staffing, skills, facilities, and services necessary to enable critical and essential business processes to continue operating at a minimum acceptable level
- Realistic estimates of the time it would take to restore minimum service levels
- Realistic estimates of the time it would take to fully recover service levels

After the business impact analysis is completed, a risk assessment is conducted to assess the extent to which a healthcare organization is vulnerable to different potential threats. For instance, a hospital in Lubbock Texas, has a higher likelihood of being susceptible to tornadoes than a hospital in Vancouver, British Columbia. After assessing the business impacts as well as the potential risks and their likelihood of occurrence, an IM/IT service continuity strategy is developed. The key elements of this strategy should describe the following:

- How the strategy will be implemented
- Arrangements made for stand-by recovery locations either via contracts with third-party vendors specializing in disaster recovery hosting services or with other organizations via reciprocal support agreements
- Risk-reduction measures (while the organization cannot do much about being located in a tornado alley, identifying a need to move the computer room from the basement of your building because it is within the 100-year flood zone to a higher floor is certainly something that can be accomplished to reduce risk)
- Detailed step-by-step procedural checklists to restore service levels (these should "be action oriented—simple checklists for teams to follow, supported by supplements containing more detailed information on each action required"; [Hiles 1992])

- Timeline for testing the plan in a realistic manner (e.g., periodically simulating a disaster and invoking your stand-by contracts to bring up one or more of your critical applications at an alternate location; this is an important element of service continuity planning, as it overcomes Clarke's [2004] criticism of symbolic plans and ensures your organization has a tried and tested approach to restore critical IM/IT dependent business processes)

The Continued Evolution of the ITIL Service Management Practices

As a framework of information technology service management practices, ITIL continues to evolve and be refined. Most recently, as this text was going to press, the ITIL framework was reconceptualized as the ITIL Service Management Lifecycle (TSO 2007). Though the individual information technology service management practices described in this chapter (release management, change management, etc.) continue to be recognized as important best practices in the management of IM/IT departments, these individual practices are now part of a lifecycle framework that emphasizes the need to view information technology services as a continual service improvement process. Figure 7.5 provides an overview of the ITIL Service Management Lifecycle and shows how the individual ITIL processes outlined in this chapter are related to the latest evolution of service management.

This new conceptualization of ITIL suggests that the delivery of services should begin with a strategy for how those services might be provided to the various businesses, customers, and users of the services. Most important, it highlights the importance of establishing policies and standards that will help effectively deliver information technology services. The financial management for information technology services, discussed in this chapter, falls into this ITIL service management lifecycle category.

The output of the service strategy lifecycle element becomes the input for the service design element, where plans to create and modify services as well as service management processes (e.g., service level management, availability management, capacity management, information technology continuity management) are addressed.

In turn, the output of the service design element becomes the input to the service transition element, in which the proactive management of the transition of a new or changed service and/or service management process (e.g., release management, change management, configuration management) is placed into production.

The output of the service transition element becomes the input for the service operation element, which involves the day-to-day operations of services and service management processes (e.g., incident management, problem management).

FIGURE 7.5
Service
Management
Lifecycle

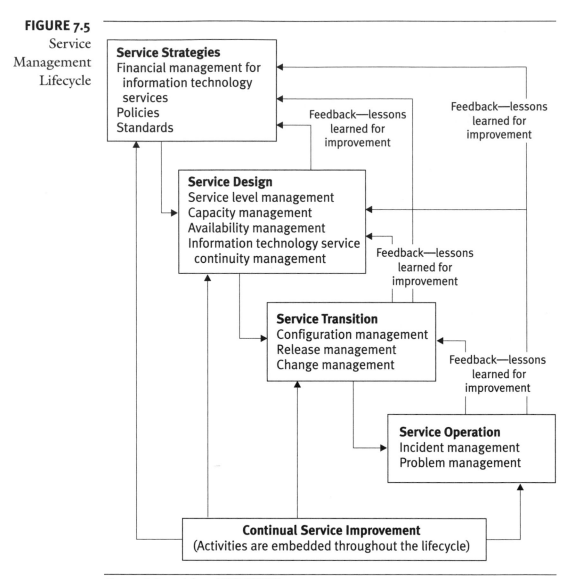

Source: Adapted from TSO (2007).

Finally, the latest evolution of the ITIL service management practices is the conceptualization of a continual service improvement element, which is to be embedded throughout all of the ITIL practices, creating feedback loops of lessons learned throughout the lifecycle that should be used to continually improve services.

Summary

Mainstream healthcare administrators have long recognized the need for efficient and effective operations throughout the healthcare enterprises that they lead. However, since few senior executives have come from IM/IT backgrounds, the internal workings of the IM/IT department have often been a "black box" to mainstream senior leadership. In this chapter, we have opened the IM/IT department black box and presented ten key processes that, when managed in a loose, informal manner, create costly unplanned work that limits the resources available for new strategic initiatives. To maximize efficiencies and effectiveness, many healthcare enterprises are adopting frameworks to enhance their internal operations. A number of frameworks were presented, including the ITIL framework, which Young and Mingay (2003) suggest is the framework best suited for IM/IT department-led process improvement efforts. ITIL categorizes the ten key IM/IT department processes into two categories: (1) service management, which includes incident management, problem management, change management, release management, and configuration management, and (2) service delivery, which includes service level management, capacity management, availability management, financial management of IM/IT services, and services continuity management. As more and more healthcare enterprises are becoming automated, demands on professional IM/IT department services will continue to increase. IM/IT departments that have implemented, or are implementing, formal process improvement frameworks like ITIL will create greater efficiencies and thereby leverage IM/IT resources toward more strategic initiatives.

Web Resources

A number of useful sources of information related to this chapter are available on the Web, including the following:

IT Service Management Forum, http://www.itsmf.com/
U.K. Office of Government Commerce, http://www.ogc.gov.uk/guidance_itil_4438.asp
ITIL Open Guide, http://www.itlibrary.org/index.php?page=ITIL

Discussion Questions

1. Why does unplanned IM/IT work increase costs?
2. Identify some process improvement frameworks that are applicable to an IM/IT department. What are the advantages and disadvantages of each?
3. Describe the five IM/IT service support processes and how they are interrelated.
4. What is a CMDB, and why is it an important component of IM/IT service support?
5. Describe the five IM/IT service delivery processes and how they are interrelated.
6. What is an SLA, and why is it an important component of IM/IT service delivery?
7. List some of the reasons given for IM/IT service continuity plan failures.

References

Agarwal, R., and V. Sambamurthy. 2002. "Principles and Models for Organizing the IT Function." *MIS Quarterly Executive* 1 (1): 1–16.

Anderson, B., and D. Peris. 2007. "Capacity Management of Computer Resources Through Performance Analysis." [Online article; retrieved 5/4/07.] http://www.isaca.org/Content/ContentGroups/InfoBytes/19981/Capacity_Man agement_of_Computing_Resources_Through_Performance_Analysis.htm

Anton, J. 2001. *Call Center Performance Benchmark Report.* No. 1347. West Lafayette, IN: Purdue Research Foundation.

Baschab, J., and J. Piot. 2003. *The Executive's Guide to Information Technology.* Hoboken, NJ: John Wiley and Sons.

Ciccolini, C., and M. McDermott. 2005. "Leveraging the ITIL Service Support Framework." [Online article; retrieved 1/3/08.] http://www.itsmwatch.com/itil/article.php/3348501

Ciotti, V., and T. Birch. 2005. "How Does Your IT Department Stack Up?" *Healthcare Financial Management* 59 (1): 44–49.

Clarke, L. 2004. "What's the Plan?" *Harvard Business Review* 82 (6): 21–22.

Farah, J. 2004. "Taking the Complexity Out of Release Management." *CM Crossroads.* [Online article; retrieved 4/25/07.] http://www.cmcrossroads.com/content/view/6741/135/

Ferranti, M. 2007. "Head of IT Finance." *CIO Magazine* 20: 16.

Field, T. 1998. "Shop Talk: Goodyear's Debra Walker on Leveraging Business-Side Experience in IS." *CIO Magazine* (11) 16: 80.

Gartner, Inc. 2001. "Describing the Capability Maturity Model." [Online article; retrieved 2/9/07.] http://www.e-strategy.ubc.ca/_shared/assets/MeasureIT-GartnersCMMmodel1278.pdf

Grajek, S., and W. Cunningham. 2007. *ITIL: An Effective Methodology of Managing IT Services,* EDUCAUSE Annual Conference, October 27. Seattle, Washington.

Hiles, A. 1992. "Surviving a Computer Disaster." *Computing and Control Engineering Journal* 3 (3): 133–35.

Holub, E. 2007. *Toolkit: How to Justify Infrastructure and Operations Staffing Size.* No. G00146650. Stamford, CT: Gartner, Inc.

IT Governance Institute. 2005. *CoBit 4.0.* Rolling Meadows, IL: IT Governance Institute.

IT Service Management Forum (itSMF). 2004. *An Introductory Overview of ITIL.* Version 1.0a. London: Office of Government Commerce.

———. 2001. *IT Service Management.* Version 2.1.b. London: Office of Government Commerce.

———. 2000. *Best Practice for Service Support.* London: Office of Government Commerce.

Kim, G. 2006. "Unplanned Work Is Silently Killing IT Departments." *Computerworld.* [Online article; retrieved 1/29/07.] http://www.computerworld.com/action/article.do?command=viewArticleBasic&articleId=110242

Library of Congress. 2002. Corporate and Auditing Accountability, Responsibility, and Transparency Act of 2002, HR 3763. [Online information; retrieved 3/3/2008.] http://thomas.loc.gov/cgi-bin/query/D?c107:3:./temp/~c10 7gMRwC9

Lutchen, M. 2004. *Managing IT as a Business: A Survival Guide for CEOs.* Hoboken, NJ: PricewaterhouseCoopers and John Wiley and Sons.

Maslow, A. 1970. *Motivation and Personality,* 2nd ed. New York: Harper and Row.

Moreira, M. 2004. "ABCs of Release Management." *CM Crossroads.* [Online article; retrieved 4/25/07.] http://www.cmcrossroads.com/content/view/6735/158/

Office of Government Commerce (OGC). 2005. *Best Practices for Service Support,* 10th impression. London: Office of Government Commerce.

Potgieter, B., J. Botha, and C. Lew. 2004. "Evidence that Use of the ITIL Framework Is Effective." Paper presented at the 17th National Advisory Committee on Computing Qualifications, Tauranga, New Zealand.

Rooney, J., and L. Vanden Heuvel. 2004. "Root Cause Analysis for Beginners." *Quality Progress* 37 (7): 45–53.

Rowland, D. 2007. "Healthcare in New Orleans: Before and after Katrina." Testimony before the Subcommittee on Oversight and Investigations, Committee on Energy and Commerce, and United States House of Representatives. [Online information; retrieved 5/14/07.] http://www.kff.org/uninsured/upload/7624.pdf

Sallé, M. 2004. "IT Service Management and IT Governance: Review, Comparative Analysis and Their Impact on Utility Computing." [Online article; retrieved 5/14/07.] http://www.hpl.hp.com/techreports/2004/HPL-2004-98.pdf

Schess, Z. 2002. "Tapped-out IT Shops Concentrate on Capacity Management." *Computerworld.* [Online article; retrieved 4/25/07.] http://www.snwonline.com/implement/tapped_out_02-18-2002.asp?article_id=99

Schick, S. 2001. "IT Departments Fall Short on Services." *Computing Canada* 27 (1): 4.

Singleton, J., E. McLean, and E. Altman. 1988. "Measuring Information Systems Performance: Experience with the Management by Results System at Security Pacific Bank." *MIS Quarterly* 12 (2): 325–37.

Smaltz, D., V. Sambamurthy, and R. Agarwal. 2006. "The Antecedents of CIO Role Effectiveness in Organizations: An Empirical Study in the Healthcare Sector." *IEEE Transactions on Engineering Management* 53 (2): 207–22.

Sundaresan, V. 2005. "Optimizing IT Service Delivery." [Online article; retrieved 1/29/07.] http://www.cioupdate.com/insights/article.php/3502581

The Joint Commission. 2003. "Using Aggregate Root Cause Analysis to Improve Patient Safety." *Joint Commission Journal on Quality and Safety* 29 (8): 434–39.

The Stationary Office (TSO). 2007. *The Official Introduction to the ITIL Service Lifecycle.* Norwich, UK: Office of Government Commerce.

Watson, R., L. Pitt, and C. Kavan. 1998. "Measuring Information Service Quality: Lessons from Two Longitudinal Case Studies." *MIS Quarterly* 22 (1): 61–79.

Young, C., and S. Mingay. 2003. *IS Process Improvement: Making Sense of Available Models.* No. DF-20–1898. Stamford, CT: Gartner, Inc.

ACHIEVING STRATEGIC COMPETITIVE ADVANTAGE

APPLICATIONS

Learning Objectives

1. List and differentiate the types of application software commonly used in healthcare organizations.
2. Discuss the evolution of medical documentation toward an electronic health record.
3. Differentiate among software applications used in healthcare enterprises by describing functionality and end users.
4. Distinguish between clinical decision support software and executive information systems.
5. Understand the use of computer applications as tools for research and medical education.

Applications are sets of software programs combined to provide a specific functionality needed within a healthcare organization. Examples of applications include systems for word processing, appointment scheduling, and laboratory test analysis.

In early development of business computing, the design and implementation of robust information systems in healthcare enterprises lagged behind most other industries. However, changes in the delivery and financing of healthcare over the last two decades have been pivotal to establishing information management as a key strategic resource in most healthcare organizations.

In the not-so-distant past, information system applications in healthcare organizations were designed as "stand alone" systems, and purchase decisions were based on maximizing desired specific functionality at acceptable costs. In the current environment, however, clinical and administrative applications are expected to integrate, sharing functionality and transferring data across various elements of the enterprise information system, and often exchanging information with systems external to the enterprise. Purchase decision criteria now include interoperability, compliance with data transmission standards, and many other complex factors. Migrating stand-alone "legacy" systems into an integrated environment has proven to be one of the most difficult challenges the healthcare organization technology leadership team encounters in building information systems. In fact, some teams conclude it would be easier to "start from scratch" than to retrofit their various systems from multiple vintages. However, this usually is not a realistic option for several reasons. Purchase and implementation costs of full-scale systems may be prohibitive, although purchase price has become almost the least important criterion in system selection. Operations and planning are dependent on data and information stored in existing systems, and migrating data archives may be difficult or even impossible. In light of the extent of technology dependence in healthcare organizations, the disruption in service delivery and business operations during a full-system transition could be tremendous.

While administrative applications typically were implemented first to manage financial affairs, now the drive for robust clinical information systems has become a top priority for most healthcare organizations. Clinical information systems not only provide direct support to patient care processes but they also populate the data repositories essential for performance measurement, external reporting, cost management, and other organizational accountability activities. Thus, the "ideal" clinical and administrative applications integrate into a comprehensive system that supports the continuum of information needs in an enterprise.

This chapter discusses the electronic health record (EHR) and selected clinical and administrative applications used in healthcare enterprises, describing key functionality and providing illustrative examples. Special features of applications designed to meet the needs of nonhospital healthcare organizations such as physician practices and home health are addressed. Additional uses of information systems in healthcare, such as medical research, education, and decision support, are discussed briefly.

Electronic Health Records

An individual's personal health record contains documentation of patient care activities and health services provided in all types of settings. For patients actively receiving health services, the health record also serves as a communication tool among care providers. For patients not currently receiving treatment, the record serves an archival function, pending a need to access the data in future episodes of care. Information maintained in health records also supports claims filed by providers for reimbursement and is an invaluable resource for clinical and health services research. Health records also are used as primary source documents for clinical and administrative performance management activities aimed at improving quality and safety of care and improving resource utilization and cost containment.

As with information in all other industries, medical and health information has grown in volume and complexity, as has the use of that information. Few healthcare organizations, even single physician practices, can survive in today's competitive environment without some level of technology-based information resources. However, the evolution of the patient medical record from its beginnings as writings on papyrus (Huffman 1972) to a seamless longitudinal record that is available electronically at all points on the continuum of care is not yet completed.

The extent of process automation and the scope of computerized data in hybrid systems vary greatly, even within one category of organizations such as hospitals or physician practices. At the lowest level of the continuum, some processes are automated and electronic files are generated. For example, patient registration and discharge information, diagnostic reports, or operative summaries may be captured through data entry, data extraction, or transcription. However, these electronic files may be printed for inclusion in a paper-based record. In other examples, documents may be scanned into an imaging system and stored electronically for viewing at workstations throughout the facility. Only a very few facilities have all, or the majority, of their health information captured, stored, and accessible electronically.

A 1991 report by the Institute of Medicine (IOM) provided major impetus to the development of EHRs (termed *computer-based patient records* in the report) by all healthcare organizations, from large medical centers to solo practice physician offices. The IOM's Committee on Improving the Patient Record called for national-level implementation of computer-based patient records, citing improvement of patient care and increased emphasis on quality improvement as key goals (IOM 1991). A revised report released in 1997 provided an update on available technology and discussed emerging issues related to privacy and confidentiality of electronic health information (IOM 1997).

As initially proposed by the IOM report and refined in later publications, the envisioned elements of a "true" EHR may be summarized as follows:

- *Electronic data capture for storage in a data repository.* Patient demographics, data generated through diagnostic and treatment events, and results of treatment are captured and accessible by all applications in the enterprise information system. Data redundancy is eliminated as data are captured once and stored for access by all appropriate applications and users.
- *"Real time" order entry and test results applications.* Results are accessible from workstations throughout the enterprise or from remote locations.
- *Administrative processes linked with clinical activities.* Scheduling, billing, referrals, and other processes that require interoperable administrative and clinical systems should be linked.
- *Electronic data interchange (EDI) with oversight agencies and strategic partners.* EDI requires compliance with national information standards and code sets.
- *Clinical decision support for diagnosis and care management.* Providers have access to diagnostic and treatment information in real time, via workstations or remote devices.
- *Performance reporting for internal use or reporting to external agencies as mandated or desired.* This requires compliance with national information standards and code sets.

- *Individual patient access to their personal records.* Incorporating safeguards to protect privacy and confidentiality while facilitating appropriate access is a significant challenge.

Progress Toward the Electronic Health Record

Despite efforts by individual organizations and integrated delivery systems as well as national funding initiatives, development of the EHR as envisioned in the 1991 IOM report remains an elusive goal. Using the terminology defined by Waegemann (1996) as a reference, many healthcare organizations have developed computerized or electronic *medical* records (use of imaging and other digitizing approaches to create a communication and archival medium for use within the organization). However, only a few large systems have created an electronic *patient* record (one that is integrated across organizations). The ultimate electronic *health* record, whereby all medical and health records related to an individual are connected via a unique identifier no matter where the actual data reside, will not be realized until national information standards and code sets are well established. While many health data standards have been implemented, they are primarily technical in nature and emerged from information technology vendor groups seeking to create interoperability between information management/information technology products for improved functionality or competitive business advantage. Much more work needs to be done related to the clinical aspects of health data. A large number of independent efforts to establish clinical standards are underway. More than 50 workgroups, including professional associations and collaborative groups, are actively engaged in such projects (Hammond and McCourt 2007).

A 2005 national survey found that 37 percent of responding hospitals had technology in place to support some components of all core EHR functionalities (Thakkar and Davis 2006). However, research using technology diffusion modeling (Ford, Menachemi, and Phillips 2006) suggests that diffusion into the small practice setting likely will not be achieved before 2024, which is well past the IOM's 2014 goal.

In the absence of regulatory guidelines for adopting technology to perform health information management functions needed to achieve the EHR, most providers respond to financial incentives and assessment of individual needs. Thus, practices vary greatly across enterprises and care delivery settings. However, technology costs and other institutional barriers may outweigh the financial incentives to adopt a given technology (Fenton and Gamm 2007; Garrett et al. 2006).

The status of progress toward electronic records can be summarized as follows:

- The Veterans Health Information Systems and Technology Architecture (VistA), which includes the Department of Veterans Affairs' (VA)

Computerized Patient Record System, likely is the most advanced health information system at the time of this writing. VistA has been adopted by a number of non-VA providers, across the United States and internationally. Additional information is available through the VA website (www.va.gov).

- Most healthcare organizations have partially automated records that include items such as laboratory results, summaries of radiology procedures, current medications, and diagnostic and treatment summaries.

- An increasing number of physician offices and group practices are installing practice management and health record systems designed for use in ambulatory care settings. Assistance and support for implementing EDI are available to physicians from the Medicare Quality Improvement Organization (QIO) Program, a support network of 53 entities directed by the Centers for Medicare & Medicaid Services. The QIOs work with medical providers and consumers to ensure quality, safety, and medical necessity of healthcare services provided to beneficiaries of the Medicare program.

- Some integrated delivery systems have developed master person indexes that provide common identifiers for all patients in the system and facilitate electronic exchange of information among all providers in the network.

- A small number of organizations, many of which are academic medical centers, are working on the development of complete electronic medical record systems, including the storage and retrieval of medical images as well as digital information.

While the EHR provides a summarizing focus for discussing the integration of health information technology and serves as the providers' interface with various applications, some categories of applications should be considered independently. A number of applications not only support the EHR but also contribute significantly to patient safety initiatives, resource efficiencies, and other strategic and operational objectives. The remainder of this chapter discusses some of the more widely implemented types of clinical and administrative systems and other applications in the healthcare field. Readers seeking a broader discussion of EHRs are referred to *The Executive's Guide to Electronic Health Records* by Smaltz and Berner (2006).

Clinical Information Systems

Clinical applications support diagnosis, treatment planning, and evaluation of medical outcomes across the continuum of care. A system may be designed to support activities related to a defined function, such as order entry, or an entire service area, such as the laboratory. Clinical applications can support quality management and cost control programs by documenting medical necessity for procedures performed. Clinical practice guidelines and other treatment proto-cols can be embedded in the application, along with programming to require clinical justification for ordering tests and procedures not addressed in the protocols, thus allowing the avoidance of unnecessary tests and procedures. Treatment plans for individual patients can be compared against evidence-based regimens used for a large number of similar patients stored in a clinical database. Incorporating evidence-based protocols into clinical decision mak-ing supports providers in delivering patient care that is both clinically effective and cost efficient.

Despite the drive for connectivity, many healthcare organizations con-tinue to maintain separate information systems for some clinical services, usu-ally either to acquire a "best of breed" system or because a legacy system cannot be fully integrated with newer installations. While the most common areas for decentralized departmental systems are pharmacy, clinical laboratory, and radiology, healthcare organizations utilize many other specific-purpose applications. Enterprise-level planning is essential when individual departmen-tal systems are used to ensure adequate system integration and the ability to transmit data across organizational units both for medical and administrative purposes.

Laboratory Automation and Laboratory Information Systems

Laboratory systems constitute one of the most common clinical computer applications in healthcare organizations. Clinical laboratory systems have two primary functions: automation of test processes and processing of laboratory data. Automation of test processing involves linking laboratory instruments directly to a computer. Signals from the test instruments are captured in (or converted to) digitized format for computer processing. The computer then carries out calculations that would be made by the lab technician in a manual system. Computer calculations can include determination of peak values, computation of the concentration of elements of the patient sample, and comparison to normal value ranges. The final results are stored in a patient laboratory data file, and test results may be printed or viewed from a workstation screen.

Although laboratory automation is most advanced in the clinical chem-istry area, information technology and systems are used extensively in other laboratory operations such as blood banks, microbiology, and virology. Lab-oratory information systems can be used independently of or in conjunction with laboratory automation systems.

A laboratory information system typically supports the following func-tions:

- Recording test requisitions
- Scheduling and tracking specimen collection and test processing
- Recording the results of completed tests

- Producing test reports for inclusion in the patient record
- Generating alerts for follow-up
- Preparing periodic summary reports of tests for a given patient
- Preparing statistical activity reports for the laboratory
- Responding to telephone inquiries for test results
- Maintaining records for quality control
- Overseeing the administration of laboratory operations, such as monitoring technologist productivity

Pharmacy Information Systems

The pharmacy is one of the most informationally complex departments in the healthcare organization and is the department that has been the focus of most error-reduction initiatives. Medication errors constitute the largest percentage of medical errors discussed in the IOM's 1999 report, *To Err Is Human: Building a Safer Health System*. The report identifies errors in all aspects of drug management—ordering, dispensing, administering, and recording—and calls for the use of computerized information and decision-support systems as aids in reducing medication and other types of medical errors.

Good records are crucial to controlling the processes associated with ordering, stocking, distributing, and administering drugs and other pharmaceuticals. Control of these processes is essential to avoid medication errors to the maximum extent possible and to manage those errors that occur. Precise records also are important for accurate billing to ensure optimum revenue generation. The volume and complexity of pharmacy services in most healthcare organizations require automated systems and information management technology.

As with other clinical applications, the two basic design approaches for pharmacy information systems are (1) a stand-alone pharmacy system and (2) integration of pharmacy activities with other institutional information system applications. Stand-alone pharmacy systems provide for control of dangerous drugs (particularly narcotics), drug ordering and inventory control, control of drug distribution to patients, storage and retrieval of drug information, construction of patient drug profiles, maintenance of the organization's formulary, and generation of charges for billing. Current drug orders and prescriptions are checked against patient profiles to ensure proper dosage, monitor contraindications, and protect against drug allergies and sensitivities.

Pharmacy systems integrated with an enterprise information system will have functionality similar to stand-alone systems for supporting pharmacy operations, but they will be linked with other systems for enhanced data management. For example, the pharmacy system will be linked with the order entry application, allowing medication orders to be entered or viewed via desktop computers or handheld devices at patient care units, outpatient clinics, and the emergency department, or even remotely. Orders are transmitted to the pharmacy, where worksheets are generated, electronic patient profiles are updated, and dispensing labels are prepared. Such systems often include automatic updating of the drug inventory and automatic generation of patient charges from the medication orders. Data and information generated by the pharmacy system also may be linked with administrative systems to track medication errors, profile ordering practices, and prepare other cost and quality analyses used for performance management.

While some commonality of functions will exist across vendor products for a category of applications, the selling point for a specific product often lies in its unique characteristics. For pharmacy systems, these desirable features often are found in the screening function (Barcia 2001). In general, screening should include drug-drug interactions, drug-food interactions, dose range checking, screening for allergies, duplicate drug protection, geriatric- and pediatric-specific screens, IV compatibility checks, and others. Although all patients benefit from the use of technology to reduce medical errors, computer protocols have special importance for pediatric patients because of the need for weight-based dosing (Kaushal, Barker, and Bates 2001).

A wide array of pharmacy software and related technology products is available in the market. Products and devices to facilitate automation of the pharmacy department and point-of-service pharmacy activities include barcode labeling, unit dose dispensers, robotic packaging, computerized medication carts, radio-frequency identification, and many others.

Medical Imaging and Radiology Information Systems

As with the clinical laboratory, radiology systems fall into two general categories: (1) automation of diagnostic and treatment procedures and (2) computerization of the information management function. *Medical imaging systems* use computer technology for image processing, image enhancement, visualization, and storage. *Radiology information system* functions include recording test requisitions, scheduling procedures, recording and reporting test results, reporting charges to the business office, and preparing management reports for the department.

Computer technology has automated much of the operation of imaging equipment, aiding technologists in positioning patients, determining exposure time, and verifying image quality. Not only does automation improve the quality of the diagnostic image, but the efficiency of the imaging process is improved as well, and rework due to poor image quality is decreased. Patient throughput is faster, which contributes to patient satisfaction.

Digital image enhancement is an increasingly important component of medical technology, particularly in computed tomography, gamma cameras, ultrasound scanners, digital subtraction angiography, and magnetic resonance imaging. Major diagnostic advancements have occurred in radiography and nuclear medicine as a result of this technology. Computers are used extensively in radiation therapy as well. Computerized treatment planning programs prepare and evaluate individual patient treatment plans using complex mathematical models in conjunction with image enhancement of the treatment site. The computer is used to analyze patient-specific data and the type, location, and size of a tumor to determine the exact dosage of radiation or radiopharmaceutical to be applied at various treatment sites while minimizing the exposure to unaffected regions of the body.

One of the most common ways to manage the storage, retrieval, distribution, and presentation of medical images is via a picture archiving and communications system (PACS). A PACS involves online storage and rapid retrieval of images transmitted over communications networks to user workstations that can display both digital information and images. Benefits of PACS include faster turnaround of images and reports, elimination of film loss, reliable retrieval of archived films, and greatly reduced storage space requirements. PACS may be used in conjunction with teleradiology communications systems to bring images from remote facilities to a central site for reading and interpretation. Teleradiology also enables physicians to call up images at workstations in remote locations, including their own homes (Luccichenti et al. 2004).

While a "filmless" radiography department sounds as appealing as a paperless medical record, the long-term stability of digital media, technology innovation, and future application upgrades must be considered in evaluating vendor PACS products. The effects of temperature extremes, exposure to water or chemicals, and other natural or human-initiated events on storage media cannot be predicted with surety. Further, one only has to consider the demise of the eight-track cassette tape and Beta video to realize that technology evolution extends to storage devices as well as processing units.

Other Service Department Systems

In addition to laboratory, pharmacy, and radiology systems described in this chapter, stand-alone and integrated applications are available for most other clinical departments and service areas of healthcare organizations. Systems are available to support clinical care and departmental management in physical therapy, pulmonary care, emergency department, operating rooms, labor and delivery, and critical care units, to mention only a few.

Order Entry and Results Reporting

Order-entry and results-reporting applications provide for efficient entry of orders for diagnostic tests and patient treatments and for subsequent reporting of test results to the ordering provider and the patient care unit. Often termed *computerized physician order entry* (CPOE) systems, these applications electronically transmit physician orders to the appropriate clinical service units. Results can be stored electronically for remote or workstation access, or printed for inclusion in a paper record. Records of charges for services provided are transmitted electronically to the appropriate business office application for processing and entry into the accounting system. Through use of drop-down menus and edit checks, the system minimizes errors in data entry as well. The physician can select from standard order sets using a touch screen or mouse/keyboard, or enter unique instructions when appropriate.

The Leapfrog Group, a voluntary organization of large purchasers of healthcare, lists CPOE as one of the three most important elements of a hospital patient safety program. Studies reported on the group's website (www.leapfroggroup.org) show that CPOE of prescriptions can reduce serious medication errors by more than 80 percent in some organizations (Leapfrog Group 2007).

Nursing Information Systems

As in other clinical care areas in healthcare organizations, information systems are an essential component of nursing practice. Stand-alone or integrated computer systems assist nurses in planning and delivering patient care, monitoring patients over the course of their treatment, and managing the administrative aspects of the nursing or patient care unit. Administrative tools include financial management, staffing and resource allocation, scheduling, activity (care) planning, and performance management reports.

Clinical management components of nursing information systems include tools for conducting and documenting the patient history and nursing assessment; charting tools to facilitate standardized progress notes, end-of-shift reporting, and data entry by exception; medication administration tools; standards of care for disease management; and information to aid in clinical outcomes analysis and improvement. Because patient data are stored in a database format, selected variables can be reported for visualization in ways that are not possible with paper charts. Vital signs can be reviewed as graphs, with data reported for designated time periods, or data points can be correlated with other selected variables, such as medication administration. Protocol-based nursing care systems incorporate uniform standards of nursing care and are capable of generating nursing orders and suggesting interventions to be considered in developing treatment plans for patients with specific diagnoses or care needs.

Point-of-care information processing is an ongoing goal of many healthcare organizations. During the 1990s, early adopters of this technology experimented with fixed computer terminals at patient bedsides or in convenient locations throughout the care unit. Wireless handheld devices have replaced these fixed units, providing more efficient and less costly data capture and access. Data entry can occur through several media. Young et al. (2001) compared the utility and efficiency of keyboard-based and pen-based portable devices used by nurses in six specialty areas of an acute care hospital. Nurses preferred pen-based devices for working with structured data, but keyboards were preferred for entering textual information.

Potential advantages for point-of-care nursing systems include the following:

1. *Reduction in nursing service costs.* Capturing or recording patient data at the bedside can improve nursing efficiency by cutting down travel time to the nursing station and decreasing the amount of time spent recording patient data.
2. *Improved quality of care.* Because nurses are able to record and retrieve data at the bedside, they can spend more time with the patient and less time at the nursing station.
3. *More timely access and improved recording of information.* The patient record is updated in real time at the bedside, and the information is accessible by all caregivers. Because information is entered immediately as it is received, the patient record is more accurate.
4. *Overall cost reduction.* Bedside patient information systems can result in fewer lost charges, because information is entered immediately after completion of a patient care activity. Length of stay could be reduced because every patient service will be delivered faster and better. The point-of-care system permits more accurate logging of nursing activity, thereby producing better data on nursing staff productivity and costs related to patient diagnosis.

Management/Administrative and Financial Systems

Most healthcare organizations began their automated information processing activities with computer systems that supported administrative operations, and in particular, financial and accounting systems. While information technology now is employed throughout healthcare organizations, a greater number of current healthcare organization applications still serve financial purposes than those applications focused on patient safety and quality improvement (Poon et al. 2006).

For many years, the healthcare field lagged behind other businesses in developing effective administrative information systems. Problems have included undercapitalization of the system development process and management failure to oversee system implementation effectively. However, the situation has changed substantially in recent years due to heightened competition, increased regulation, and changing payment mechanisms affecting the entire field. Healthcare managers have come to rely on their information systems as essential tools for effective competition and, in some cases, survival.

The same focus on moving toward interconnectivity and interoperability in clinical systems can be observed in administrative and financial systems designed for use in healthcare organizations. Enterprise resources planning (ERP) systems are bundled applications that integrate operational information derived from financial, human resources, materials management, and other function-based areas into a single database used to achieve business management objectives (Legnick-Hall and Legnick-Hall 2006). These systems connect inventory and facilities management, resource scheduling, accounting and financial management, and other business events in a real-time environment.

Although the trend appears to be moving toward these "single vendor solutions," implementation of enterprise resource planning applications has occurred in fewer than 20 percent of hospitals (Raths 2006). Again as with clinical systems, the future market for ERP applications will emerge from the need to update legacy software. However, a large number of vendors continue to develop and market applications that will operate as stand alones or that can be integrated or interfaced with other applications. The following administrative applications incorporated in an ERP are discussed below:

- Financial information systems
- Human resources information systems
- Resource utilization and scheduling systems
- Materials management systems
- Facilities and project management systems
- Office automation systems

Financial Information Systems

In the current competitive and regulatory environments, healthcare organizations must have timely and accurate financial information to monitor and guide operational performance. In the face of answering demands for accountability and cost containment while still providing high-quality services, managers are acutely aware of the importance of sound financial management in guiding operational performance. Financial information systems support operational activities such as general accounting, patient accounting, payroll, contract management, and investment management. Financial systems also provide information to management for controlling and evaluating organizational performance. Analysis of current and historical information helps in projecting future financial needs of the organization.

Financial information systems require input from transaction-processing systems, external sources, and strategic organizational plans (see Figure 8.1). Transaction-processing systems record the organization's routine activities, collecting information from other administrative subsystems, including payroll, accounts payable, accounts receivable, general ledger, and inventory control. These transactions are the basis for many financial reports required by management. To support effective financial decisions, financial systems also need external information such as government statistics, inflation rates, and information about the marketplace. An organization's strategic plan should contain financial goals and objectives that help provide the framework for preparation of financial reports.

A fully integrated financial information system brings related information together for planning, monitoring, and control. Individual financial subsystems include the following:

- Payroll preparation and accounting, linked to a human resources information system
- Processing of accounts payable, linked to purchasing and inventory control systems
- Patient accounting, patient and third-party billing, and accounts receivable processing
- Cost accounting and cost allocation of non-revenue-generating activities and general overhead expense
- General ledger accounting
- Budgeting and budget control
- Internal auditing
- Financial forecasting
- Investment monitoring and analysis
- Financial statement preparation
- Financial reporting for operating supervisors, executive management, board members, external regulators, and third-party financing agencies

The development of a financial information system depends on the existence of a good accounting system. Sophisticated cost accounting, essential in today's environment, enables the financial information system to generate accurate information on resources used to deliver services. In a managed care environment, both providers and managed care organizations need cost information to help negotiate rates and monitor contract performance. Integrated financial reporting based on a solid cost accounting system provides information for product costing, analysis of labor productivity, inventory control, and examination of the productivity of capital.

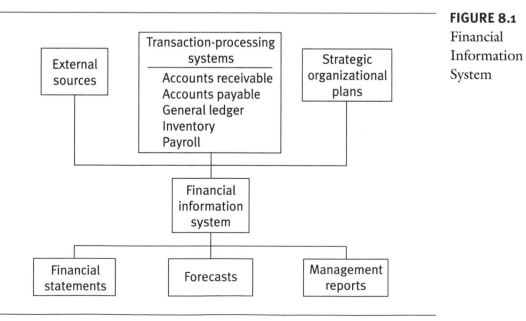

FIGURE 8.1

Financial Information System

Increasingly, payment for healthcare is based on either a fixed payment per case (such as diagnosis-related groups) or a fixed payment per person per month (capitation payment systems). For effective management in this environment, a financial information system must have the capability to convert or link cost and net revenue information among multiple units of payment.

Human Resources Information Systems

Employees of a healthcare organization constitute its most important resource. Most organizations spend 60 percent to 70 percent of their operating budget on employee salaries and benefits. Thus, a good human resources information system (HRIS) is very important to assist management in personnel planning, staffing, and productivity analysis. The functions of an HRIS include the following:

- Maintaining, updating, and retrieving information from a database of employee permanent records
- Providing automatic position control linked to the budget
- Producing labor analysis reports for each cost center
- Producing reports for analyzing personnel problems, such as turnover and absenteeism
- Maintaining an inventory of special skills and certifications of employees
- Producing labor cost allocations with linkage to the payroll system
- Providing information on employee productivity and quality control, assuming that appropriate labor standards have been developed
- Comparing compensation and benefit packages to outside industry norms

An automated database of employee information used in conjunction with an HRIS might include the following components (Austin, Johnson, and Palestrant 1998, 83):

- Personnel information, such as name, address, Social Security number, birth date, and marital status
- Job-related information, such as job title, department, employment date, date of last promotion, and salary history
- Benefits information, such as medical insurance coverage, life and disability insurance coverage, and pension plan data
- Miscellaneous information, such as special skills, physical limitations, disciplinary actions, awards, and bonuses

The availability of computerized employee record files creates a security issue. Because protecting the employee's right to privacy is essential, organizations need to establish software and hardware security systems and set policies for accessing and updating electronic personnel files. (See Chapter 5 for discussion on data security policies.)

In addition to supporting operational work in the human resources department, a well-designed HRIS will produce reports for management planning and control (see Figure 8.2). For example, HRIS management reports can be used to monitor turnover rates, unfilled positions, labor costs, employee productivity, and utilization of benefits. Attitudes of employees and physicians can be monitored through periodic satisfaction surveys.

Some larger hospitals and multi-institutional healthcare organizations have developed automated databases to support recruitment of physicians. Such systems can identify staff needs, plan searches, and schedule interviews with candidates for appointment to the medical staff.

Computer systems also are available to maintain records related to physician credentials and practice privileges in the organization. These systems are important for monitoring quality standards and for maintaining documentation required by accreditation surveyors.

Resource Utilization and Scheduling Systems

Under current fixed price and capitation payment systems, cost containment and efficient resource utilization are pivotal to success. External mandates for utilization review by regulatory agencies and insurance companies are more than balanced by internal drivers for ensuring that resource utilization is optimized. Managers must ensure that services are available when needed and that personnel and technology are efficiently allocated and scheduled. These efficiency needs are met through computerized monitoring and scheduling systems.

Information systems monitor inpatient occupancy rates, clinic and emergency department activity, and utilization of individual service facilities such as the operating suite. Patient scheduling systems are used for advance booking and scheduling of facilities, both for patient and physician convenience and for efficient allocation of resources, particularly staffing.

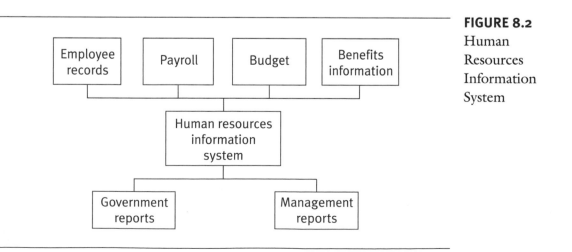

FIGURE 8.2

Human Resources Information System

Advance bed booking and preadmissions systems are particularly useful in situations where most of the admissions are elective (e.g., a specialized surgical facility). Advance booking also provides time for necessary precertification for managed care patients and others covered by insurance plans that require review and certification of medical necessity for procedures and inpatient admission. Preadmission information systems can be linked to individual physicians' offices as well. Computer programs can project the average length of stay for each elective admission once historical data (including diagnosis, surgical procedure, age of patient, and sex of patient) have been accumulated. After admissions are scheduled and the data are entered into the computer's master files, the system keeps track of projected occupancy levels for each day.

Admissions monitoring and scheduling systems improve staffing and workflow in healthcare organizations. These systems can reduce daily fluctuations in a hospital's census and improve employment of flexible staffing systems. Acute care general hospitals must maintain an accurate accounting of bed census and occupancy if they are to survive. Census information helps compare projected income against projected budgets. Administrators can also track demands for specific services and adjust staffing levels and scheduling of facilities as demand patterns change.

Computer programs are also available for scheduling operating rooms in hospitals and ambulatory surgery centers. These systems are designed to improve operating room utilization, contain costs, facilitate planning, and aid in the scheduling of specific surgical procedures. Outpatient clinic appointment and scheduling systems are common in organizations with a large volume of outpatient activity.

Resource utilization and scheduling systems may operate at the department level, but enterprisewide scheduling systems that meet multiple objectives, including balanced schedules, optimum staffing, and management of resources across the enterprise, are beginning to enter the market.

Baldwin (2001) suggests that desirable capabilities of an enterprisewide scheduling system include the capability to

- Recognize that certain procedures should be preceded or followed by other procedures;
- Automatically order needed supplies and material;
- Automatically verify insurance status;
- Automatically produce timely patient reminders; and
- Suggest how to reassign staff as workloads expand or contract.

Materials Management Systems

Computer systems assist healthcare organizations in more effective management of supplies and materials. These systems include computerized purchasing, EDI with suppliers, inventory control, use of bar-code devices for encoding supplies and materials, and computerized menu planning and food service management.

In a typical materials management system, requisitions for supplies and materials are entered into the computer and matched against budgetary authorization for financial control. Overdrafts on supply accounts are flagged and sent to the appropriate supervisor for follow-up action. Once requisitions are cleared, the computer generates purchase orders. As materials are received, receipt notices are entered into the computer and matched against an open order file. Many automated purchasing systems also include direct linkage to the accounts payable system if system integration has been planned. Some systems also provide the capability for automatic reordering of selected items (see Figure 8.3).

Purchase orders can be transmitted electronically to suppliers. Modern systems of supply chain management link healthcare organizations to vendor information systems using Internet technology. Supply chain applications are designed to reduce processing costs and obtain materials on a "just in time" basis, thus reducing the need to carry a large inventory.

Coding standards are an important element of automated purchasing and materials management systems. Expanded use of bar codes for all types of medical supplies and pharmaceuticals can be anticipated as purchaser-vendor relationships in healthcare continue to develop.

Computerized menu-planning systems store and analyze data on patients' nutritional and dietary requirements, food items in inventory and their costs, and decision rules for selecting from among alternative menus. Decision criteria might include patient preferences or visual appearance of food in addition to nutritional adequacy and cost.

Facilities and Project Management Systems

Computerized systems can help organizations plan, manage, and maintain physical facilities. Examples include preventive maintenance systems, energy management systems, and project scheduling and control systems (particularly useful in construction and remodeling projects).

Preventive maintenance project management systems help extend the life of equipment and facilities and reduce costly failures. Potential benefits include the following:

- Cost savings through reduced inventory of spare parts for equipment repair
- Reduced staffing of housekeeping and maintenance department personnel
- Improved risk management through better record keeping on equipment maintenance and reduction of safety hazards

Energy conservation has become an important cost-saving strategy for the healthcare field as it has for all major industries. Computer packages have been developed to assist in monitoring energy use. Actual utilization figures are compared against calculated requirements, and the computer model points out possibilities for reduced consumption.

FIGURE 8.3
Materials
Management
System

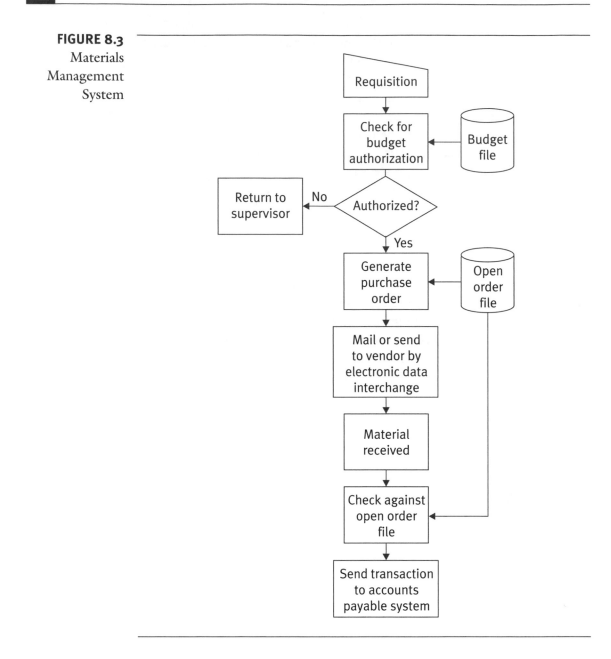

Healthcare organizations frequently are involved in capital construction and major remodeling projects. Computer systems have been developed to aid in project management. One such system, Program Evaluation and Review Technique, assists in project scheduling and control. System users identify (1) all activities required to complete the project; (2) the relationships of these activities to one another, including those that can be carried out simultaneously and those that must follow a time sequence; and (3) time estimates for completing each activity. These data are used to generate a diagram of activities that shows the critical path for project completion. As activities are completed, actual completion times can be entered back into the calculation, and more accurate schedules can be prepared for the remaining work. The system is an excellent tool for dynamic scheduling and control of major projects. For more detailed coverage of project management, see Chapter 4.

Office Automation Systems

Office automation helps to coordinate and manage people and workflow, link organizational units and projects, and coordinate work in the organization across levels and functions. Healthcare organizations use a variety of computing tools to carry out general office functions, such as word processing, electronic mail, project management, meeting scheduling, and maintenance of calendars for management personnel. These activities may be conducted using desktop workstations, laptop computers, or a variety of handheld devices.

Managing documents can consume 40 to 50 percent of an office staff's time when all functions are considered—that is, document creation, storage, and retrieval; desktop publishing; and converting documents to other forms. Use of systems for integrated word processing, scheduling, electronic filing of documents, and message/document transmission can dramatically improve efficiency and reduce the costs of office operations.

Office systems can link parts of the organization together by scheduling meetings using electronic calendars and communication via electronic mail (e-mail). E-mail systems link offices and/or individuals, allowing electronic files to be forwarded to others or archived in a shared storage area for access by members of a workgroup.

Many organizations have expanded the concept of office automation to include *groupware*, a combination of software and hardware that enables managers to share information in an interactive networked environment. This software/hardware combination facilitates real-time interaction among members of the group to improve problem solving and project management. Typical groupware activities include the following:

- E-mail
- Teleconferencing
- Interactive two-way compressed video conferencing
- Relational databases (used to search for data and information)
- Document editing and management
- Group calendars and scheduling

Mobile computing using laptops and handheld devices, wireless technology, and the Internet have changed the way people work together. Workgroups and teams can work collaboratively anywhere—in a conference room or in geographically separated offices—with full access to necessary programs and files. Audio and video conferencing allow real-time interaction among team members. The virtual office can be as productive as the traditional office.

Information Systems for Nonhospital Healthcare Organizations

As changes to payment models in the 1980s led to changes in delivery models during the 1990s, nonhospital healthcare organizations began implementing information systems to manage clinical services and business operations. The vendor sector quickly began designing and marketing software products to meet the special information needs of these organizations. Organization types that fall under this category include ambulatory clinics, physician practices, home health agencies, long-term care (LTC) facilities, and many others. These applications typically include multiple modules that meet the healthcare organizations' needs for clinical documentation, operations management, and financial management.

Ambulatory Care Information Systems

Increasingly, healthcare is being delivered in outpatient and ambulatory care settings. Information systems that support ambulatory care and assist primary care providers in their practices have become a niche market. The availability of powerful and inexpensive microcomputers and practice management software packages has brought this technology within the reach of even small medical groups and solo practitioners.

A typical practice management system (Slovensky et al. 2006) includes modules to support such business functions as the following:

- Operations management (scheduling, reminders, billing, authorizations, etc.)
- Services (e-mail, groupware)
- Claims processing
- Document processing, spreadsheets, and databases
- Transcription
- Personnel management
- Inventory management
- Waste management
- Energy management

Clinical applications in medical practices include EHRs, prescription management, and disease management resources. Patient applications, an emerging software market, include electronic communication, monitoring, educational resources, and telehealth applications. Various vendor products offer full-service suites or selected modules based on the practice's needs.

Automating practice functions increases operational efficiency and reduces errors in information processing, both of which contribute to patient satisfaction. Automating or using Web-based patient communication for services such as call-backs, prescription renewals, and similar activities can be helpful as well.

Office practice computers can be linked to local hospitals in addition to serving the management needs of the practice. Many hospitals or integrated delivery systems have developed computer linkages with physician offices to enable clinicians to pre-admit patients; order diagnostic tests; and query the patient information system for lab results, progress notes, and other current clinical information. Healthcare organizations use such linkages as incentives to attract physicians to use their facilities in a highly competitive environment.

Long-Term Care Information Systems

The LTC industry has been a late adopter in implementing computer systems, in part because software vendors have been slow to develop products tailored to the needs of nursing homes and continuing care communities. This situation is changing as the scope and volume of healthcare delivered in subacute- and postacute-care facilities increase. Typical requirements for LTC systems include census management, initial and periodic resident assessments, documentation of care services provided, documentation of physician orders, nutritional assessments and menu planning in the dietary department, and pharmacy applications.

The ability to communicate clinical information between caregivers and the admitting physician is especially important, as the physician usually is not physically present on a daily basis. Remote access to clinical documentation facilitates timely intervention in an acute episode and contributes to better health outcomes.

As LTC care facilities become components of larger integrated delivery systems, electronic sharing of clinical and administrative information with hospitals, clinics, ambulatory care facilities, and other system components becomes a business essential.

Home Health Care Information Systems

Home health care services have expanded rapidly in recent years as an alternative to more costly institutional care. As service volume has increased and the scope of services expanded, information systems have been developed specifically to meet the needs of home care provider organizations.

Many home health agencies use laptop computers and other remote access devices for on-site documentation of patient care. Home health nurses and other caregivers enter information directly at the treatment sites for uploading to the centralized data repository. Relevant data can be accessed during a service visit by any provider. These systems reduce the amount of administrative work needed to document care, allowing visiting nurses and home health aides to spend more time with patients.

Electronic devices also can transmit clinical information for routine health monitoring between visits via telephone lines or the Internet. Patients and family members follow the treatment plan, take and record measurements as indicated, and submit data for evaluation by the clinical personnel overseeing their care.

Other Information System Applications in Healthcare

Information systems support most processes in healthcare. While many applications can be categorized by their use for a defined function, many serve the needs of multiple providers and managers in disparate service areas. Clinical information may be combined with administrative information or used for an administrative purpose exclusively. Alternatively, administrative information may be applied in the delivery of clinical care.

Clinical Decision-Support Systems

Clinical decision support (CDS) systems are computer-based information systems designed to assist physicians and other providers in diagnosis and treatment planning. CDS systems fall into two categories: (1) passive systems, which collect, organize, and communicate patient data to the physician, including data on the patient's medical history, physical examinations, and diagnostic tests performed, and (2) active decision support systems, which use medical data stored in the computer to suggest diagnoses and treatment protocols.

Passive systems use the computer to organize clinical data for interpretation and analysis by the physician. They make clinical information more readily available and usable but do not process the information for further analysis. The clinical information systems described earlier in this chapter (computer-based patient records, laboratory, pharmacy, radiology, and other clinical services applications) are examples of passive CDS systems in that they capture clinical data and make them available to caregivers. These applications become more useful to clinicians for decision support when they are fully integrated and can provide complete medical information (both current data and historical information on the patient) through simple, user-friendly access from a computer workstation.

Active CDS systems employ the computer to provide direct assistance to the physician in diagnosis and treatment planning. They combine patient-specific data with generalized medical knowledge to reach a conclusion or make a recommendation to the caregiver. Active clinical decision support systems generally fall into three categories: expert systems, systems that employ probabilistic algorithms, and reminder/alert systems (Elson and Connelly 1995).

Expert systems also contain three major components—a knowledge base, patient-specific information, and an inference engine. A *general knowledge base* of medical information is obtained from a panel of experts in a given medical specialty. This knowledge base is matched against *patient-specific information* retrieved from the healthcare organization's clinical database. A *rule-based inference engine* generates conclusions for consideration by the physician. The system is dependent on the quality of the expert knowledge base and the "reasoning power" of the rules used by the inference engine.

Probabilistic algorithms employ statistical probabilities, which include the element of randomness, rather than knowledge collected from expert human beings. Expert knowledge is based on a combination of academic preparation and experiential learning.

Clinical reminders and alerts are incorporated into clinical computer applications to alert the caregiver to potential medical conditions or other problems that should be given attention. Examples include pharmacy systems that alert the physician to potentially negative interactions between two drugs prescribed for the same patient and systems that suggest that certain drugs or treatments should not be employed when specific laboratory results contraindicate their use.

Computers can aid decision making by simplifying access to data needed to make decisions, providing reminders and prompts, assisting in order entry, assisting in diagnosis, and reviewing new clinical data to issue alerts when important patterns are recognized. Systems are more likely to be successful when they give patient-specific suggestions, save time, and are incorporated into the regular workflow of the organization. Payne (2000) describes two examples of successful systems. In the treatment of HIV-infected patients, Beth Israel Hospital in Boston demonstrated that clinicians who received patient-specific alerts and reminders instituted treatment far more rapidly than clinicians who did not. At LDS Hospital in Salt Lake City, a computer-assisted management program for antimicrobials has reduced excessive drug dosage and drug allergies. The system has resulted in shorter length of stay and lower hospital costs for patients treated with the program.

Researchers at the University of Alabama at Birmingham (Berner et al. 2006) found that physicians using a decision support rule accessed via a handheld device (a personal digital assistant, or PDA) made better prescribing decisions than those who did not have the PDA for CDS access. The study, a randomized controlled trial, examined ordering practices for nonsteroidal anti-inflammatory drugs (NSAIDs). Physicians accessing the rule were more likely to order NSAIDs that were considered "safer" when considering gastrointestinal risk factors.

Executive Information Systems

The "business" corollary to clinical decision support systems is the executive information system (EIS). Sometimes referred to collectively as "business intelligence," EISs include systems designed to access and merge internal and external data into meaningful information reports. Executives identify critical environmental trends and facility performance indicators related to strategic objectives to guide their information capture and analysis. Data to support the EIS may be extracted from clinical and administrative databases serving the healthcare enterprise as well as public and proprietary data repositories. Important features of an effective EIS are the ability to query databases to construct user-defined reports and "drill down" capability to achieve the desired level of data granularity (Xu et al. 2003; Watson et al. 1995).

Evidence-Based Medicine and Disease-Management Systems

Evidence-based clinical practice guidelines are intended to assist clinicians and healthcare organizations in standardizing decisions about the care of individual patients to achieve cost and quality benefits. Accumulated evidence from clinical research is used to formulate statements of the "right" things to do for patients with a given diagnosis or condition. Ideally, guidelines ensure that patients receive appropriate diagnostic tests and treatments in an efficient and cost-effective manner. Guidelines are assumed to lower treatment costs by avoiding unnecessary tests. Hundreds of guidelines have been developed and are archived in the National Guideline Clearinghouse sponsored by the Agency for Healthcare Research and Quality (www.ahrq.gov). Although managed care organizations and health insurers have used such guidelines "with considerable success in reducing costs, lengths of stay, and utilization rates" (Woolf and George 2000, 761), practice guidelines are not without significant limitations. Among these limitations are differences in local standards of care, access to recommended technologies, and unique patient characteristics.

One approach to providing "evidence" to aid clinicians in decision making has been to share performance data among a benchmark group (Kiefe et al. 2001). Data collected during a reporting period are shared in an aggregate, graphic format. Physicians can identify clinical practices used by higher-performing colleagues on key outcome metrics to improve their own performance.

Disease management information systems and software products are designed to assist healthcare organizations in designing processes to provide quality care at the most reasonable cost possible. For the most part, they are disease specific and focus on high-volume, high-cost chronic conditions such as asthma, diabetes, and congestive heart failure. The typical approach is to involve patients in self-management of their condition and to create monitoring and feedback processes that encourage compliance with treatment plans. The information system may include capturing blood or urine test data, blood pressure readings, and other clinical information in the patient's home and transmitting it to the healthcare organization via digital telephony or other remote monitoring devices. Communication between patients and providers may be via telephone or the Internet. While routine patient monitoring assists in daily decision making, analyzing aggregated data can guide case managers and physicians in modifying treatment plans for better long-term clinical outcomes.

Computer-Assisted Medical Instrumentation

Computers or microprocessors are an important component of most sophisticated pieces of medical equipment used for instrument control, image enhancement, or processing of medical data. Computer systems interface directly with patient-monitoring devices in critical care units of the hospital. Patient-monitoring systems employ the computer for continuous surveillance of a patient's vital signs and periodic display of physiological data for use by trained monitoring personnel.

The first step in the process is acquiring data from monitoring equipment attached to the patient and converting the data for computer processing and display. Data are stored and made available for periodic display or display on demand. Computer programs enhance the measured data through structured analysis of clinical data in accordance with programmed decision rules. Trend data are followed to monitor changes in patient vital signs over time. Patient-monitoring systems can operate at the individual patient bedside, at a central station designed to monitor a small number of intensive care beds, or at a remote location linked back to the critical care unit by telecommunication equipment. Many of these systems also have electronic linkages for transmission of clinical data to the centralized computer-based medical record.

Computer systems have been designed for processing and interpretation of data from various diagnostic devices. Computerized signal processing is used in electrocardiograms, electroencephalograms, and pulmonary function testing. In fact, virtually every piece of modern medical equipment used for diagnostic testing and treatment now contains a microprocessor that helps control, enhance, and interpret the results of the testing or treatment process.

Telemedicine

Telemedicine is the application of computer and communications technologies to support healthcare provided to patients at remote locations. Telemedicine often involves telephone and online communication between a primary care physician, nurse practitioner, or physician's assistant who is treating patients in a rural area, and specialty physicians located at a distant medical center. Audio communications and video conferencing equipment are used in conjunction with computer access to patient records to establish primary diagnoses or provide expert consultation and second opinions. The systems often employ teleradiology for transmission of medical images for review by specialty physicians. Telemedicine systems can save travel time and costs for patients in addition to service delivery cost savings.

The University of California Davis Medical Center engaged in a demonstration project that serves patients with congestive heart failure. Patients use a portable telemedicine unit in their home that is connected by telephone lines to a terminal at the medical center some 10 miles away. A nurse at the center listens to heart and lungs, monitors blood pressure and pulse, and checks for ankle swelling. Each home unit costs about $5,000, which is less than the average cost of one hospital admission that could be avoided by use of the system (Sandberg 2000).

The University of Texas Medical Branch's Electronic Health Network, self-described as "the largest telemedicine system in the world" (UTMB 2007), provides medical services to indigent populations and correctional facilities across Texas, in addition to corporate and school programs. One of its more interesting programs has been to provide telemedicine services to National Science Foundation researchers in Antarctica.

Although telemedicine applications have increased in recent years, issues related to reimbursement for remote services, state licensure of health professionals when the system crosses state borders, patient privacy protection, and government regulation remain (Thompson 2006). And, clinical outcome benefits achieved through various telemedicine applications differ, as do cost savings. However, home-based telemedicine has been shown to be effective for chronic disease management, and telemedicine applications for surgical and neonatal intensive care units have achieved success (Hersh et al. 2001). In general, patients report satisfaction with telemedicine applications (Mair and Whitten 2000).

Computer Applications in Medical Research and Education

Information systems and medical databases are used extensively to support biomedical education and research. Computerized patient records serve as the basis for epidemiological studies of a variety of diseases and their potential linkages to social and environmental factors. In addition, computers are used to support medical, dental, nursing, and allied health education, using such techniques as computer-aided instruction and patient management simulation.

Computers are an integral component of most medical research projects. Effective project design requires close collaboration among clinicians, biostatisticians, and information systems specialists. Some research projects would not be possible without the high-speed computational capabilities and data storage capacity of large computer systems. An excellent example is the Human Genome Project, which mapped all the genes of the *Homo sapiens* species. One element of the map detailed all sequences of DNA chemical bases, an astounding three billion pairs. Analytical work of this magnitude is inconceivable without super-computing capabilities.

Hospitals, medical libraries, and individual clinicians use personal computers to access references to the medical literature and full-text online documents. The most widely used bibliographic system is MEDLINE, developed at the National Library of Medicine, which currently provides links to almost 11 million records (medline.cos.com). Articles from thousands of biomedical journals are indexed, stored in computer files, and available for searching and retrieval using standard medical subject headings and key word searches. The

Internet is used extensively to retrieve clinical information from a wide variety of specialty databases and sponsored websites.

Computers are an important tool for the education of clinicians. Computer-based medical education is designed to involve the student actively in the learning process. Projects range from presentation of information to students at computer terminals to sophisticated simulations of clinical problems. Microcomputer-based simulation programs are used to teach clinical problem solving. Students are presented initial cues and additional information on request as they proceed through a diagnostic process. Final diagnosis, patient management, and follow-up plans selected by the students are entered, and the system responds with a comparison to the "ideal" solution and critiques the process followed.

Summary

Most healthcare organizations began using electronic data processing by developing or purchasing financial information systems. Financial applications remain essential, but from a broader perspective, healthcare organizations use computers and information systems to support all administrative operations, including human resources management, resource utilization and scheduling, materials management, facilities and project management, and office automation in addition to financial activities.

Clinical services applications support the various clinical service departments of a healthcare organization or integrated delivery system. Common clinical services applications include laboratory information systems, pharmacy systems, and radiology information systems. PACS provide online storage and retrieval of medical images transmitted to user workstations. Information systems also support clinical care and departmental management in areas such as physical therapy, pulmonary medicine, emergency department, operating rooms, labor and delivery, and critical care. Across the healthcare field, the number of clinical systems installed continues to increase as governing boards and healthcare managers recognize their importance for continuous improvement of patient care quality, cost control, and reduction of medical errors.

Medical records are central to all patient care activities, whether maintained in paper format or electronically. However, the development of a completely electronic longitudinal health record remains an elusive goal. Although healthcare organizations may have many required elements in place locally, the implementation of standard code sets and transaction protocols is a significant barrier to full system interoperability.

As more healthcare is delivered in outpatient and other nonhospital settings, development of information systems specific to these delivery sites has accelerated. Typical functions for ambulatory settings include (1) patient scheduling and appointments, (2) electronic medical records and medical management, (3) patient and third-party billing, (4) managed care contract management, and (5) electronic communication with other providers in a network of care. LTC systems support census management, residential care documentation, pharmacy, and other areas of operation in skilled nursing facilities. Home health nurses often use laptop computers or other remote-access devices to document care at the location where it is provided.

Applications developed to assist physicians and other providers in the delivery of high-quality care include CDS systems and evidence-based medicine programs. These tools aid in diagnosis and treatment planning and compare treatment plans to established "best practices" using large databases.

Computers have become an integral component of medical equipment for instrument control, image enhancement, and medical data processing. These foundation applications evolved into sophisticated integration of computer and communications technology in telemedicine applications that support patient care at remote locations.

Information systems are used extensively to support biomedical education and research. Automated databases of patient records support epidemiological studies of disease linkage to social and environmental factors. Computer-assisted instruction and patient management simulation programs support the education of physicians, dentists, nurses, and other allied health personnel.

Simply stated, no aspect of healthcare delivery or health services management is untouched by computers and information systems. The computer, in its various forms, has become a ubiquitous tool used by clinician providers and managers alike. Technology evolution has resulted in powerful machines whose functional capabilities are optimized through judicious selection of application software to meet business and care delivery needs.

Web Resources

Additional information about the topics addressed in this chapter is available from several reliable websites.

Students interested in current information about EHRs are referred to www.ahima.org, the website of the American Health Information Management Association. In addition to the resources included in its Body of Knowledge, a special section of the website is devoted to e-HIM guidelines.

Health Level Seven (HL7) (www.hl7.org) is a leading healthcare standard-developing organization. HL7 is working as a coordinating agent for various active standard-setting groups.

Information about vendors of information technology products and information systems management services is available from *Healthcare Informatics* magazine at www.healthcare-informatics.com.

Information about vendors of software, services, and medical equipment is available from KLAS Enterprises at http://www.healthcomputing.com/VendorDirectory/.

Discussion Questions

1. Why are administrative systems more evolved than clinical systems?
2. What are the primary uses of an individual's personal health record?
3. Using Waegemann's (1996) framework, what are the distinguishing features of an EHR when compared with electronic medical records?
4. What aspects of clinical applications support quality management and cost control programs?
5. Describe various functionalities of pharmacy information systems that can aid in reducing medication errors.
6. Distinguish between features of medical imaging systems that support test automation and those that support department and information management.
7. What is the value in integrating order entry systems with pharmacy or diagnostic service systems?
8. List and describe various input devices used in point-of-care systems.
9. What challenges do legacy systems pose for enterprise system integration?
10. How are transaction processing systems employed in financial information systems?
11. What are the key functions of a human resources information system?
12. How can centralized scheduling systems contribute to the financial "bottom line"?
13. What are the key components of groupware as a resource to the management team?
14. What are the typical elements of a physician practice management system?
15. Describe the basic documentation requirements for an LTC information system. How do they differ from those for an information system used in an inpatient facility?

References

Austin, C. J., J. A. Johnson, and G. D. Palestrant. 1998. "Information Systems for Human Resources Management." In *Essentials of Human Resource Management in Health Services Organizations*, edited by M. D. Fottler, S. R. Hernandez, and C. L. Joiner. Albany, NY: Delmar Publishers.

Baldwin, F. D. 2001. "Book 'em. Enterprisewide Scheduling Presents Challenges, but CIOs Will Find It Worth the Effort." *Healthcare Informatics* 18 (9): 37–42.

Barcia, S. M. 2001. "Reducing Medication Errors." *Health Management Technology* 22 (1): 26.

Berner, E. S., T. K. Houston, M. N. Ray, J. J. Allison, G. R. Heudebert, W. W. Chatham, J. I. Kennedy, G. L. Glandon, P. A. Norton, M. A. Crawford, and R. D. Maisiak. 2006. "Improving Ambulatory Prescribing Safety with a Handheld Decision Support System: A Randomized Controlled Trial." *Journal of the American Medical Informatics Association* 13 (2): 171–79.

Elson, R. B., and D. P. Connelly. 1995. "Computerized Decision Support Systems in Primary Care." *Primary Care* 22 (2): 365–84.

Fenton, S. H., and L. D. Gamm. 2007. "Evaluation and Management Documentation and Coding Technology Adoption." *Perspectives in Health Information Management* 4: 7.

Ford, E. W., N. Menachemi, and M. T. Phillips. 2006. "Predicting the Adoption of Electronic Health Records by Physicians: When Will Health Care be Paperless?" *Journal of the American Medical Informatics Association* 13 (1): 106–12.

Garrett, P., A. Brown, S. Hart-Hester, E. Hamadain, C. Dixon, W. Pierce, and W. J. Rudman. 2006. "Identifying Barriers to the Adoption of New Technology in Rural Hospitals: A Case Report." *Perspectives in Health Information Management* 3: 9.

Hammond, W. E., and B. McCourt. 2007. "Making Sense of Standards." *Journal of AHIMA* 78 (8): 60–61.

Hersh, W. R., M. Helfand, J. Wallace, D. Kraemer, P. Patterson, S. Shapiro, and M. Greenlick. 2001. "Clinical Outcomes Resulting from Telemedicine Interventions: A Systematic Review." *BMC Medical Informatics and Decision Making* 1 (November): 5.

Huffman, E. K. 1972. *Medical Record Management.* Berwyn, IL: Physicians' Record Company.

Institute of Medicine (IOM). 1999. *To Err Is Human: Building a Safer Health System.* Washington, DC: National Academies Press.

———. 1997. *The Computer-Based Patient Record: An Essential Technology for Health Care,* revised ed. Washington, DC: National Academies Press.

———. 1991. *The Computer-Based Patient Record: An Essential Technology for Health Care.* Washington, DC: National Academies Press.

Kaushal, R., K. N. Barker, and D. W. Bates. 2001. "How Can Information Technology Improve Patient Safety and Reduce Medication Errors in Children's Health Care?" *Archives of Pediatric Adolescent Medicine* 155 (9): 1002–7.

Kiefe, C. I., J. J. Allison, O. D. Williams, S. D. Person, M. T. Weaver, and N. W. Weissman. 2001. "Improving Quality Improvement Using Achievable Benchmarks for Physician Feedback: A Randomized Controlled Trial." *Journal of the American Medical Association* 285 (22): 2871–79, 2921–22.

Leapfrog Group. 2007. "Computer Physician Order Entry Fact Sheet." [Online information; retrieved 2/8/07.] http://www.leapfroggroup.org/media/file/Leapfrog-Computer_Physician_Order_Entry_Fact_Sheet.pdf

Legnick-Hall, C. A., and M. L. Legnick-Hall. 2006. "HR, ERP, and Knowledge for Competitive Advantage." *Human Resource Management* 45 (2): 179–94.

Luccichenti, G., N. Ngo Dinh, F. Cademartiri, G. Evangelisti, A. Paolillo, and S. Bastianello. 2004. "Teleradiology System Accessible Through a Common Web Browser." *Radiologica Medica* 108 (5–6): 542–48.

Mair, F., and P. Whitten. 2000. "Systematic Review of Studies of Patient Satisfaction with Telemedicine." *British Medical Journal* 320: 1517–20.

Payne, T. H. 2000. "Computer Decision Support Systems." *Chest* 118: 47S–52S.

Poon, E. G., A. K. Jha, M. Christino, M. M. Honour, R. Fernandopulle, B. Middleton, J. Newhouse, L. Leape, D. W. Bates, D. Blumenthal, and R. Kaushal. 2006.

"Assessing the Level of Healthcare Information Technology Adoption in the United States: A Snapshot." *BMC Medical Informatics and Decision Making* 5 (6): 1.

Raths, D. 2006. "Making ERP Work: Healthcare Providers Are Taking a Closer Look at Enterprise Resource Planning." *Healthcare Informatics* 23 (6): 16.

Sandberg, L. 2000. "Managing Congestive Heart Failure with Telemedicine." *Health Management Technology* 21 (7).

Slovensky, D. J., J. M. Trimm, R. L. Garrie, and P. E. Paustian. 2006. *Information Management*, vol. 6 of the Medical Practice Management Body of Knowledge Review. Englewood, CO: Medical Group Management Association.

Smaltz, D. H., and E. S. Berner. 2006. *The Executive's Guide to Electronic Health Records*. Chicago: Health Administration Press.

Thakkar, M., and D. C. Davis. 2006. "Risks, Barriers, and Benefits of EHR Systems: A Comparative Study Based on Hospital Size." *Perspectives in Health Information Management* 3: 5.

Thompson, J. N. 2006. "The Future of Medical Licensure in the United States." *Academic Medicine* 91 (12) (Supplement): S36–S39.

University of Texas Medical Branch (UTMB). 2007. "UTMB Electronic Health Network." [Online information; retrieved 2/17/07.] http://www.digitalmedical services.com/EHN_Services.htm

Waegmann, C. 1996. "The Five Levels of Electronic Health Records." *MD Computing* 13 (3): 199–203.

Watson, H., R. Watson, S. Singh, and D. Holmes. 1995. "Development Practices for Executive Information Systems: Findings of a Field Study." *Decision Support Systems* 14: 171–84.

Woolf, S. H., and J. N. George. 2000. "Evidence-Based Medicine: Interpreting Studies and Setting Policy." *Hematology Oncology Clinics of North America* 14 (4): 761–84.

Xu, X. M., B. Lehaney, S. Clarke, and Y. Duan. 2003. "Some UK and USA Comparisons of Executive Information Systems in Practice and Theory." *Journal of End User Computing* 15 (1): 1–19.

Young, P. M., R. M. Leung, L. M. Ho, and S. M. McGhee. 2001. "An Evaluation of the Use of Hand-held Computers for Bedside Nursing Care." *International Journal of Medical Informatics* 62 (2–3): 189–93.

THE KNOWLEDGE-ENABLED ORGANIZATION

Learning Objectives

1. Describe the impact of knowledge on quality of care.
2. Articulate the differences between knowledge and information.
3. Define *sensemaking* and describe how it can be applied to healthcare organizations.
4. Define *knowledge management*.
5. Articulate what it means to "bake in" knowledge into organizational workflows, and provide some examples of how that is being done in the healthcare field.
6. List some reasons why healthcare organizations invest in enterprise data warehousing, data mining, and data analytics capabilities.

The Institute of Medicine (IOM 1999) suggests that each year up to 98,000 patients die as a direct result of errors made in the course of their care. Other more recent studies suggest that the actual number of deaths in the United States that are attributable to medical errors may be significantly higher (e.g., HealthGrades 2004). A key contributing cause of these errors, the IOM report concludes, is a lack of relevant information, and a follow-up IOM (2001) report specifically recommends significant investments in healthcare information technology to achieve its six goals of making healthcare safe, effective, patient centered, timely, efficient, and equitable.

Another factor is the exponential expansion of medical knowledge, making it virtually impossible for a physician to stay abreast of the latest medical information (AMA 2006). Finally, many physicians perceive that the impact of managed care practices has essentially limited the amount of time they spend with a patient and the amount of cognitive time they spend thinking about diagnoses and treatment options on any given patient (Morrison and Smith 2000).

These dynamics create increasing decision complexity, which affects what a caregiver notices and what a caregiver ignores. Weick (1995) notes that "information load is a complex mixture of the quantity, ambiguity, and variety of information that people are forced to process. As [information] load increases, people take increasingly strong steps to manage it. They begin with omission, and then move to greater tolerance of error, queuing, filtering, abstracting, using multiple channels, escape, and end with chunking." Weick's seminal work suggests that to adequately overcome complexity and information load, organizations must put in place deliberate systems of *sensemaking*—the ability to more accurately make sense of any given situation. Leading healthcare organizations are adopting sensemaking strategies to reduce medical errors and increase operational efficiency. Knowledge management principles and practices adopted in a sensemaking environment help optimize decision making with the limited time and ambiguous information available to contemporary providers (Middleton et al. 2004).

Knowledge Management

While a relatively new concept to healthcare delivery organizations, knowledge management is being successfully used by many other industries, particularly industries that gain from reusing knowledge (e.g., consulting firms) or quickly leveraging new discoveries into new products and services (e.g., manufacturing research and development). From Peter Senge's (1990) *The Fifth Discipline* to Nonaka and Takeuchi's (1995) *The Knowledge Creating Company* to Davenport and Prusak's (1998) *Working Knowledge*, ample resources are available to inform the healthcare field about the basics of knowledge management and how to apply its principles within a complex organizational setting. The key underlying tenet of the seminal knowledge management literature is that when individuals within organizations have the knowledge they need to be able to make decisions and accomplish their individual jobs, organizational efficiency and effectiveness are significantly improved. Often, however, they do not, and errors and suboptimal outcomes follow.

Knowledge management is the organizational practice of explicitly and deliberately building, renewing, and applying relevant intellectual assets to maximize an enterprise's effectiveness (Wiig 2000). Knowledge management practices seek to leverage as much of the information and knowledge that exists within and beyond an organization as possible. Smaltz and Cunningham (2005, 126) suggest that "this knowledge can either be in explicit form (such as in databases, spreadsheets, presentation slides, or documents or other media) or in tacit form (such as the 'know-how' in an individual's head). The task of knowledge managers is to explicitly and deliberately build the organizational processes and toolsets that bring this knowledge asset to bear on the thousands of daily tactical and strategic decisions that are made each day in a healthcare organization."

Building the Knowledge-Enabled Healthcare Organization

One mistake that many healthcare organizations make is that they expect to achieve better decision making, more efficient operations, and better healthcare outcomes by simply providing more and more data to caregivers and administrators. As noted from Weick (1995), such approaches merely increase the information load on caregivers, thereby making it more difficult to arrive at quality decisions. In response, leading healthcare organizations are taking systematic and deliberate steps to reduce the information load on caregivers by focusing attention on the data and information that truly matter in a given situation. They accomplish this primarily by using the following two practices:

1. "Baking in," or embedding, knowledge into clinical and administrative workflows (e.g., via alerts, reminders, evidence-based order sets, and "click through" capability to relevant medical literature and evidence)
2. Achieving excellence in data warehousing, data mining, and analytics (often evidenced through frontline patient safety dashboards, real-time process and outcomes reporting, and real-time feedback loops between patient care systems such as an electronic medical record and the organization's data warehouse)

Knowledge-Enabled Workflows

There are literally thousands of workflows in the typical twenty-first-century healthcare organization. Some examples of workflows include the process of admitting a patient to the hospital, a patient appointment in an outpatient clinic, or assessing a patient's condition in the emergency room. On the surface, these seem fairly innocuous examples, but consider the implications of missing information, too much information, or ambiguous information on any of these workflows. Being alerted that a patient is allergic to amoxicillin, is currently already taking a beta-blocker for an unrelated condition, or is epileptic can make a profound difference in the treatment plan initiated by the caregiver team, not to mention the patient outcome. Table 9.1 provides some examples of how healthcare organizations are baking in knowledge into their workflows to increase patient safety and ensure more quality outcomes for the services they provide.

While not infallible, the practice of placing relevant knowledge directly within the workflow creates an organizational system that will maximize quality decision making, reduce medical errors, and significantly increase the quality of care provided to patients (Bates et al. 1998; Berner and La Lande 2007).

Excellence in Data Warehousing, Data Mining, and Analytics

Contemporary healthcare organizations produce mass quantities of data often housed within siloed, transaction-based systems. For instance, within a typical hospital laboratory system sit vast quantities of test results; within a pharmacy system sit vast quantities of drug orders for various patients at various points in time; within an electronic medical record sits a growing body of text reports and notes describing signs, symptoms, and diagnoses for various patients.

TABLE 9.1
Baking In
Healthcare
Knowledge with
Workflow
Examples

Types of Baked-In Knowledge	Workflow Example
Alerts	Within an electronic medical record system, an alert is triggered when a provider orders for a patient a new drug that interacts negatively with another drug that either the physician has ordered previously or the patient is already taking.
Reminders	On a nursing unit, a nurse is reminded that a patient is due for another dose of a particular medication at a prescribed time.
Evidence	Within an electronic medical record system, the organization provides "click-through" capability to access relevant medical literature (often via an electronic subscription service) pertinent to the current patient situation.
Order sets	Within an electronic medical record system, physicians often place orders for various drugs or treatments. Creating order sets is the practice of prepopulating orders into groups that evidence has shown to be effective together; rather than having to place individual orders, a physician may select an entire order set.
Automatic billing codes	During an outpatient visit, evaluation and management codes are automatically generated to facilitate billing via information that the caregiver team annotates in the electronic medical record.

To aid organizational efforts to holistically assess patient outcomes, patient safety, and organizational efficiencies, these data must be aggregated into a data warehouse to facilitate analysis, thereby aiding continuous process improvement efforts. Smaltz and Cunningham (2005, 118) note that

> enterprise data warehouses essentially provide a homogeneous location for the data that heterogeneously resides in your various information systems. . . . The way an enterprise data warehouse typically functions is that data collected from the main transaction-based systems (appointing and scheduling, laboratory, pharmacy, and the like) is copied over to the data warehouse for use in organizational analyses and performance measurement activities. Once in the data warehouse, it serves as the one-stop shopping for management engineering studies, operations research studies, clinical process studies, and other decision support processes. Most recently, enterprise data warehouses have enabled the new field of data mining (large variable data set correlation and associative studies).

Figure 9.1 depicts a typical hospital data warehouse. Data from various source systems are acquired and transferred to the data warehouse. The data integration is accomplished via a process commonly known as extraction,

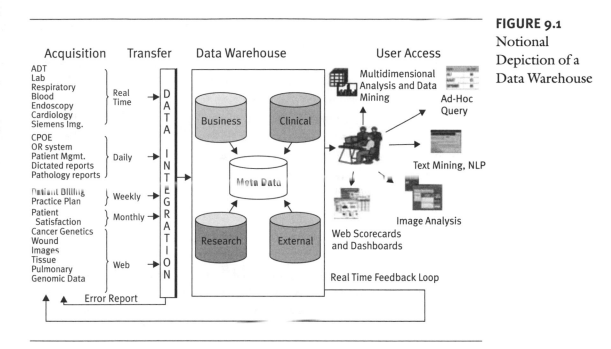

FIGURE 9.1
Notional
Depiction of a
Data Warehouse

transformation, and load (ETL). Because the data formats within the source systems on the left are often quite heterogeneous, the ETL process transforms the data into homogeneous data fields for ease of management and further analysis. When data quality errors are encountered during the extraction and transformation stages, action is taken to improve the data quality within the source system, as opposed to within the data warehouse itself. The actual data warehouse may be organized into logical groups of data marts. A data mart is a logical subset of the data that resides within a data warehouse, often organized into logical groupings. In this example, the data warehouse is made up of business, clinical, research, and external (benchmarking) data marts.

The organization benefits from the data warehouse by being able to accomplish a variety of data queries and multidimensional analyses and can support management dashboards and scorecards designed to focus organizational attention on metrics-driven approaches to improvement. Pioneering healthcare organizations are also creating real-time feedback loops whereby novel groupings of data from the data warehouse are fed back into source systems (often via web portals) to facilitate real-time quality improvements.

Smaltz and Cunningham (2005, 115) note that

> most organizations would agree that realization of investments in IM/IT fall[s] short when attempting to truly assess population health, to manage disease processes within that population, to analyze variation in practice patterns among physicians, to determine the efficacy of long-term health promotion programs, to gauge the benefit of outsourcing to other healthcare providers, or, in some cases, to gain a true picture of their own organizations' performance in spite of

the mounds of data available to do so. Interestingly, the IT functionality (for the most part) currently exists to create these capabilities. However, responsibility for ensuring that the IT assets are used effectively and efficiently has primarily fallen on users who, in general, know little about the systems or their full capabilities (beyond what they need to know to accomplish transactions within their responsibility), making it impossible to achieve full realization of IT benefits. While some might call for more training or for vendors to make information systems easier to use (which certainly is beneficial), *organizations cannot avoid investing in people, processes and capabilities that are expressly focused on leveraging enterprise-wide data, information and knowledge . . . if they want to truly achieve and sustain superior clinical and business results.*

Healthcare delivery organizations are increasingly adding transaction based applications, such as electronic health records systems, with the potential to create large volumes of data (Smaltz and Berner 2007). When they make these investment decisions, they also typically ensure that they invest in the requisite people and process redesign to gain full benefit from the applications that they implement. Ironically, our anecdotal observations suggest that few healthcare delivery organizations are adequately investing in the people and processes needed to leverage the data these systems create. As healthcare delivery organization profit margins continue to be challenged by increasingly difficult reimbursement mechanisms, data warehousing, data mining, and analytics will increasingly become vital in efforts to analyze business and clinical processes and outcomes and to maximize efficiencies and effectiveness.

Summary

Medical knowledge is increasing at a rate impossible for physicians and caregivers to comprehend and retain. Furthermore, physicians and caregivers are often faced with limited time to make clinical decisions with imperfect information about their patients. The practice of knowledge management attempts to systematically and deliberately take steps to reduce the information load on physicians and caregivers by focusing attention on the data and information that truly matter in a given situation. Knowledge management also attempts to create organizational competencies that leverage the hordes of data produced from the myriad of healthcare applications. Healthcare delivery organizations' knowledge management foci are typically in two key areas:

1. Baking in knowledge into clinical and administrative workflows
2. Excellence in data warehousing, data mining, and data analytics

While quality in the delivery of healthcare has been highlighted as a systemic problem within the U.S. healthcare system, organizations can, at least in part, overcome such systemic problems by investing in resources focused on building a knowledge-enabled organization. Gartner, Inc. suggests that data integration, management, and access will be the single greatest source of competitive advantage for life science organizations (Helfrish 2002). Healthcare organizations would be well served to invest more resources focused on creating a knowledge-enabling core competency.

Web Resources

Resources available on the web for concepts presented in this chapter include the following:

- Brint Institute's index of knowledge management sources, http://www.brint.com/km/
- Google Scholar index of knowledge management articles, http://scholar.google.com/scholar?hl=en&q=Knowledge%20Management
- Healthcare Information and Management Systems Society Knowledge, Management Special Interest Group, http://www.himss.org/ASP/sigs_knowledge.asp
- *Inside Knowledge* magazine, http://www.kmmagazine.com
- eKnowledge Center, http://www.eknowledgecenter.com/
- Knowledge Management Professional Society (KMPro), http://kmpro.org/

Discussion Questions

1. What is the impact of knowledge on quality of care?
2. What, if any, are the major differences between knowledge and information?
3. What is *sensemaking*, and how can it be applied to healthcare organizations?
4. Define knowledge management.
5. What does it mean to bake in knowledge into organizational workflows?
6. What are some of the ways that knowledge can be baked into information technology–enabled workflows?
7. Why should an organization invest in enterprise data warehousing, data mining, and data analytics capabilities?

References

American Medical Association (AMA). 2006. *Preliminary Report on the American Medical Association Initiative to Transform Medical Education.* [Online report; retrieved 6/28/07.] http://www.ama-assn.org/ama1/pub/upload/mm/377/2006results.pdf

Bates, D., L. Leape, D. Cullen, N. Laird, L. Petersen, J. Teich, E. Burdick, M. Hickey, S. Kleefield, B. Shea, M. Vander Vliet, and D. Seger. 1998. "Effect of Computerized Physician Order Entry and a Team Intervention on Prevention of

Serious Medication Errors." *Journal of the American Medical Association* 280 (15): 1311–16.

Berner, E., and T. La Lande. 2007. "Overview of Clinical Decision Support Systems." In *Clinical Decision Support Systems*, 2nd ed., edited by E. Berner. New York: Springer.

Davenport, T., and L. Prusak. 1998. *Working Knowledge*. Boston: Harvard Business School Press.

HealthGrades. 2004. "HealthGrades Quality Study: Patient Safety in American Hospitals." [Online article; retrieved 1/4/08.] http://www.healthgrades.com/media/english/pdf/HG_Patient_Safety_Study_Final.pdf

Helfrish, J. 2002. "A Data Management Foundation Strategy for Drug Discovery Through Manufacturing in the Biopharmaceutical Industry." *American Laboratory* (September): 20–23.

Institute of Medicine (IOM). 2001. *Crossing the Quality Chasm: A New Health System for the 21st Century*. Washington, DC: National Academies Press.

———. 1999. *To Err Is Human: Building a Safer Health System*. Washington, DC: National Academies Press.

Middleton, B., G. Christopherson, R. Rocha, and D. Smaltz. 2004. "Knowledge Management in Clinical Systems: Principles and Pragmatics." Paper presented at the International Medical Informatics Association Medinfo 2004 conference, San Francisco, September 11.

Morrison, I., and R. Smith. 2000. "Hamster Health Care: Time to Stop Running Faster and Redesign Health Care." *British Medical Journal* 321: 1541–42.

Nonaka, I., and H. Takeuchi. 1995. *The Knowledge Creating Company*. Oxford, UK: Oxford University Press.

Senge, P. 1990. *The Fifth Discipline: The Art & Practice of the Learning Organization*. New York: Doubleday.

Smaltz, D., and E. Berner. 2007. *The Executive's Guide to Electronic Health Records*. Chicago: Health Administration Press.

Smaltz, D., and T. Cunningham III. 2005. "Data Rich, Information Poor: Building a Knowledge-Enabled Organization." In *The CEO-CIO Partnership: Harnessing the Value of Information Technology in Healthcare*, edited by D. Smaltz, J. Glaser, R. Skinner, and T. Cunningham III. Chicago: Healthcare Information and Management Systems Society.

Weick, K. 1995. *Sensemaking in Organizations*. Thousand Oaks, CA: Sage Publications.

Wiig, K. 2000. "Knowledge Management: An Emerging Discipline Rooted in a Long History." In *Knowledge Horizons: The Present and the Promise of Knowledge Management*, edited by C. Depres and D. Chauvel. Woburn, MA: Butterworth-Heinemann.

IM/IT VALUE

Learning Objectives

1. Specify why making information management/information technology (IM/IT) investment decisions based upon realized value rather than upon "anecdote, inference, and opinion" leads to better outcomes.
2. Describe five changes that make today's IM/IT investment decisions more challenging than in the past.
3. Provide examples of IM/IT costs and outcomes changes that will "always" be adopted and examples that will "never" be adopted.
4. Analyze how the major techniques used for evaluation of IM/IT investment differ.
5. List the eight key steps in cost evaluation.
6. Analyze why certain types of IM/IT applications are less likely to be performed.
7. Describe value realization and total cost of ownership methodologies.

Up to this point in the book, the discussions surrounding healthcare information management/information technology (IM/IT) have explicitly recognized that the organization, financing, and delivery of healthcare services are different from other goods and services. While the authors consider this to be fundamentally true, some aspects of healthcare, and especially healthcare IM/IT, should adhere to core business processes. IM/IT can be considered an input into the "production" process just as are inputs of nursing time, allied health staff, medical supplies, and physician services. In that context, the decisions regarding how much and what type of IM/IT inputs to use should fall under a valuation paradigm. Johnston, Pan, and Middleton (2002) make this point strongly in their argument for finding value from healthcare information technologies.

Firmly establishing value in many healthcare investments has proven to be a challenge, however. Clinical technologies have increasingly been subject to critical valuation, or benefits received relative to costs incurred, and this notion has taken hold for IM/IT as well (Board 2004; Miller et al. 2005; Wiley and Daniel 2006). Issues related to data collection, methodology, and application make the realization of value from and widespread use of evidence-based management a challenge. The health economics literature is replete with methodologies of cost, cost-benefit, and cost-effectiveness analysis and quality-adjusted life years (Chaudhry et al. 2006; Gold et al. 1996; Rahimi and Vimarlund 2007; Shekelle, Morton, and Keeler 2006; Simon and Simon 2006; Warner and Luce 1982). Most of these studies involve developing the methodology for assessing complex medical applications, and only a few are applied. In addition, large organizations have become sources for clinical intervention evaluations (see University HealthSystem Consortium at www.uhc.edu or Blue Cross and Blue Shield Technology Evaluation Center at www.bcbs.com/betterknowledge/tec/). Surprisingly, only a few studies look specifically at IM/IT interventions (Chaudhry et al. 2006; Rahimi and Vimarlund 2007; Shekelle, Morton, and Keeler 2006; Simon and Simon 2006). Some very dated studies still serve the literature well (Glandon and Shapiro 1988). The Center for Information Technology Leadership (www.citl.org) now serves as one of the sources of information regarding IM/IT value.

Because of the complexity of the problem and the lack of comprehensive data, healthcare executives have largely been forced to make decisions about IM/IT investments based on cursory evidence at best, and occasionally based on instinct or hope at worst. In the words of Johnston, Pan, and Middleton (2002), IM/IT decisions are often based upon "anecdote, inference, and opinion." Inevitably, this approach produces decisions that may not yield the hoped-for benefits. As a result, health IM/IT may fall short in addressing the problems plaguing healthcare.

As organizations struggle to meet patient and community health needs and improve quality with increasingly tight budgets, performing strict value assessment of all investments has become increasingly important. To give some idea of the magnitude of the issue at an individual hospital level, according to an American Hospital Association (AHA 2007) survey, in 2006, the median hospital spent $5,556 per bed for health information technology capital and $12,060 for operating costs of health information technology. This translates to more than $1 million in capital expenditures for a 200-bed hospital and nearly $2.5 million in operating costs. Among the hospitals responding to the survey, 54 percent reported that capital costs were a significant barrier to information technology adoption, and 32 percent reported that operating costs were a significant barrier to adoption. Financial barriers exceeded interoperability, acceptability by clinical staff, availability of qualified staff, and inadequate technology in importance as perceived barriers to adoption.

As the government and competitive pressures induce care delivery organizations to implement interoperable electronic health records (EHRs) that enable the exchange of information within and across institutions, these organizations must still focus on value creation. Early evidence indicates that the financial benefits of interoperable EHRs to the healthcare system may be substantial. Walker and colleagues (2005) estimate that healthcare information exchange and interoperability (HIEI) may generate upwards of $77 billion in savings to the U.S. healthcare system once fully implemented. Providers will come to expect electronic information exchange. They increasingly work in healthcare delivery teams consisting of physicians, nurses, pharmacists, therapists, and others who require a real-time exchange of information. Finally, consumers will demand new delivery modes for their care and expect coordination of care across provider segments. Consequently, the ability to assess value will be crucial for the IM/IT leader of the future, and information technology will play a vital role in that value delivery.

This chapter first outlines why the evaluation problem is more complex today because of the systems nature of healthcare delivery. It then presents what is known about how IM/IT investments are analyzed and provides a framework for conducting these analyses. Next, it details value realization as a method to implement evaluation, and it ends with selected findings from cost evaluation studies.

Systems Challenges

Despite these costs, at one level, healthcare information technology is essential for the provision of high-quality care in today's environment. However, technology acquisition is not an all-or-nothing proposition. Questions of scale, scope, application, integration, and timing must be addressed, all of which make the decision complex. Do you wait another year? Do you purchase and install some applications and not others? How do you ensure that the appropriate mix of information technologies is selected? Furthermore, once that set of decisions is made, how do you implement so that costs stay at the expected level and the benefits promised are actually realized? In the face of these questions, some have come to challenge the wisdom of assumed value, and even benefits of healthcare IM/IT investments (Carr 2003; Koppel 2005; Koppel et al. 2005; Loomis et al. 2002).

If these considerations did not make this problem difficult enough, the interdependence of providers in a healthcare "system" complicates the decision further. As detailed in Chapter 1, problems of cost, quality, and access plague those responsible for healthcare delivery. In a general discussion regarding the transformation of the U.S. healthcare system, Adams and colleagues (2007) identify the following five features that make today's challenges different from challenges in the past:

1. Globalization
2. Consumerism
3. Aging and overweight populations
4. Diseases that are more expensive to treat
5. New medical technologies and treatments

To respond successfully to these challenges, Adams and colleagues argue that value decisions must extend beyond individual organizational considerations to the perspective of society as a whole. For example, medical tourism will become common as the financial incentives for care delivered outside of the United States will eventually drive select care overseas (see Table 10.1).

Their recommendations for successful transformation of the healthcare system include many features, but most important, they argue that there will be different perspectives on value. The U.S. healthcare system will transform from one that emphasizes individual value and cost containment to one with an emphasis on balancing "stakeholder value across dimensions (cost, quality, access and choice)" (Adams et al. 2007, 42). The latter emphasis will usher in a transformation from the current state of data management to electronic, evidence-based, standard, shared and interoperable information (Adams et al. 2007). Similarly, Enthoven and Tollen (2005) make the point that to address cost and quality concerns, rather than introduce competition to the healthcare market, healthcare organizations need to consider moving away from market changes that foster independent competing business units. To capture potential cost savings and quality improvements, in their opinion, the U.S. government should encourage organizations within local and regional markets to form "integrated delivery systems, with incentives for teams of professionals to provide coordinated, efficient, evidence-based care, supported by state-of-the-art information technology" (Enthoven and Tollen 2005, 420).

Evaluation Problem

At the most fundamental level, business decisions faced by the chief information officer (CIO), and indirectly by the chief executive officer (CEO) and board of trustees, come down to a challenge of deciding among competing alternatives. The questions they must ask are, does the investment in IM/IT increase, have no effect, or decrease organizational outcomes, and does it increase, have no effect, or decrease costs to the organization?

TABLE 10.1
Cost of Key Procedures in Six Countries

Procedure	United States	Mexico	Costa Rica	India	Thailand	Singapore
Angioplasty	$33,000	$13,125	$14,500	$7,800	$9,200	$12,500
Heart bypass	$37,000	$14,400	$13,600	$6,650	$11,000	$13,500
Hip replacement	$45,000	$9,400	$13,000	$6,500	$8,000	$9,000
Knee replacement	$21,000	$10,500	$9,500	$6,500	$8,500	$10,000
Laparoscopic hysterectomy	$19,000	$4,275	$6,500	$2,238	$4,500	$4,500
Laparoscopic prostatectomy	$27,500	$16,800	$11,500	$5,900	$9,500	$16,000

Source: Adams et al. (2007). Reprint courtesy of International Business Machines Corporation, copyright 2006 © International Business Machines Corporation.

Table 10.2 presents a simple paradigm from which decisions can be made. The matrix consists of nine cells, or potential outcome/cost combinations, and, in some cells, the decision to adopt the technology or not to adopt it is straightforward. For example, if adopting the technology results in a reduction in outcomes and at the same time an increase in costs (cell 3), most CIOs will never adopt. Similarly, if outcomes improve with the new technology and costs are reduced (scenario 7), the decision to adopt is straightforward (always). Combinations of costs and outcomes that place the organization in scenarios 2, 3, or 6 are never adopted. Similarly, combinations of costs and outcomes that place the organization in scenarios 4, 7, or 8 are always adopted.

The interesting cases involve combinations of costs and outcomes that place the organization on the diagonal in scenarios 1, 5, or 9. For these cases, a methodology must be put in place to more rigorously measure the magnitude of the changes in outcomes and the magnitude of the changes in costs. Formal benefit-cost or cost-effectiveness analyses need to be applied to assess the relative changes for these three cases: both outcomes and costs increase, neither benefits nor costs change, and both benefits and costs decrease.

Benefit-Cost and Cost-Effectiveness Analyses

A number of studies have documented the use of conventional benefit-cost, cost-effectiveness, or cost-utility analysis in healthcare (e.g., Gold et al. 1996). The discussions that follow are not significantly concerned with differentiating among these techniques. A full history of the concepts is beyond the scope of this book. In simple terms, *benefit-cost analyses* are applied when all aspects of the costs related to a technology and benefits of that technology are measured in monetary terms. The outcome from these analyses might be presented as $3 in benefits for every $1 in cost ($3/$1). The decision calculus then enables leadership to select among alternatives that have the highest ratio.

For many healthcare applications, some of the outcomes or benefits may be difficult or objectionable to put into financial terms. Loss of life, for example, can be quantified in financial terms (Viscusi 2004), but not everyone is comfortable making those assessments. *Cost-effectiveness analyses* were developed for technologies that resulted in outcomes that could not

Cost	Outcome Effect		
	Improve	No Change	Worsen
Increase	1 ?????	2 Never	3 Never
No change	4 Always	5 ?????	6 Never
Decrease	7 Always	8 Always	9 ?????

TABLE 10.2
Technology Cost and Outcome Effect Decision Matrix

be quantified (Weinstein and Stason 1977). In this case, one might estimate the costs associated with extending life for an additional year. The outcome from these analyses might be presented as $10,000 cost per life year saved ($10,000/life year). In this case, considering alternative technologies, leadership would adopt the technology with the *lowest* cost per life year saved.

Cost-utility analysis extends this measurement challenge even further by recognizing that the quality of life year extended might not always be the same. That realization led to a host of attempts to adjust the life years saved by some notion of the utility, value, or quality of that life (see, e.g., the Centers for Disease Control and Prevention website on quality of life measurement and findings at www.cdc.gov/hrqol/index.htm).

For example, if the outcome was an additional year of life, but that year was spent by the patient in pain or confined to a nursing home bed, the value of that life year might not be as great as nine months of pain-free or fully functional extended life.

The key to using any of these formal methods of cost evaluation involves a series of eight steps (see Glandon and Shapiro 1988; Gold et al. 1996; Warner and Luce 1982).

Steps in Using Methods of Cost Evaluation

Step 1: Identify study objectives. While this step may be obvious to many, clearly identifying study objectives may be the most important step in the analysis. Without knowing precisely what the organization desires or what the proposed IM/IT application or technology is designed to do, the outcomes of the evaluation will be meaningless. At a fundamental level, the decision comes down to whether the organization is looking narrowly at the financial benefits and costs associated with the decision or whether it is considering broader organizational or social benefits and costs. From the perspective of information technology, social costs might include those incurred by physicians or others who are not employees of the organization but who matter to decision makers. An otherwise strong IM/IT system may fail if the burden on the users is not fully measured.

Step 2: Specify alternatives. The relevant alternatives to the proposed technology must be clearly articulated; otherwise, a valid decision cannot be attained. Make the decision relative to the best alternative to ensure that the optimal choice is made. Not using credible alternatives in judging the proposed technology risks participants losing faith in the outcomes. A common error is to compare a proposed IM/IT solution with the status quo. The status quo is often not relevant when adopting an EHR, for example. Comparisons should be required among alternative vendors rather than the current state of health record management.

Step 3: Develop a framework for analysis. This is often called the theoretical framework or model, and one might have a tendency to ignore it. Developing the framework is important, however, because it puts the technology into the broader systems context and defines how the inputs to the technology are related and how the outcomes are used by the system. Developing the framework forces you to understand how the technology affects the total healthcare delivery system so that the direct and indirect (unintended consequences) costs and benefits to your system can be clearly identified and measured (Han et al. 2005). Returning to the EHR example, the framework for analysis forces a full understanding of the information flow from the bedside or the physician's office to the electronic record, of how that information is stored, catalogued, and retrieved from the record, and of what its end uses are designed to be. Without that full understanding, crucial components of costs and benefits might be ignored or shortchanged.

Step 4: Measure costs. Cost assessment is essential to the benefit-cost analysis. While identification and measurement of costs is relatively straightforward for big-ticket items such as direct labor, equipment, and supplies, fully identifying indirect or opportunity costs associated with the intervention takes more time. The concept of *total cost of ownership* is an operational device designed to aid in defining and collecting relevant startup (one time) and recurring costs (Smaltz and Berner 2006; Hickman and Kusche 2006). The EHR might shift some of the burden of data collection, analysis, and reporting. Unless that added burden results in easily measurable increases in time or supply use, it can often be overlooked. Management, in particular, can easily be affected by added data availability. The electronic record facilitates more analysis in an attempt to make better evidence-based decisions. While this may result in benefits associated with better decision making, it may also result in added time spent understanding the data that are generated. Managers may find they spend more time preparing and poring over reports at the expense of other tasks.

Step 5: Measure benefits. As with cost identification, good evaluation requires clear identification of all benefits associated with the technology. Ignoring key benefits can clearly lead to underestimating the net effect of technology. Johnston, Pan, and Middleton (2002) argue that many researchers take a narrow view of benefits, or, in their term, *health information technology (HIT) value.* They argue one should consider organizational, financial, and clinical benefits. Identifying these benefits is facilitated if the framework for analysis is done correctly. A related issue with regard to benefits is that they must be realized and not necessarily speculative, assumed, or hypothetical.

Step 6: Factor in lifecycle and discounting. Most IM/IT projects have a pattern of costs and benefits that vary over the product's lifecycle. Typically, costs are incurred early in a project cycle as resources are expended to purchase equipment, hire staff, and train staff. Conversely, the benefits or value to the organization accrue over time. Understanding that cycle with respect to the organization's technology is important for making valid comparisons. Although the CIO or IM/IT decision maker may not be as concerned with the timing issue as others in the healthcare organization, the timing of incurred benefits and costs cannot be ignored. In fact, considering alternatives with the same net costs and benefits, one should select that project with the distribution of costs skewed toward the future rather than that project with the distribution of benefits skewed toward the present.

Step 7: Deal with uncertainty. By the nature of IM/IT investments, uncertainty exists regarding the estimates of both their costs and their value or benefits. Despite leadership's best efforts, they may find that these estimates are inaccurate. For example, with the EHR, physicians may not readily adopt the new technologies and systems as planned. In these cases, the costs of developing and implementing the system would be the same, but the measured benefits will be much lower. One would never assume exceedingly high levels of avoidance by the medical staff. If physicians do not adopt, the evaluation of the EHR would most likely appear unsatisfactory. To deal with uncertainty, most will look at the estimates being used and develop a best-case and worst-case scenario. For example, in the EHR example, you are assuming benefits with 80 percent of your medical staff fully participating. To test best case, you might estimate benefits with 90 percent medical staff participation (base estimate + 10 percent). You would then test worst case by estimating benefits with 70 percent medical staff participation (base estimate − 10 percent). This process is often called *sensitivity analysis*. If performing this approach to dealing with uncertainty yields estimates that do not change your overall evaluation of the technology, you have added confidence to your decision. If you find that at extreme values your overall evaluation of the technology changes, you might want to return to your framework and your assumptions to be certain they are accurate.

Step 8: Consider equity. This step has its origins in the federal government's use of benefit-cost analysis for evaluating alternative government interventions. However, it has application to individual healthcare organizations as well. Equity considerations require examination of not just what the costs and benefits are for the organization but also who receives those benefits and costs. Again from the perspective of the EHR, if the benefits accrue to the institution, its employees, and its patients, but the costs are largely borne by those involved in using the technology (physicians), the EHR strategy is likely to fail (Landro 2003). For social investment decisions, you might consider compensating those bearing the costs from the gains made in the use of the technology. Healthcare organizations have no way available to compensate cost bearers, and legal restrictions may limit their compensation.

Challenges to Evaluation

Despite the prevalence of IM/IT mechanisms in place in healthcare organizations, much evidence exists that IM/IT value is not easy to attain or ensure. Early assessments of the "state of the art" (Glandon and Shapiro 1988) suggested that more work was needed in this area. High-profile failures occurred, such as Cedars-Sinai Medical Center in Los Angeles ending its effort to convert to a computerized physician order entry (CPOE) system in January 2003

(Chin 2003). The cause of this extreme failure is uncertain. Failure most probably occurs at the implementation stage, although failure of that magnitude may have had many causes.

In the late 1980s, some key findings on reasons for poor evaluations of technology suggest why IM/IT value does not always ensue from these significant investments. First, much of the technology was found to be selected for the wrong reasons, such as keeping up with the competition. While there might be good reasons to adopt technology that your competition is using, that alone is not sufficient reason to implement an information technology system or application. Second, knowledge, time, and money may prohibit adequate evaluation. The CIO and his or her managers just may have been too busy to spend the time conducting evaluations to determine value from the investment. Finally, in many cases, the technology in place was determined to be a poor decision, which might help in future decisions but will have no impact on the original decision going forward. This "water under the bridge" argument might keep leaders who are living in the past from investigating prior failures seriously (Glandon and Shapiro 1988).

Related to these items are the following two fundamental impediments to maximizing IM/IT value:

1. *Documentation.* The comprehensive, reliable data on the clinical or business outcomes related to the technology and the true, full costs associated with selecting, purchasing, implementing, hiring staff, training staff, training users, and so forth, are difficulty to obtain, synthesize, and report. It takes time and money to determine if the value from your IM/IT investments actually exists. More on this issue, called the total cost of ownership, is presented in the next section.
2. *Interdependence.* Even if data have been defined and collected, the pervasive nature of the influence of many IM/IT investments across functional areas in the organization makes determination of value difficult at best. Many systems have both direct and indirect cost and outcome effects across a wide number of portions of the organization; thus, assigning value to a particular investment is a major undertaking.

Glandon and Buck (1994) identified these fundamental challenges to effectively maximize value from IM/IT investments. They developed a model of information systems that separates application and function (see Table 10.3) and suggest where more rigorous evaluation might exist.

Assessing and ensuring value at the *operational level* has the greatest chance of success. Investments to improve Admissions, Discharge and Transfer (ADT) or general ledger applications have a greater chance of clearly linking the technology change to a measurable outcome. The well-defined and limited scope of such application reduces the severity of the measurement challenges. Outcomes at the operational level are generally characterized as

TABLE 10.3	Information Requirement	Function	
Information Systems by Function and Information Requirement		Clinical	Business
	External systems	Physician recruitment and retention Contracting	Legal actions Cost containment
	Administrative systems	Case mix Incomplete chart reporting Care planning patient scheduling	Absence and turnover control Revenue statistics Wage and salary planning Capital spending
	Operational systems	Admission, discharge, and transfer Census reporting	Inventory control General ledger Accounts payable

Source: Adapted from Glandon and Buck (1994). Used with permission.

intermediate compared to outcomes of the healthcare organization as a whole. For example, ADT outcomes might include time to admit a patient to a bed from the emergency department as an intermediate outcome. This outcome may depend upon the ADT system, but ultimate outcome of patient mortality, morbidity, or satisfaction is less likely to be influenced by the ADT system.

Investments applied to *administrative systems* are less clear in terms of value assessment. These systems influence the efficiency and effectiveness of institutional operations and often contain some of the quantifiable elements inherent in operational systems. However, they often apply to cross-functional areas within the organization, making their impact more difficult to quantify. In administrative systems, then, it is less clear than in operational-level systems that outcomes, benefits, and costs are attributable to the new technology. Outcomes for administrative systems are generally intermediate, as are the outcomes for operational applications, but should apply more broadly than operational systems. For example, systems designed to improve incomplete chart reporting can have somewhat measurable outcomes, such as delinquent report rates. This outcome has broader impact because medical staff, nursing, ancillary systems, as well as quality assurance and accreditation preparation, all bear costs or benefit from changes in this outcome.

Finally, investments applied to *strategic planning* have the greatest difficulty with respect to value determination. All of the inputs used in these systems are cross functional, which implies that data must be gathered from diverse units across the institution and often from outside of the institution. Outcomes are generally final from the perspective of the healthcare organization as a whole; thus, they are very difficult to measure, and attribution is always a challenge. For example, systems to support physician recruitment might be expected to lead to greater market share and improved physician retention. However, many external factors influence these outcomes, leading to greater uncertainty with respect to the value of this type of IM/IT investment. For example, you might have improved physician recruitment by operating a well-functioning system. However, your market share and physician retention may suffer because a specialty hospital moved into your market and siphoned off key physicians and associated patients. The outcomes are poor from the organization's perspective.

Probably the best example of this type of challenge is with the introduction of the EHR strategy. Smaltz and Berner (2006) outline the interrelated nature of benefits and challenges the EHR system faces. Because EHR is not a thing but a comprehensive strategy, it is difficult to value. It is an "organizational, cultural transformation project that just happens to have a technology component" (Smaltz and Berner 2006, 16). Examination of just the benefits section of an EHR strategy described by these authors reveals how investment in this process spans the organization and creates difficulties in financial documentation. The descriptions in Table 10.4 by major benefit category and subcategory demonstrate that benefits are not confined to a single operational unit.

Value Realization

The IT Governance Institute (2006, 5) developed a multipart initiative to support IM/IT value realization in response to a perceived need for "organizations to optimize the realisation of value" from investments. The comprehensive framework assists users in measuring, monitoring, and maximizing

TABLE 10.4 Descriptions of EHR Benefits by Category: Demonstration of System Nature of EHR

Category	Subcategory	Description Example of Impact
Improve efficiency		Improve efficiency of the clinical patient care–related processes
	Access to information	Getting information when and where it is needed
	Organization of the data	Patient data entered one time
	Claims processing	By allowing the clinical data to drive billing processes
Improve monitoring		Enables individual provider profiles of performance as well as aggregate profiles
Improve clinical processes		Real-time clinical decision support
	Quality improvement	Clinical and financial outcomes can be more easily monitored and linked
	Disease management	Aggregate data across patients

Source: Smaltz and Berner (2006).

realized value from IM/IT investments. Rather than a simple "cookbook" approach, this framework employs a holistic approach to value realization. While not fundamentally different from the benefit-cost analysis and cost-effectiveness analysis methodologies described above, this framework is more attuned to practicing IM/IT leadership decision making.

The IT Governance Institute approach starts by asking the following four questions, posed originally by Thorp (2003):

1. *Strategic Question: Are we doing the right thing?* Is the investment aligned with our broader business vision, is it consistent with our principles, and does it contribute to our strategic objectives?
2. *Architecture Question: Are we doing it the right way?* Is the investment aligned with our information technology architecture and consistent with our architecture principles?
3. *Value Question: Are we getting the benefits?* Do we have a clear understanding of the expected benefits, and do we have a process for realizing the benefits?
4. *Delivery Question: Are we getting it done the right way?* Do we have effective and disciplined management, delivery, and change management processes with technical and business resources to deliver the promise of the technology investment?

In the context of these four questions, the institute uses a three-part strategy to maximize return on IM/IT investment (the first two elements are developed in detail in earlier chapters of this book, and the third is discussed below):

1. *Value governance.* Optimizes the value of an organization's information technology–enabled investments by establishing the governance, monitoring, and control framework; providing strategic direction for the investments; and defining the investment portfolio characteristics (see Chapter 3, "IM/IT Governance and Decision Rights")
2. *Portfolio management.* Ensures that an organization's overall portfolio of information technology–enabled investments is aligned with and contributing optimal value to its strategic objectives by establishing and managing resource profiles, defining investment thresholds, evaluating and prioritizing new investments, managing the overall portfolio, and monitoring and reporting on portfolio performance (see Chapter 4, "The IM/IT Portfolio Management Office")
3. *Investment management.* Ensures that IM/IT investments deliver outcomes at reasonable costs while also managing associated risk.

To accomplish the investment management aspect of obtaining a return on IM/IT investment, the IT Governance Institute proposes that the organization engage in an eight-step process. In this framework, implementing the investment management process requires detailed information gathering; assessment of benefits, costs, and risks; selecting the investment vehicle; and monitoring outcomes. This process is geared to the corporate environment, as opposed to the government or social perspective detailed above. Figure 10.1, taken from the IT Governance Institute (2006), outlines these eight steps.

1. Building the Fact Sheet

The first step in the process is to gather all of the information relevant for making the appropriate IM/IT business decision. The IT Governance Institute provides a model form for collecting the necessary data, but the experience of the authors suggests that each organization should implement a collection form that works in its environment. The key point is that no category of information can be ignored. At a minimum, the following categories of information need to be assembled (IT Governance equivalent terms are given in parentheses):

- *Congruence (Alignment).* The investment must be consistent with documented business strategy (see Chapter 3), current IM/IT management practices, and government regulatory constraints (current and anticipated).
- *Business outcomes.* The investment must deliver an organizational need to achieve intermediate and final outcomes. These outcomes need to be documented and measurable.
- *Financial benefits.* Input for financial benefits should document cost saving, revenue enhancements, capacity/volume growth, or risk mitigation deriving from the investment decision. These include the tangible revenue enhancements or cost reductions in capital, operations, or risk.
- *Indirect benefits (Nonfinancial benefits).* As in the benefit-cost assessment discussed above, some benefits are not easily quantified in financial terms, but must be seriously considered nonetheless.
- *Costs (Resources and expenditures).* All categories of equipment, human resources, supplies, consultants, and other resources necessary for this IM/IT investment must be documented.
- *Sensitivity (Risk).* Alternatives that quantify the risk in the investment must be identified. Understanding the best-case and worst-case scenarios for the investment helps the organization select an investment that meets its tolerance for risk.
- *Model (Assumptions and constraints).* Understanding how the IM/IT investment will accomplish the desired outcomes, with associated benefits and costs, helps to determine the reasonableness of the subsequent analyses. The logic of the empirical claims for outcomes, benefits, and costs depends crucially on the assumptions employed. These must be articulated clearly.

FIGURE 10.1

Steps in Information Technology Business Case Development

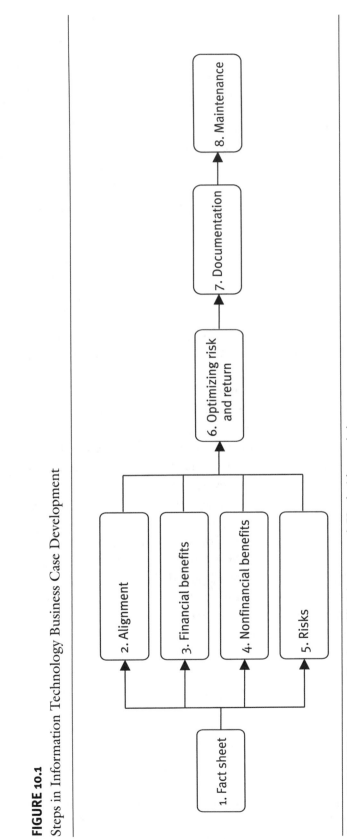

2. Alignment Analysis

Investment alternatives abound, necessitating decision making. The selected option needs to optimize net benefits from the scarce resources available. Alignment helps to ensure that the IM/IT-related investments support the organization's strategic business objectives. This might include direct contribution to the objectives of the current organization or to the broader system or contribution to a future vision for the organization. The investment must also be consistent with existing enterprise architecture. Assuming that this architecture has been selected as a guideline to achieve the current vision, each investment must be chosen carefully so as not to move away from that guideline.

3. Financial Analysis

To gain acceptance in the healthcare corporate environment, IM/IT investments must pass conventional financial analysis constraints. Discounting of financial benefits and costs is an essential technique. The final decision will require the project to have a positive discounted net value (positive net present value, or NPV) and perhaps have better NPV than alternative investments so that the organization selects the best investment.

4. Nonfinancial Benefit Analysis

The nonfinancial aspects of business processes must also be considered, especially in not-for-profit healthcare organizations. Building positive relations with constituencies external to the IM/IT function may create value for the organization. Alternatively, negative relations can destroy value. Consideration of the external or indirect effects of the investment may not fully offset poor financial considerations but may influence a decision that is otherwise close.

5. Risk Analysis

Not every organization tolerates risk in the same way, and not all investment opportunities carry the same risks. Assessing and documenting these risks in outcomes, financial benefits, and resource use or costs are integral steps in the value assessment process. Both delivery risk and benefits risk are inherent in any IM/IT investment. One must ask if the investment delivers on the anticipated business processes, human resources, technology, and organizational changes being proposed. Likewise, the outcomes and financial benefits promised may not in fact occur. In simple terms, the IM/IT investment may not perform as promised. The IT Governance Institute (2006) provides many examples of both delivery and benefit risks.

6. Optimizing Risk and Return

As stated in Chapter 4, the program planning office (portfolio management office) must assess and review the IM/IT investment proposal in the context of other applications and broad business needs. The key is that all proposals have the same sets of information collected and reported and that assessment is done in a comparable manner. The best decision will evolve if valid comparisons are made by those with the incentive to maximize value to the organization.

7. Document Business Case

Nothing can be more important than transparency in decision making. Documentation of data and information, assessment techniques, and findings all add to the open framework for decisions. This "open architecture" helps to create a culture of critical assessment so important to good decision making. The tendency to not reveal information as a mechanism to protect those making the decision may lead to poorer outcomes and to greater consequences should those outcomes fail to meet standards.

8. Feedback Mechanism

The single view of IM/IT investment value as presented by the value realization effort is a necessary first step for healthcare organizations, but IM/IT investment needs, organizational priorities, staffing constraints, and other environmental changes occur continuously. The information collected, assumptions made, benefits observed, and costs incurred should be reviewed periodically throughout the lifecycle of the investment. While many decisions cannot be "undone," midcourse adjustments in investment scale and scope are often possible. If the organization veers off course as a result of an investment, having a feedback mechanism enables the organization to adjust to minimize loss. Physician order entry provides a good example of the potential value of feedback. Faced with resistance to the widespread adoption of this technology, a temporary solution might be to implement in only parts of the organization. You can identify clinical areas or key supportive medical staff leaders and implement only in select areas. This avoids some of the resistance and provides you with areas more likely to be successful. Full implementation might occur later, but you have avoided the costly failure of the entire project.

To close this discussion, a number of investigators and thought leaders have found that the methods for realizing IM/IT value are often difficult to implement. As Johnston, Pan, and Middleton (2002) suggest, IM/IT investment decisions continue to rely upon "anecdote, inference and opinion" rather than evidence. They argue that IM/IT leadership must support a comprehensive assessment of value using existing data. Toward that end, Bates and colleagues (2003) propose "ten commandments" to follow for effective clinical decision support. While they are specifically interested in making evidence-based medicine a reality, these commandments also enhance realization of the IM/IT value realization described above. Four of the ten items are particularly important for IM/IT value and are provided:

1. *Speed is everything.* Providers will not accept a system that does not respond quickly to their inquiries. System design for rapid access appears to be essential for information technology effectiveness.
2. *Fit into the user's workflow.* The IM/IT investment must support the providers' and other users' current practice processes to be readily accepted. They will not use a system that does not fit seamlessly.
3. *Simple interventions work best.* The IM/IT investment with grand plans to alter the practice of medicine may not be as effective as a simple solution.
4. *Monitor impact, get feedback, and respond.* The feedback mechanism appears to be essential for success. Even the best systems may not integrate in the manner anticipated; thus, being flexible and adaptable may be keys to success.

IM/IT Value Findings

Impact of Specific IM/IT Investments on Patients

Many studies have been conducted on specific IM/IT investment value recognition. Three studies illustrate this process. A common characteristic is that this literature tends to report only narrow analyses of impacts of IM/IT investments. The desire for academic rigor results in such narrow scope. IM/IT managers need broader evaluations to make decisions for the organization; therefore, two additional studies report organizational value of IM/IT investments.

The first study discussed, by Hillestad and colleagues (2005), presents a national simulation study of the potential cost savings from health IM/IT investments, specifically adoption of an electronic medical record (EMR). Table 10.5, from the Hillestad et al. (2005) study, suggests that in the near term, savings may total as much as $21.3 billion per year (year 5), more of which is derived from inpatient care than from outpatient care. Once adoption reaches the authors' anticipated 90 percent, savings could amount to more than $77 billion per year (again, more of this savings is derived from inpatient care). The savings in inpatient care come from reductions in length of stay followed by reductions in nursing time. On the outpatient side, most of the savings come from reduced/appropriate drug use.

In addition to these cost savings, benefits or value from IM/IT investments are derived from improved patient safety and health outcomes. Hillestad and colleagues (2005) estimate that the safety benefits of CPOE are seen at the national level for both inpatient and outpatient care. Inpatient care savings resulting from an estimated 200,000 adverse drug events eliminated amount to $1 billion per year once fully implemented. Outpatient care savings resulting from an estimated two million events avoided amount to $3.5 billion per year. In both settings, the bulk of the study participants were over age 65, thus the findings might not be generalizable to other participants.

TABLE 10.5
Short-Term and
Long-Term
Annual Cost
Savings from
HIT, by
Selected Major
Categories

	Short Term Year 5 (in billions)	Percent of Total	Long Term Year 15 (in billions)	Percent of Total
Outpatient				
Transcription	$0.4	1.9	$1.7	2.2
Chart pulls	$0.4	1.9	$1.5	1.9
Laboratory tests	$0.5	2.3	$2.0	2.6
Drug usage	$3.0	14.1	$11.0	14.2
Radiology	$0.8	3.8	$3.3	4.3
Total outpatient savings	$5.2	24.4	$20.4	26.3
Inpatient				
Nursing time	$3.4	16.0	$13.7	17.7
Laboratory tests	$0.8	3.8	$2.6	3.4
Drug usage	$1.0	4.7	$3.5	4.5
Length of stay	$10.1	47.4	$34.7	44.8
Medical records	$0.7	3.3	$2.4	3.1
Total inpatient savings	$16.1	75.6	$57.1	73.7
Total HIT cost savings	$21.3	100.0	$77.4	100.0

Note: Numbers and percentages do not sum to totals because of rounding.
Source: Hillestad et al. (2005). Used with permission.

Near-term preventive care can benefit from HIT intervention as well. This study generated estimates for two vaccination programs (influenza and pneumococcal vaccination) and three screening programs (breast cancer, cervical cancer, and colorectal cancer screening). The findings are highly positive from a health outcome perspective and depend heavily upon assumptions regarding current compliance rates in the defined population, compliance rates for the specific vaccination and screening programs, and costs. Taking the midpoints of the estimated effects, pneumococcal vaccination resulted in a median reduction of 21,000 deaths per year (15,000 to 27,000), 2.25 million median bed days eliminated (1.5 million to 3.0 million), and 150,000 median workdays restored (100,000 to 200,000). These effects came at a program cost of about $90 million per year. At the same time, however, the program generated median financial benefits estimated at $750 million per year ($500 million to $1 billion).

The second study used here to illustrate value findings, by Pizziferri and colleagues (2005), examines the issue of an EHR and physician clinic time with patients. The study broke time down into a number of key components so that the total time and contributing factors to any time change could be examined. Overall, they found no difference in time spent in direct care, indirect care (reading, writing, or other activities), administrative activities, or miscellaneous activities. From a value perspective, this is only one small consideration but an important element with regard to physician acceptance of the

EMR. Pizziferri and colleagues (2005) recommend that future investigations examine the impact of the EMR on nonclinic time spent.

The third study presented here, by Poissant and colleagues (2005), involves a comprehensive review of studies examining physician and nurse documentation time as a result of implementation of an EHR. Generally, they reported that neither bedside nor central nursing station use of EHR reduced nursing documentation time by more than 20 percent. Physician documentation time increased by 17 percent for bedside technology and by more than 200 percent for central nursing station terminals. This analysis of time impact again raises some significant questions regarding system impact. This study did not examine the cost of the EHR or the direct cost impact.

Consistent with the assertion that IM/IT leadership must reach out to the entire organization in its efforts to invest in IM/IT, studies are now being published that assess the value of IM/IT investments in terms of their impact on the organization as a whole.

Impact of IM/IT Investments on Organizations

Iansiti and colleagues (2005) demonstrate that IM/IT matters at least in mid-size firms. Their research does not measure the impact of any specific technology intervention or even overall dollars spent. It uses an index of what "IT actually does for a business" to measure impact. The study's authors created an "IT scorecard" to assess IM/IT capability in the functional areas of sales/marketing, finance, operations, empowered professionals, and information technology infrastructure. They found that greater capability generates business process scalability, which enables firms to do the following:

- Improve process knowledge and standardization
- Streamline operations, allowing the firm to grow without expanding the labor force
- Become flexible enough to take advantage of/respond to new opportunities
- Enhance management's access to critical business indicators used in decision making

Similarly, Menachemi and colleagues (2006) demonstrate a robust relationship between information technology adoption and hospital financial performance, at least for hospitals in Florida. Their findings suggest that overall and operational improvement followed from information technology adoption. This outcome was observed for their categories of clinical, administrative, and strategic information technology.

Summary

Healthcare IM/IT should adhere to core business processes. In that context, the decisions regarding how much and what types of IM/IT resources an organization uses should fall under a valuation paradigm. Finding value in any healthcare investment has proven to be a challenge, however, because data collection, methodology, and application make the use of evidence-based management difficult. Because of the complexity of the problem and the lack of comprehensive data, healthcare executives have largely been forced to make decisions about IM/IT investments based on cursory evidence at best and occasionally based on instinct or hope at worst. As a result, health IM/IT may fall short in helping to address the problems plaguing healthcare.

The median hospital spent $5,556 per bed for health information technology capital and $12,060 for operating costs of health IM/IT in 2006, according to the AHA (2007) underscoring the fact that this is not a small problem. From a healthcare IM/IT leadership perspective, however, healthcare information technology is essential for the provision of high-quality care in today's environment, so the decision to invest in IM/IT must be faced. Many factors make such decisions difficult, including the scaling of information technology and the systems nature of information technology. For example, technology acquisition is not an all-or-nothing proposition; questions of scale, scope, application, integration, and timing are involved. The interdependence of providers in a healthcare "system" complicates the decision further. Care delivery organizations will implement interoperable EHRs to enable the exchange of information across venues while still focusing on value creation.

The early evidence coming out of IM/IT investment studies is that the financial benefits to the healthcare system may be substantial. Walker and colleagues (2005) estimate that HIEI may generate upwards of $77 billion in savings to the U.S. healthcare system once fully implemented. Providers will come to expect electronic information exchange as they increasingly work in teams that require a real-time exchange of information. Finally, consumers will demand new delivery modes for their care and expect coordination of care across provider segments. Consequently, the ability to assess value will be crucial for those leading the IM/IT functions of the future.

Business decisions faced by the CIO and indirectly by the CEO and board come down to a challenge of deciding among competing alternatives, leading to the evaluation challenge. The questions that must be asked are whether the IM/IT investment increases or decreases organizational outcomes, and whether it increases or decreases costs to the organization. Economists have frameworks for assisting in making these decisions, called benefit-cost analyses, cost-effectiveness analyses, and cost-utility analyses.

Further, business models suggest a similar evaluation process for value realization that consists of conceptualizing, capturing, analyzing, and reporting detailed financial and nonfinancial information. The IT Governance Institute (2006) has developed a detailed value realization process that can direct IM/IT leadership to achieve their goals.

A number of challenges hinder the efforts to maximize the value of health IM/IT investments, including lack of proper, detailed documentation of key information and conceptual problems of assigning benefits and costs to a particular investment. These investments garner benefits from and impose costs throughout the organization, thus posing problems of assignment to uniquely evaluate the net effect of any single investment. These impacts are now extending even outside of the confines of the traditional organizational entity. Obtaining that data and generating reliable estimates of net value are problematic at best.

Web Resources

This chapter relies upon a number of reliable sources for additional information.

Cost analyses for healthcare technologies can be found at the University HealthSystem Consortium (www.uhc.edu) and Blue Cross and Blue Shield Technology Evaluation Center (www.bcbs.com/betterknowledge/tec/). Specific IM/IT intervention evaluations can be found at the Center for Information Technology Leadership (www.citl.org).

Quality of life measurements can be found at the Centers for Disease Control and Prevention website, www.cdc.gov/hrqol/index.htm.

Discussion Questions

1. Explain why obtaining value from health IM/IT investments is so important in today's healthcare environment.
2. How valid and reliable do you think IM/IT investment decisions are currently? Why?
3. What is the system nature of healthcare, and why does it affect value estimation?
4. Define *medical tourism* and explain why it is both a threat and an opportunity to U.S. healthcare organizations.
5. What do you think will drive adoption of interoperable EHRs—cost savings or consumer preferences? Why?
6. What is the evaluation problem faced by health IM/IT investment decision makers? Why does Table 10.2 help in understanding that problem?
7. Why do we not observe examples of all of the cells in Table 10.2?
8. Compare and contrast benefit-cost, cost-effectiveness, and cost-utility analyses. Which do you prefer, and why?
9. List and assess the eight steps in conducting benefit-cost analysis, cost-effectiveness analysis, or cost-utility analysis.
10. What is value realization? In what ways is it similar to and different from economic evaluation techniques?

11. Explain the four questions proposed by the IT Governance Institute, and explain why they are important.

12. Describe how the nature of the IM/IT investment application affects the quality and nature of the value determination.

References

Adams J., E. Mounib, A. Pai, N. Stuart, R. Thomas, and P. Tomaszewicz. 2007. "Healthcare 2015: Win-Win or Lose-Lose? A Portrait and a Path to Successful Transformation." IBM Global Business Services, IBM Institute for Business Value. [Online information; retrieved 1/4/08.] http://www-931.ibm.com/tela/servlet/Asset/169464/Healthcare2015-Win-win_or_lose-lose.pdf

American Hospital Association (AHA). 2007. *Continued Progress: Hospital Use of Information Technology*. Chicago: American Hospital Association.

Bates, D. W., G. J. Kuperman, S. Wang, T. Gandhi, A. Kittler, L. Volk, C. Spurr, R. Khorasani, M. Tanasijevic, and B. Middleton. 2003. "Ten Commandments for Effective Clinical Decision Support: Making the Practice of Evidence-Based Medicine a Reality." *Journal of the American Medical Informatics Association* 10 (6): 523–30.

Board, A. 2004. *Prioritizing IT Investments: Toward a Disciplined Approach amid Heightened Competition for Capitol*. New York: Advisory Board Company.

Carr, N. 2003. "IT Doesn't Matter." *Harvard Business Review* 81 (5): 41–49.

Chaudhry, B., J. Wang, S. Wu, M. Maglione, W. Mojica, E. Roth, S. C. Morton, and P. G. Shekelle. 2006. "Systematic Review: Impact of Health Information Technology on Quality, Efficiency and Costs of Medical Care." *Annals of Internal Medicine* 144 (10): 742–52.

Chin, T. 2003. "Doctors Pull Plug on Paperless System." *AMNews* February 17. [Online article; retrieved 1/4/08.] http://www.ama-assn.org/amednews/2003/02/17/bil20217.htm

Enthoven, A., and L. Tollen. 2005. "Competition in Health Care: It Takes Systems to Pursue Quality and Efficiency." *Health Affairs*. Web Exclusive (W5-420-433). [Online article; retrieved 1/4/08.] http://content.healthaffairs.org/cgi/content/abstract/hlthaff.w5.420

Glandon, G. L., and T. Buck. 1994. "Cost-Benefit Analysis of Medical Information Systems: A Critique." In *Evaluating Health Care Information Systems: Methods and Applications*, edited by J. Anderson, C. Aydin, and S. Jay. Thousand Oaks, CA: Sage Publications.

Glandon, G. L., and R. J. Shapiro. 1988. "Benefit-Cost Analysis of Hospital Information Systems: The State of the (Non) Art." *Journal of Health & Human Resources Administration* 11 (1): 30–92.

Gold, M., J. Siegel, L. Russell, and M. Weinstein. 1996. *Cost-Effectiveness in Health and Medicine*. New York: Oxford University Press.

Han, Y. Y., J. A. Carcillo, S. T. Venkataraman, R. S. Clark, R. S. Watson, T. C. Nguyen, H. Bayir, and R. A. Orr. 2005. "Unexpected Increased Mortality After Implementation of a Commercially Sold Computerized Physician Order Entry System." *Pediatrics* 116 (6): 1506–12.

Hickman G., and K. Kusche. 2006. "Building the EHR Total Cost of Ownership (TCO) Model." Healthcare Information and Management Systems Society Webinar, Chicago, April 27.

Hillestad, R., J. Bigelow, A. Bower, F. Girosi, R. Meili, R. Scoville, and R. Taylor. 2005. "Can Electronic Medical Record Systems Transform Health Care? Potential Health Benefits, Savings, and Costs." *Health Affairs* 24 (5): 1103–17.

Iansiti, M., G. Favaloro, J. Utzschneider, and G. Richards. 2005. "Why IT Matters in Midsized Firms." Harvard Business School Working Paper, No. 06–013. Boston: Harvard Business School Press.

IT Governance Institute. 2006. *Enterprise Value: Governance of IT Investments, the Business Case.* Rolling Meadows, IL: IT Governance Institute.

Johnston, D., E. Pan, and B. Middleton. 2002. *Finding the Value in Healthcare Information Technologies.* Boston: Center for Information Technology Leadership.

Koppel, R. 2005. "Computerized Physician Order Entry Systems: The Right Prescription?" *LDI Issue Brief* 10 (5): 1–4.

Koppel, R., J. P. Metlay, A. Cohen, B. Abaluck, A. R. Localio, S. E. Kimmel, and B. L. Strom. 2005. "Role of Computerized Physician Order Entry Systems in Facilitating Medication Errors." *Journal of the American Medical Association* 293 (10): 1197–1203.

Landro, L. 2003. "Doctors Need Incentives to Embrace Technology." [Online article; retrieved 3/1/06.] http://online.wsj.com/article/sb105777796472723600.html

Loomis, G. A., J. S. Ries, R. M. Saywell, Jr., and N. R. Thakker. 2002. "If Electronic Medical Records Are So Great, Why Aren't Family Physicians Using Them?" *Journal of Family Practice* 51 (7): 636–41.

Menachemi, N, J. Burkhardt, R. Shewchuk, D. Burke, and R. Brooks. 2006. "Hospital Information Technology and Positive Financial Performance: A Different Approach to Finding an ROI." *Journal of Healthcare Management* 51 (1): 40–58.

Miller, R. H., C. West, T. M. Brown, I. Sim, and C. Ganchoff. 2005. "The Value of Electronic Health Records in Solo or Small Group Practices." *Health Affairs (Millwood)* 24 (5): 1127–37.

Pizziferri, L., A. Kittler, L. Volka, M. Honourb, S. Guptaa, S. Wang, T. Wang, M. Q. Lippincott, Q. Lia, and D. W. Bates. 2005. "Primary Care Physician Time Utilization Before and After Implementation of an Electronic Health Record: A Time-Motion Study." *Journal of Biomedical Informatics* 38: 176–88.

Poissant, L., J. Pereira, R. Tamblyn, and Y. Kawasumi. 2005. "The Impact of Electronic Health Records on Time Efficiency of Physicians and Nurses: A Systematic Review." *Journal of the American Medical Informatics Association* 12 (5): 505–16.

Rahimi, B., and V. Vimarlund. 2007. "Methods to Evaluate Health Information Systems in Healthcare Settings: A Literature Review." *Journal of Medical Systems* (5): 397–432.

Shekelle, P. G., S. C. Morton, and E. B. Keeler. 2006. "Costs and Benefits of Health Information Technology." Evidence Report/Technology Assessment #132. Prepared for Agency for Healthcare Research and Quality #06-E006.

Simon, S. J., and S. J Simon. 2006. "An Examination of the Financial Feasibility of Electronic Medical Records (EMRs): A Case Study of Tangible and Intangible Benefits." *International Journal of Electronic Healthcare* 2 (2): 185–200.

Smaltz, D. H., and E. S. Berner. 2006. *The Executive's Guide to Electronic Health Records*. Chicago: Health Administration Press.

Thorp, J. 2003. *The Information Paradox: Realizing the Business Benefits of Information Technology*. Toronto: McGraw-Hill Ryerson.

Viscusi, W. 2004. "The Value of Life: Estimates with Risk by Industry and Occupation." *Economic Inquiry* 42 (1): 28–49.

Walker, J., E. Pan, D. Johnston, J. Adler-Milstein, D. Bates, and B. Middleton. 2005. "The Value of Health Care Exchange and Interoperability." *Health Affairs*. Web Exclusive (W5–10-W5–18). [Online article; retrieved 2/1/08.] http://content.healthaffairs.org/cgi/content/full/hlthaff.w5.10/DC1

Warner, K., and B. Luce. 1982. *Cost-Benefit and Cost-Effectiveness Analysis in Health Care: Principles, Practice, and Potential*. Chicago: Health Administration Press.

Weinstein, M., and W. Stason. 1977. "Foundations of Cost-Effectiveness Analysis for Health and Medical Practice." *New England Journal of Medicine* 298: 716–21.

Wiley, V., and G. Daniel. 2006. *An Economic Evaluation of a Payer-Based Electronic Health Record Within an Emergency Department*. Wilmington, DE: HealthCore, Inc.

GLOSSARY OF TECHNICAL TERMS

Administrative information system. An information system that is designed to assist in the performance of administrative support activities in a healthcare organization, such as payroll accounting, accounts receivable, accounts payable, facility management, intranets, and human resources management.

Algorithm. A step-by-step procedure for performing a task. Computer algorithms consist of logical and mathematical operations.

Analog signal. The representation of data by varying the amplitude, frequency, and/or phase of a waveform. *See also* Digital signal.

Application service provider (ASP). An organization that contracts with a healthcare facility to provide access to applications that are available online.

Applications program. A program that performs specific tasks for the computer user, such as payroll, order entry, or inventory control.

Artificial Intelligence (AI). A discipline that attempts to simulate human problem-solving techniques in a computer environment. *See also* Expert system.

Asynchronous transfer mode (ATM). A networking technology that segments data into small fixed-length cells, directs the cells to the appropriate destination, and reassembles the data.

Bandwidth. A measure of the data-carrying capacity of a transmission medium. The higher the bandwidth, the larger the volume of data that can be moved across networks.

Bar-code label. A printed form or plastic card containing a sequence of vertical bars and spaces that represent numbers and other symbols. The contents can be read automatically by specially designed computer input devices.

Bar-code scanner. An input device that allows a computer user to scan a bar code label and transfer its contents to a computer.

Bit. A binary digit (0 or 1) that is part of a data byte. In most computer systems, eight bits make up one byte.

Bridge. An interface that connects two or more networks that use similar protocols.

Browser. A software application that enables users to view and interact with information on the World Wide Web.

Bus. (1) The physical network topology in which all workstations are connected to a line directly. (2) Within a computer, the signal path that links the central processing unit with primary memory and with input/output devices.

Byte. The smallest addressable piece of information in a computer's memory, typically consisting of eight bits, used to signify a letter, number, or symbol.

CD-R (compact disk—recordable). An optical disk used for mass storage of computer data onto which it is possible to write additional data in multiple sessions, as long as subsequent "writes" are made to different areas of the disk.

CD-ROM (compact disk—read-only memory). An optical disk used for mass storage of computer data on a read-only basis.

CD-RW (compact disk—rewritable). An optical disk used for mass storage of computer data for which it is possible to record over old, redundant data or to remove selected files from the disk.

Cellular digital packet data (CDPD). A network, similar to that used by cellular telephones, in which the user is transmitting or receiving data rather than voice messages.

Central processing unit (CPU). The component in a computer that performs calculations, makes logical decisions, and supervises and coordinates the various functional units of the system.

Chief information officer (CIO). The job title for the head of the information management and technology group within an organization.

Client/server architecture. A computing configuration in which users interact with their machines (called "clients") and one or more other machines (called "servers"), store data, and do much of the computing.

Clinical data repository. A database that consists of information from various sources of care and from various departments and/or facilities. The database may represent a longitudinal description of an individual's care.

Clinical (or medical) information system. An information system that provides for the organized storage, processing, and retrieval of information to support patient care activities.

Closed system. A completely self-contained system that is not influenced by external events. *See also* Cybernetic system; Open system; System.

Computer programming. The process of coding a set of instructions or steps in a given data processing language that directs the computer and coordinates the operation of all hardware components.

Computer virus. A computer program that intentionally tries to alter application programs, operating systems, and/or data files on a computer hard drive or floppy disk. Viruses may be intentionally or unintentionally transmitted from one computer to another by floppy disks, communication links, or downloading from the Internet.

Computerized physician order entry (CPOE). A process of electronic entry of physician instructions or orders regarding the diagnosis and treatment of the physician's patients.

Consumer Price Index (CPI). An index measuring the weighted average price of consumer goods and services purchased by consumers. The weights are the proportion of spending on the goods or services.

CPU. *See* Central processing unit.

Cybernetic system. A self-regulating system that contains the following automatic control components: sensor, monitor, standards, and control unit. *See also* Closed system; Open system; System.

Data. Raw facts and figures collected by the organization from clinical encounters, empirical observations, or research. Data in and of themselves often have little value and take on meaning only after sorting, tabulation, and processing into a more usable format (information).

Database. A series of records, containing data fields, stored together in such a way that the contents are easily accessed, managed, and updated.

Database management system (DBMS). Software that enables the creation and accessing of data stored in a database.

Data dictionary. A file that contains the name, definition, and structure of all the data fields and elements in a database.

Data field. One piece of information stored in a data record as part of a database.

Data record. A group of individual fields, corresponding to a real-world entity, that are stored together in a database.

Data redundancy. A situation in which the same data item appears in several files of a healthcare organization's computer system.

Data warehouse. A data warehouse enables the collection and organization of disparate data sources into an integrated subject-oriented view of the data to facilitate decision making.

Decision support system. A system designed to support the decision-making process of an individual or organization through the use of data retrieval, modeling, and reporting.

Deterministic system. A system in which the component parts function according to completely predictable or definable relationships with no randomness present.

Digital signal. The representation of data as a series of on-off pulses (1s and 0s). *See also* Analog signal.

Digital versatile disk (DVD). A secondary storage medium, similar in appearance to a compact disk (CD), available in read-only, recordable, and rewritable formats. A DVD can store data on both of its sides and is available in capacities ranging from 4.7 gigabytes to 17 gigabytes.

Disk drive. A secondary data-storage device that uses a magnetically coated disk as the storage medium. The disk drive consists of a mechanism to provide rotation of the disk (spindle), a read/write head to establish and detect magnetic patterns on each disk surface being accessed, and a mechanism to position the head appropriately for access.

Distributed processing. A computer network topology in which the workload is spread out through a network of computers that can be located in different organizational units.

Documentation. Written information that provides a description and overview of a computer program or system and detailed instructions on its use.

Dumb terminal. A device that can provide input to and display output from a central computer but cannot perform any independent processing.

DVD. *See* Digital versatile disk.

E-health applications. Healthcare software applications delivered through the Internet and related technologies.

Electronic data interchange (EDI). The transfer of structured information between two computers.

Electronic health record (EHR). The EHR consists of an individual's medical records from all locations and sources. Stored in digital format, it facilitates the storage and retrieval of individual records with the aid of computers.

Electronic mail (e-mail). The electronic communication of messages between two or more people over computer networks.

Encryption. The scrambling of an electronic transmission by using mathematical formulas or algorithms to protect the confidentiality and security of communications.

Ethernet. The trade name for a logical network topology that is used to control how devices on the network send and receive messages. The goal is to avoid "collisions" resulting from two devices attempting to send messages simultaneously.

Evidence-based management (EBM). A movement to explicitly use the current, best-available scientific evidence for managerial decision making.

Executive information system (EIS). An organized data storage, retrieval, and reporting system that is designed to provide senior management with information for decision making.

Expert system. A decision support system that can approximate a human decision maker's reasoning processes. It can assist in reaching a decision, diagnosing a problem, or suggesting a course of action.

Fiber-distributed data interchange (FDDI). A network consisting of two identical fiber-optic rings connected to local area networks and other computers.

Fiber-optic medium. A communication transmission medium that uses light pulses sent through a glass cable at high transmission rates with no electromagnetic interference.

Firewall. Hardware and/or software that restricts traffic to and from a private network from the general public Internet network.

Flowchart. A graphical representation of the steps and sequences that compose a project, process, or computer program. The graphical representation consists of symbolic shapes, legends, and connecting flow lines.

Front-end processor. The processor with which application users interact directly. In a client/server network, the front-end processor would correspond to the client.

Gantt chart. An illustration of a project schedule that includes the start and finish dates of a project. Depending upon the complexity, it may include terminal elements, summary elements, the work breakdown structure, and the dependency relationships between activities.

Gateway. The interface between two networks that use dissimilar protocols to communicate.

Graphical user interface. A particular interface between the human user and the computer to manage the functioning of the software and hardware that employs icons (graphical symbols on the monitor screen) to represent available operating system commands.

Gross domestic product (GDP). A measure of an economy's size. For any single country, GDP is the total market value of all goods and services produced. Economists measure GDP as the sum of consumption, investment, and government spending on goods and services, and the net of exports minus imports.

Hard disk. One of several rigid platters, coated with a thin magnetic film, contained within an enclosure known as a hard-disk drive. These platters serve as random access secondary storage devices.

Hardware. The physical components of a computer system.

Health Insurance Portability and Accountability Act (HIPAA). Federal legislation passed in 1996 to make health insurance more portable. The administrative simplification provisions of HIPAA establish standards for electronic transmission of administrative information related to health insurance claims. The privacy protection regulations are designed to limit the nonconsensual use and release of private health information.

Health Level Seven (HL7). A standard for data formatting that helps to facilitate the exchange of data among disparate systems within and across software vendors.

Home page. The first Web page associated with a particular site. *See* Web page.

Host. A computer to which other, smaller computers in a network are connected and with which it can communicate.

Hub. A hardware device with multiple user ports to which computers and input/output devices can be attached.

Information. Data or facts that have been processed and analyzed in a formal, intelligent way so that the results are directly useful to clinicians and managers.

Input. Data fed into a computer system, either manually (such as through a keyboard or bar-code device) or automatically (such as in a bedside patient monitoring system).

Integrated system. A set of information systems or networks that can share common data files and can communicate with one another.

Internet. An open network of computer networks that permit people and computers to communicate and share applications through standard open protocols.

Internet Protocol (IP). An addressing scheme that identifies each machine on the Internet and is made up of four sets of numbers separated by "dots."

Interoperability. The ability of health information systems to effectively transmit and share medical information across organizations.

Intranet. A private computer network contained within an organization that uses Internet software and transmission standards (TCP/IP).

ISDN (integrated services digital network). A network that uses a local telephone company branch exchange to allow separate microcomputer workstations, terminals, and other network nodes to communicate with a central computer and with each other.

Knowledge management. The organizational practice of explicitly and deliberately building, renewing, and applying relevant intellectual assets to maximize an enterprise's effectiveness.

LAN. *See* Local area network.

Laptop computer. A powerful microcomputer that is characterized by its small size, light weight, portability, and range of capabilities.

Laser printer. A high-speed, high-quality printer that can function with several graphic formats and type-font options.

LCD (liquid crystal display) screen. An output device, originally associated with laptop computers, that is thin, is lightweight, and makes use of liquid crystal technology to form the output.

Legacy systems. Computer applications, running in parts of the organization, that were designed to meet specific operational needs. Usually developed independent of a broad organizational information management/information technology plan and often not compatible with newer integrated systems.

Lifecycle. The sequence of specification, design, implementation, and maintenance of computer programs. For models of computer hardware, the lifecycle is the sequence in market status of development, announcement, availability, and obsolescence.

Local area network (LAN). A computer network providing communication among computers and peripherals within an organization or group of organizations over a limited area. The network consists of the computers, peripherals, communication links, and interfacing hardware.

Magnetic storage. Online or offline data storage in which each data character is stored as a 0 or 1 in magnetic form. Magnetic storage includes magnetic disks and tapes.

Mainframe. A term used to describe relatively large computer systems, which normally have very large main memories, specialized support for high-speed processing, many ports for online terminals and communication links, and extensive auxiliary memory storage.

Master patient index. A relational database containing all of the identification numbers that have been assigned to a patient anywhere within a healthcare system. The master patient index assigns a global identification number as an umbrella for all patient numbers, thus permitting queries that can find all appropriate data for a particular patient regardless of where that person was treated within the system.

Menu. A list of options, displayed on a monitor, to allow the user to select the function to be performed or another, more specific menu. Programs operated through the use of menus are said to be *menu driven*.

Microcomputer. A relatively small computer system, with the microprocessor, main memory, disk drives, CD-ROM, and interface cards and connectors installed in a small case or box. *See* Microprocessor.

Microprocessor. A CPU contained on a single semiconductor chip.

Middleware. System architecture in which applications are connected to and distributed by networked systems.

Minicomputer. A computer with capabilities somewhere between those of a microcomputer and of a mainframe computer. *See also* Mainframe; Microcomputer.

Modem (modulator/demodulator). A data communication device that modulates signals from output devices for transmission on a data link and demodulates signals destined for input devices coming from the transmission link.

Multiplexing. The process of combining two or more signals into a single signal, transmitting it, and then sorting out the original signals. The devices that combine or sort out signals are called *multiplexers*.

Network. A collection of computer and peripheral devices interconnected by communication paths. *See also* Local area network; Wide area network.

Network computer. A low-cost personal computer having minimal equipment and designed to be managed and maintained by a central computing function.

Network controller. A mini- or microcomputer that "directs" the communication traffic between the host and the terminals and peripheral devices.

Network interface card (NIC). A plug-in board used in microcomputers and workstations to allow them to communicate with a host computer and other nodes in a local area network.

Open system. A system whose components are exposed to everyone and can thus be modified or improved.

Operating system. A set of integrated subroutines and programs that control the operation of a computer and manage its resources.

Optical disk. A disk in which data are written and read by a laser. Optical disk types include a number of variations of CDs and DVDs. *See also* CD-R; CD-ROM; CD-RW; DVD.

Output. Any data or information that a computer sends to a peripheral device or other network.

Outsourcing. Delegation of responsibility of a noncore operation to an external entity. The organization contracts with outside experts to perform specific tasks that were once performed internally. Examples could include software development and accounts receivable collection.

Parallel processing. The use of multiple CPUs linked together generally for the purpose of more efficiently completing complex tasks.

PC. *See* Personal computer.

Peer networks. A decentralized computing environment in which each computer on the network has either data or some hardware resource that it can make available to the other users on the network.

Peripheral devices. A general term used to refer to input, output, and secondary storage devices on a computer.

Personal computer (PC). Name commonly used to refer to a microcomputer.

Picture archiving and communications system (PACS). A device that provides online storage and retrieval of medical images for transmission to user workstations.

Portfolio management office (PMO). A centralized organization dedicated to improving the practice and outcomes of projects via holistic management of all projects. This includes the professional management and oversight of an organization's entire collection of projects. *Project management office* and *program management office* are used interchangeably with *portfolio management office*.

Program. An ordered set of instructions that a computer executes to obtain a desired result.

Programming language. A software system having a specific format, or syntax, used for writing computer programs.

Project management. The planning, organizing, directing, and controlling of company resources to accomplish the organization's goals and objectives related to a distinct initiative, such as the implementation of an information system application.

Protocols. Rules and conventions for communication between computers.

Radio-frequency identification (RFID). An automatic identification method that relies on storing and remotely retrieving data using devices called transponders or RFID tags. The RFID tag can be applied to a product, an animal, or a person for the purpose of identification using radiowaves.

RAM. *See* Random access memory.

Random access memory (RAM). Storage that permits direct access to the data stored at a particular address.

Read-only memory (ROM). Storage that contains permanent instructions or data that cannot be altered by ordinary programming.

Real time. Describes a computer or process that captures data, performs an operation, or delivers results in a time frame that humans perceive as instantaneous.

Relational database. A type of database that stores data in individual files or tables, with data items arranged in rows and columns. Two or more tables can be linked for the purposes of ad hoc queries if at least one data item (the "key") is common in each of the tables.

ROM. *See* Read-only memory.

Router. A device located at a gateway that manages the data flow between networks. *See also* Gateway.

Software. The programs that control the operation of a computer, including application programs, operating systems, programming languages, development tools, and language translators.

System. A network of components or elements joined together to accomplish a specific purpose or objective. Every system must include input, a conversion process, and output. *See also* Closed system; Cybernetic system; Open system.

Systems analysis. The process of collecting, organizing, and evaluating facts about information system requirements, processes, and the environment in which the system will operate.

Telecommunications. Transmission of information over distances through wired, optical, or radio media.

Telemedicine. A rapidly developing application of clinical medicine that employs communications and information technologies to assist delivery of care (consulting, medical procedures, or examinations).

Terminal. A device consisting of a monitor and keyboard that allows a computer user to perform processing on a host computer directly. *See also* Dumb terminal.

Terminal-host system. A centralized computer network configuration in which dumb terminals are connected to a large central host computer, typically a mainframe, and all of the computing is taking place on the host computer. *See also* Host; Mainframe; Terminal.

Thin client. System architecture in which most processing is performed on a server remote from the end user or client.

Three-tier architecture. Configuration in which the user interface resides with the client, the relational databases reside on one server, and the application programs reside on a second server. This configuration offers faster information processing and distribution than a two-tier system.

Throughput. The total time span from collection of the first data element to the preparation of the final report in a given system.

Total cost of ownership. An operational device designed to aid in defining and collecting relevant startup (one time) and recurring costs of purchase. These include the costs of training support personnel and the users of the system, costs associated with planned or unplanned failure or outage, diminished performance incidents, costs of loss of reputation and recovery from security breaches, costs of disaster preparedness and recovery, floor space, electricity, development expenses, testing infrastructure and expenses, quality assurance, boot image control, marginal incremental growth, decommissioning, electronic waste handling, and more.

Transaction processing systems. Application programs that form the bulk of the day-to-day activities of an organization, such as financial, clinical, admissions, and business office systems.

Transmission Control Protocol/Internet Protocol (TCP/IP). A collection of data communication protocols used to connect a computer to the Internet. TCP/IP is the standard for all Internet communication.

Two-tier client/server architecture. All back-end functions (database management, printing, communication, and applications program execution) are performed on a single server.

VDT. *See* Video display terminal.

Video display terminal (VDT). Often known as a "monitor," the VDT displays the output text and/or graphics created by a computer.

Web browser. Software that enables a user to view and interact with information stored on the Web.

Web page. A file that contains text, graphics, or other multimedia information that indicates how the information is to be formatted when the page is displayed. A "home page" is the first Web page of a particular site.

Wide area network (WAN). A network in which long distance lines allow computers and local area networks to communicate.

Windows. Operating system that allows data from two or more programs to be displayed on a video display terminal at the same time. The use of graphical user interfaces supports a user-friendly environment and allows for multitasking of software applications.

Workstation. (1) A microcomputer connected to a larger host computer in which some independent processing is performed. (2) A high-end microcomputer with a large amount of primary storage, a fast processor, a high-quality sound card, high-resolution graphics, a CD-RW drive, and in many cases a DVD drive.

World Wide Web (www). The collection of text, graphics, and multimedia stored in databases all over the world that can be accessed via the Internet.

INDEX

ABOUT THE AUTHORS

Gerald L. Glandon, Ph.D., is professor and chair of the Department of Health Services Administration at the University of Alabama at Birmingham (UAB). He is the interim program director for the Health Informatics Program and directs the Center for Health Services Continuing Education at UAB. Dr. Glandon has had a career in research, health administration education, and academic administration. His primary research interests have been technology evaluation (especially information technology), the economics of aging, patient and physician satisfaction, and assessment of organizational performance. He has published in such journals as *JAMA*, *Journal of Gerontology: Social Sciences, Medical Care, Hospital and Health Services Administration*, and *Health Services Research* as well as numerous books and book chapters.

Over the years, Dr. Glandon has kept his research and practice skills current by consulting with academic health centers, external agencies, and organizations. He has also worked in international health with engagements in Albania, Turkmenistan, Uzbekistan, Kazakhstan, Yemen, and Saudi Arabia. He has both developed and delivered management education in these countries and provided healthcare strategic analysis to Ministries of Health and to individual hospitals. Prior to coming to UAB, he had been program director of the Department of Health Systems Management at Rush-Presbyterian–St. Luke's Medical Center in Chicago.

Detlev H. (Herb) Smaltz, Ph.D., FHIMSS, FACHE, is the chief information officer of the Ohio State University (OSU) Medical Center. In addition, he serves as an associate vice president for health sciences, leading collaborative initiatives between the three mission areas of the medical center: research, academics, and patient care.

Dr. Smaltz has over 20 years of experience in healthcare management, with 17 of those years as CIO/CKO at various-sized organizations. He is a Fellow of the Healthcare Information & Management Systems Society (FHIMSS) and recently completed a three-year term on the HIMSS Board of Directors. He is also a Fellow in the American College of Healthcare Executives (FACHE) and served as the Co-Founding President of the Central European Healthcare Executives, an ACHE affiliated group.

Dr. Smaltz also holds certifications in knowledge management from the Knowledge Management Certification Board (KMCB) and in total cost of ownership from Gartner Research. In addition, he has served as an adjunct professor at Capital College in Laurel, Maryland, an associate professor at University of Alabama at Birmingham, and as an adjunct faculty at OSU. He is a widely published author.

Dr. Smaltz earned a B.S. in management information systems from the University of Tampa in 1985, an M.B.A. from OSU in 1992, and a Ph.D. in information and management science from Florida State University in 1999.

Donna J. Slovensky, Ph.D., RHIA, FAHIMA, is a professor in the Department of Health Services Administration in the School of Health Professions at the University of Alabama at Birmingham (UAB). She holds secondary appointments in the Department of Management, School of Business, and the Graduate School at UAB. Dr. Slovensky is a scientist with UAB's Center for Outcomes and Effectiveness Research and Education, a scholar with the Lister Hill Center for Health Policy, and a Fellow in the American Health Information Management Association (AHIMA).

Dr. Slovensky has more than 30 years of experience as an educator, teaching undergraduate and graduate students in health information management, healthcare management, and health administration and business. In addition to teaching, Dr. Slovensky has consulting experience in a variety of healthcare organizations, including inpatient and ambulatory facilities, home health programs, physician practices, and health professions academic programs.

Dr. Slovensky directs the HSA Department's undergraduate healthcare manager program in the Department of Health Services Administration and serves as the interim associate dean for academic affairs in the School of Health Professions. Current professional activities include service on the AHIMA Council on Certification, committees with the American Association of University Programs in Health Administration, and service on editorial and review boards for publishers of books and journals targeted at healthcare management professionals and educators. Her publications include journal articles, textbook chapters, and cases on topics related to healthcare management and health information management.

Dr. Slovensky earned her Ph.D. in health services administration from UAB.